A BLOOMSBURY REFERENCE BOOK

www.bloomsbury.com

First published in Great Britain 2004
Reprinted 2005

Bloomsbury Publishing Plc
38 Soho Square
London W1D 3HB

British Library Cataloguing-in-Publication Data

A catalogue record for this book is available from the British Library

ISBN 0 7475 6975 4

Text processing and computer typesetting by Bloomsbury
Printed and bound in Italy by Legoprint

Eating out
in five languages

General editor
Simon Collin

Editorial team

Cécile Guinard	Sarah Lusznat
Louise Miller	Lourdes Melcion
Loredana Riu	Doris Schweighofer

Text processing and proofreading
Daisy Jackson

For the first edition:

Françoise Laurendeau	Paolo Sciarrone
Rupert Livesey	Lourdes Melcion

BLOOMSBURY

Contents

Introduction

If you have ever ordered from a menu written in another language without being completely sure what you were asking for, then you need this pocket dictionary!

We have compiled this book to provide an essential pocket companion for any traveller who likes to know what they are ordering and eating, or who likes to try out new or local dishes. And unlike many other menu readers, the text has translations to and from English, so that you can both translate a menu and ask for a favourite dish or a particular ingredient. We have included 2,000 terms for each language, and our aim has been to cover general menu and restaurant terms as well as names of dishes, ingredients and drinks.

At the start of each section there is a section of useful English phrases translated into the other language . These have been selected to help you to find a restaurant, ask for the table that you want, order your meal, pay the bill – and, if necessary, complain.

We have also included helpful phrases for vegetarians, who traditionally have a difficult time eating out in some parts of Europe. Because it can often be difficult to find out exactly what is in a dish, we have also included phrases to help anyone with a common food allergy or intolerance, for example to gluten or nuts.

Finally, as you travel you will doubtless find new local dishes and local names for ingredients – in our experience, this is particularly so with local names for different types of fish. If you find interesting new terms that are not in this book, we would love to hear from you; please let us know and we will try to include the terms in future editions. Send any new terms (or comments on local variations of expressions) to: .

In the meantime - Bon appetit!, Guten Appetit!, Bon appetito!, ¡Que aproveche!

Useful French Phrases

Types of restaurant

une auberge	*hotel-restaurant, usually in the country*
un bar	*serves alcoholic drinks*
un bistrot	*café-restaurant, serves drinks and simple meals*
une brasserie	*café-restaurant, choice of beer and simple meals*
un café	*serves alcoholic drinks and coffee, some serve ice cream*
un café-restaurant	*serves alcoholic drinks, serves meals*
une cafétéria	*self-service restaurant providing simple meals*
un restaurant	*proper dining room; quality can vary*
un restaurant d'autoroute	*motorway restaurant, often a cafeteria*
un restaurant gastronomique	*high quality food, though sometimes no choice of menu, often more expensive*
un salon de thé	*shop selling cakes with a few tables to have tea or coffee*

Tipping

Tipping is relatively straightforward: bills are often stamped 's.t.c.' (service, taxes, compris) and it means what it says – all service and taxes included. The only exception perhaps is to leave the small change in the saucer at a bar (if you are eating at the bar rather than at a table).

Menu

Menus are usually split into five sections; shorter menus might have just three sections: entrée, plat principal and dessert:

potage or hors-d'oeuvre	*soup or starter*
entrée	*first course*
plat principal	*main course*
fromage	*cheese course*
dessert	*dessert*

Meals and eating times

07:00 - 09:00	petit déjeuner *breakfast*
12:00 - 14:00	déjeuner *lunch*
19:30 - 22:30	dîner *dinner*

Restaurant rating scheme

Toques (chef's hats) (five toques = de luxe, one toque = fourth-class);
Michelin stars (three-stars = exceptional, one-star = very good)

Getting to a restaurant

Can you recommend a good restaurant?	*Quel restaurant nous recommandez-vous?*
I would like to reserve a table for this evening	*J'aimerais réserver une table pour ce soir*
Do you have a table for three/four people?	*Avez-vous une table pour trois/quatre (personnes)?*
We would like the table for 8 o'clock	*Nous aimerions réserver une table pour 20 heures*
Could we have a table....?	*Auriez-vous une table de libre...?*
by the window	*près de la fenêtre*
outside	*dehors/à l'extérieur*
on the terrace	*sur la terrasse*
in the non-smoking area	*dans la section non-fumeurs*
in the smoking area	*dans la section fumeurs*
What time do you open?	*A quelle heure ouvrez-vous?*
Could you order a taxi for me?	*Pourriez-vous me faire venir un taxi?*

Ordering

Waiter/waitress !	*Garçon! / Mademoiselle !*
What do you recommend?	*Que nous proposez-vous?*
What are the specials of the day?	*Quels sont les spéciaux du jour?*
Is this the fixed-price menu?	*C'est le menu à prix fixe?*
Can we see the à-la-carte menu?	*Vous avez aussi un menu à la carte?*
Is this fresh?	*Est-ce frais?*
Is this local?	*Est-ce une spécialité de la région?*
I would like a/an …	*J'aimerais un/une...*
Could I/we have ... please?	*Pourriez-vous me/nous donner...*
an ashtray	*un cendrier*
the bill	*l'addition*
our coats	*nos manteaux*
a cup	*une tasse*
a fork	*une fourchette*
a glass	*un verre*
a knife	*un couteau*

the menu	*le menu*
a napkin	*une serviette*
a plate	*une assiette*
a spoon	*une cuillère*
a toothpick	*un cure-dents*
the wine list	*la carte des vins*
May I have some ...?	*J'aimerais avoir/pourriez-vous m'apporter*
bread	*du pain*
butter	*du beurre*
ice	*de la glace*
(slice of) lemon	*une tranche de citron*
milk	*du lait*
pepper	*du poivre*
salt	*du sel*
sugar	*du sucre*
water	*de l'eau*
I would like it ...	*Je le/la préférerais/je l'aimerais*
baked	*cuit(e) au four*
fried	*frit(e)*
grilled	*grillé(e)*
poached	*poché(e)*
smoked	*fumé(e)*
steamed	*(cuit(e)) à la vapeur*
boiled	*cuit(e) à l'eau/à l'anglaise*
roast	*rôti(e)*
very rare	*bleu*
rare	*saignant(e)*
medium	*à point/rose*
well-done	*bien cuit(e)*

Useful phrases for vegetarians

I am ...	*Je suis ...*
vegetarian	*végétarien (-ienne)*
lacto-ovo-vegetarian	*lacto-ovo-végétarien (-ienne)*
lacto-vegetarian	*lacto-végétarien (-ienne)*
vegan	*végétalien (-ienne)*
I don't eat ...	*Je ne mange pas ...*
I don't eat meat, pork or chicken	*Je ne mange pas de viande, de porc ou de poulet*
I don't eat fish	*Je ne mange pas de poisson*
I eat eggs, milk and cheese	*Je mange des oeufs, du lait et du fromage*
I don't eat eggs, milk or cheese	*Je ne mange pas d'oeufs, de lait ou de fromage*
I don't eat suet/lard/dripping	*Je ne mange pas de suif/de saindoux/de graisse de viande*
Do you have any vegetarian dishes?	*Avez-vous des plats végétariens?*

Is there a vegetarian restaurant near here?	*Y a-t-il un restaurant végétarien près d'ici?*
Is this cheese made with rennet?	*Ce fromage est-il fabriqué avec de la présure animale?*
Do you have a rennet-free cheese?	*Auriez-vous des fromages sans présure?*
Do you serve this dish without meat/eggs/cheese?	*Pourriez-vous préparer ce plat sans viande/oeufs/fromage?*
Does this sauce/soup contain beef/chicken/fish/meat stock?	*Est-ce que cette sauce/soupe contient du bouillon de boeuf/poulet/poisson/ viande?*
Does this dish contain gelatine/aspic?	*Est-ce que ce plat contient de la gélatine/de l'aspic?*
Does this contain organic ingredients?	*C'est bien un plat biologique?*
Do you use GM foods/MSG?	*Utilisez-vous des aliments GMO/du glutamate de sodium?*

Useful phrases for people on special diets etc.

I am diabetic	*Je suis diabétique*
Does this dish contain nuts?	*Est-ce que ce plat contient des noix?*
I am allergic to …	*Je suis allérgique à ...*
I have a peanut/seafood/ wheat allergy	*Je suis allergique à l'arachide/aux fruits de mer/au blé*
I don't eat wheat/gluten	*Je ne mange pas de blé/de gluten*

Drinks

Can I see the wine list, please?	*Puis-je avoir la carte des vins s'il vous plaît?*
I would like a/an...	*J'aimerais avoir*
aperitif	*un apéritif*
another	*un deuxième; encore un(e)*
I would like a glass of …	*Puis-je avoir un verre de/d'*
red wine	*vin rouge*
white wine	*vin blanc*
rose wine	*vin rosé*
sparkling wine	*vin mousseux*
still water	*eau plate*
sparkling water	*eau gazeuse*
tap water	*eau du robinet*
With lemon	*avec du citron*
With ice	*avec de la glace*
With water	*avec de l'eau*
Neat	*sans eau ni glace*
I would like a bottle of....	*Donnez-moi une bouteille de*
this wine	*ce vin-ci*
house red	*de vin rouge maison*
house white	*de vin blanc maison*
Is this wine ...?	*Est-ce un vin ...?*
very dry	*très sec*

dry	*sec*
sweet	*doux/sucré*
local	*de la région*
This wine is	*Le vin...*
not very good	*n'est pas très bon*
not very cold	*n'est pas très frais*
corked	*est bouchonné*
I would like a …	*J'aimerais un/une ...*
fruit juice	*jus de fruits*
lemonade	*limonade*
non-alcoholic beer	*bière non alcoolisée*
non-alcoholic wine	*vin non alcoolisé*
low-alcohol beer	*bière peu alcoolisée*
low-alcohol wine	*vin peu alcoolisé*
non-alcoholic beverage	*boisson non alcoolisée*
decaffeinated coffee/tea	*thé/café décaféiné*
soft drink	*boisson non alcoolisée*

Complaints

This is not what I ordered	*Ce n'est pas ce que j'ai commandé*
I asked for …	*J'ai commandé...*
Could I change this?	*Est-ce que je peux le changer pour autre chose?*
The meat is …	*La viande...*
overdone	*est trop cuite*
underdone	*n'est pas assez cuite*
tough	*est dure*
I don't like this	*Je n'aime pas ça*
The food is cold	*Tout est froid*
This is not fresh	*Ce n'est pas frais*
What is taking so long?	*Pourquoi est-ce si long?*
This is not clean	*Ce n'est pas propre*

Paying

Could I have the bill?	*Pourrez-vous m'apportez l'addition?*
I would like to pay	*Garçon, l'addition*
Can I charge it to my room?	*Vous l'ajoutez à ma note d'hôtel?*
We would like to pay separately	*Chacun paye sa part*
There's a mistake in the bill	*Je crois qu'il y a une erreur sur la facture*
What's this amount for?	*Ce montant représente quoi?*
Is service included?	*Le service est-il compris?*
Do you accept traveller's cheques?	*Acceptez-vous les chèques de voyage?*
Can I pay by credit card?	*Vous acceptez les cartes de crédit?*

Numbers

0	*zéro*	15	*quinze*
1	*un(e)*	16	*seize*
2	*deux*	17	*dix-sept*
3	*trois*	18	*dix-huit*
4	*quatre*	19	*dix-neuf*
5	*cinq*	20	*vingt*
6	*six*	30	*trente*
7	*sept*	40	*quarante*
8	*huit*	50	*cinquante*
9	*neuf*	60	*soixante*
10	*dix*	70	*soixante-dix*
11	*onze*	80	*quatre-vingt(s)*
12	*douze*	90	*quatre-vingt-dix*
13	*treize*	100	*cent*
14	*quatorze*	200 etc.	*deux cents etc.*

French-English

à consommer avant use by
à emporter take home
à l'extérieur outside
à l'intérieur, dans inside
A la tienne Cheers!
A la vôtre! Cheers!
abats giblets
abattis *[de volaille]* giblets, offal
abricot apricot
absinthe absinthe
accompagnement *[garniture]* trimmings
acide sharp
addition bill, *[US]* check
agneau lamb
agnelet spring lamb
agrumes citrus
aiglefin haddock
   aiglefin fumé *[haddock]* smoked haddock
aïgo bouido Provençal garlic soup served over pieces of bread
aigre sour
aigre-doux (-douce) sweet and sour
aiguillat dogfish
ail garlic
aillé(e) garlicky
ailloli, aïoli garlic-flavoured mayonnaise
airelle blueberry
airelle rouge small cranberry
alcool alcohol
   alcool *[fort]* spirits
algue seaweed
aligot de Lozère potato, cheese and garlic purée
alimentation small shop selling general groceries
aliments pour bébés baby food
allumettes matches
   allumettes au fromage (fine) cheese straws
   pommes allumettes matchstick potatoes
alose shad
alouette lark *[bird]*
   alouette sans tête beef olive
aloyau *[faux-filet]* sirloin
amande (douce) almond
   aux amandes with almonds
   pâte d'amandes almond paste
amandine almond tart
amer (amère) bitter
américaine, sauce the cooking liquor from lobster mixed with the lobster coral and cream
amidon starch
amoricaine, à l' with brandy, white wine, onions, and tomatoes

13

amuse-gueule *[hors-d'oeuvre]*   hors-d'oeuvre; *[US]* appetizer
ananas   pineapple
anchoïade   anchovy dipping sauce
anchois   anchovy
   anchois de Norvège   sprat
andouille, andouillette   sausage made of chitterlings, pork meat, onions, seasoning, etc.
aneth   dill
ange de mer   angel fish
anglaise, à l'   plain boiled *[vegetables]*
anglaise, sauce   *see* **crème (à l')anglaise**
anglaise, sauce à l'   thin crème à l'anglaise sauce
angélique   angelica
anguille   eel
   anguille fumée   smoked eel
anis   aniseed
anone *[pomme canelle]*   custard apple
apéritif   aperitif
arachide   peanut
arêtes *[de poisson]*   bones *[fish]*
Armagnac   brandy
aromatisé   flavoured
arôme   smell
arôme *[d'un vin]*   bouquet
arroser   baste
arrow-root   arrowroot
artichaut   artichoke
   fond d'artichaut   artichoke heart
asperge   asparagus
   pointes d'asperges   asparagus tips
aspic   aspic
assaisonné   seasoned
assaisonnement   seasoning
assez   enough
assiette   plate
   assiette anglaise, assiette de viandes froides   assorted cold meat; *[US]* cold cuts
   assiette de viandes grillées   mixed grill
aubergine   aubergine; *[US]* eggplant
   aubergines à la niçoise   aubergine with olive oil, garlic, tomatoes, and black olives
au gratin   with a topping of cheese and breadcrumbs
aumônière   pouch-shaped pancake filled with fruit salad, ice cream, etc.
autruche   ostrich
aveline   filbert
avocat   avocado
   avocat gratiné au four   baked avocado gratin
   avocats gratinés au parmesan   baked avocado and cheese gratin
avoine   oats
avoir faim   (to be) hungry
avoir soif   (to be) thirsty
baba au rhum   rum baba
bacon   bacon
baguette *[pain]*   French bread
baguettes *[chinoises]*   chopsticks
baies   berries
ballottine   faggot

bambou bamboo
banane banana
   bananes flambées banana flambé
   banane verte *[plantain]* plantain
bar *[loup de mer]* sea bass
barbue brill
bardane burdock
barquette small tart *[shaped like a boat]*
basilic basil
basquaise, à la Basque style, with ham, red peppers, tomatoes
bâtonnets batons *[of carrots, etc.]*
baudroie *[lotte de mer]* monkfish
bavarois Bavarian cream
bavette flank (of beef)
bavette, bavoir (child's) bib
bayonnaise, à la braised in Madeira wine
béarnaise, sauce hollandaise sauce but thicker and with tarragon. Served
   warm with grilled meat and fish
bécasse woodcock
bécassine snipe
béchamel, sauce béchamel a basic white sauce made from butter, flour and
   seasoned milk
beignet *[pâte frite et sucrée]* doughnut, fritter
   beignet viennois doughnut
   beignet fourré à la confiture jam doughnut
   beignet de bananes banana fritter
   beignets de légumes vegetable fritter
   beignet de pommes apple fritter
belon type of oyster from Brittany
Bercy, sauce chopped shallots cooked in butter with white wine and fish
   stock added
bergamote bergamot
bette chard
betterave beetroot
   betteraves rouges à la crême creamed beetroot
beurre butter
   avec (du) beurre; au beurre with butter
   sans beurre without butter
   beurre blanc sauce of white wine, vinegar, shallots, butter
   beurre clarifié *[cuisine indienne]* ghee
   beurre d'anchois anchovy butter
   beurre de cacah(o)uètes/d'arachides peanut butter
   beurre de cacao cocoa butter
   beurre de truffes truffle butter
   beurre fondu melted butter
   beurre noir browned melted butter with vinegar and seasoning
   beurre noisette brown butter
   beurre sans sel unsalted butter
biberon baby's bottle
bien cuit(e) well done
bière beer
   bière (à la) pression draught beer
   bière anglaise blonde ale
   bière anglaise pression bitter (beer)
   bière blonde lager
bifteck steak; *[US]* beefsteak
bigarade, sauce sauce made from the remains of duck with Seville orange
   and lemon juice

bigorneau winkle
biologique organic
biscotte crispbread, rusk
biscuits *[gâteaux secs]* biscuits; *[US]* cookies
    biscuits à la cuillère sponge fingers
bisque de homard lobster bisque
blanc d'oeuf egg white
blanchaille whitebait
blanchi(e) blanched
   blanchir to blanch
blanc-manger blancmange
blanquette de veau veal stew in cream sauce
blé wheat
   blé complet wholewheat
   blé concassé bulgur wheat, bulgar wheat
   blé noir *[sarrasin]* buckwheat
blennie butterfish
blette chard
bleu very rare (meat)
blinis blinis
boeuf beef
   boeuf (à la) bourguignonne see **bourguignonne**
   boeuf de conserve corned beef
   boeuf en daube beef casserole
   boeuf stroganoff beef stroganoff
   rôti de boeuf *[rosbif]* roast beef
boire drink *[verb]*
boisson drink
   boisson chaude hot drink
   boisson fraîche cold drink
   boisson (gazeuse) non alcoolisée soft drink
boîte (de conserve) tin; *[US]* can
   en boîte tinned; *[US]* canned
bol bowl
bombe bombe
bon marché cheap
bonbon sweet; *[US]* candy
bon(ne) good
bonne femme cooked with leeks and potatoes
bonite bonito; skipjack tuna
bordeaux rouge claret, red Bordeaux
bordelaise, à la with red wine, bone marrow, mushrooms and artichokes
bouchée (feuilletée) vol au vent
   bouchée à la reine chicken vol au vent
boucherie chevaline butcher's selling horsemeat
boudin blanc sausage of finely ground white meat
boudin noir black pudding
bouillabaisse Provençal fish stew
bouilloire kettle
bouillir to boil
bouilli(e) *[cuit(e) à l'eau, à l'anglaise]* boiled
bouillon broth, stock
   bouillon de boeuf beef stock, beef broth
   bouillon de légumes vegetable stock
   bouillon végétarien vegetable stock
boulangerie bakery
boule flat round loaf with coarse crust

French-English

boule de glace   scoop of ice cream
boules de picoulat   Catalan dish of pork meatballs in a bean casserole
boulette de pâte   dumpling
boulette de viande   meat ball
bouquet garni   bouquet garni *[mixed herbs]*
bouquet *[crevette rose]*   prawn
bourgeoise, à la   cooked in family style
bourguignonne, à la   with red wine, mushrooms, small onions and bacon
bourrache   borage
bourride   Provençal fish dish with garlic mayonnaise
bouteille   bottle
   bouteille d'eau (minérale)   bottle of (mineral) water
   bouteille de vin   bottle of wine
braisé(e)   braised
braiser   to braise
branche   stick, stalk
brandade de morue   salt cod purée
brasserie   café-restaurant serving simple meals and beer; brewery
brebis   ewe
brème   bream
brème de mer   sea bream
brési   air-dried beef from Franche-Comté
brik   North African pasty filled with egg, tuna and vegetables
brioche   brioche
Brocciu   Corsican cream cheese made with sheep or goat's milk
broche, à la   grilled on a skewer over a flame
brochet   pike
brochette   skewer
brocolis   broccoli
brugnon *[nectarine]*   nectarine
brûlé(e)   burnt
brûler   to burn
brune, sauce   *see* **demi-glace**
buccin   whelk
bûche de Noël   Christmas log
buffet   buffet
buffle   buffalo
cabécou   goat's or ewe's milk cheese, often served warm
cabillaud   (fresh) cod
cacah(o)uète   peanut
cacao   cocoa, chocolate
café   café
café   coffee
   café au lait   coffee with milk
   café complet   continental breakfast
   café crème, un crème   (large) coffee with cream or milk
   café décaféiné   decaffeinated coffee; decaf
   café express   espresso, expresso coffee
   café filtre   filter coffee
   café instantané   instant coffee
   café liégeois   iced coffee served with cream or whipped cream
   café noir   black coffee
   café moulu   ground coffee
   café soluble   instant coffee
   petit crème   (small) coffee with cream of milk
caféine   caffeine
   sans caféine *[décaféiné]*   caffeine-free, decaffeinated

cafetière   coffee pot
caille   quail
   oeufs de caille   quails' eggs
caissier   cashier
cake   fruit cake
calmar *[encornet]*   squid
Calvados   apple brandy
camomille *[infusion de, tisane de]*   camomile (tea)
canapés   canapés
canard   duck *[domestic]*
   canard (à la) rouennaise   duck stuffed with its own liver, in a red wine sauce
   canard à l'orange   duck with oranges
   canard de Barbarie   Barbary duck
   canard sauvage   wild duck
caneton   duckling
canette   duckling *[female]*
canneberge   cranberry
cannelle   cinnamon
cannelloni   cannelloni
   cannelloni aux champignons   mushroom cannelloni
cantaloup   cantaloup (melon)
cappuccino   cappuccino coffee
câpres   capers
carafe   carafe
   carafe d'eau   carafe of water, jug of water
caramel   caramel
   caramel (au beurre)   toffee
carbon(n)ade de boeuf   beef braised with onions and beer
carbonara   carbonara
cardamome   cardamom
cari   curry
carotte   carrot
   carottes Vichy   carrots stewed in butter, sugar and seasoning
carpaccio   wafer-thin slices of raw beef or tuna
carpe   carp
carré   rack
   carré *[d'agneau, de porc, etc.]*   rack of ribs
   carré d'agneau   rack of lamb
carrelet   plaice
carte   menu
   carte, à la   each menu item is priced separately
carte des vins   wine list
carthame   safflower
cartilage *[croquant]*   gristle
carvi   caraway
casher   kosher
cassate   cassata
casserole   casserole
cassis   blackcurrant
cassoulet   casserole from Languedoc, with haricot beans, pork, sausage or goose
   cassoulet végétarien   vegetarian bean casserole
catalane, à la   with tomatoes, black olives and garlic
cavaillon   honeydew melon
caviar   caviar
   caviar d'aubergine   puréed roasted aubergines

cédrat citron
céleri celery
céleri-rave celeriac
cendrier ashtray
cèpe cep; porcini mushroom
céréales (froides) (breakfast) cereal
cerfeuil chervil
cerise cherry
   cerise confite glacé cherry
   cerise noire black cherry
cervelas saveloy
cervelle brains
   cervelle de veau calf's brains
chaise chair
   chaise haute highchair
chambré(e) at room temperature
champagne champagne
champignon mushroom
   champignons à l'ail garlic mushrooms
   champignons de Paris button mushrooms
   champignons farcis stuffed mushrooms
   champignons sauvages wild mushrooms
chandelier candlestick
chandelle candle
changer *[de]* to change
chanterelle chanterelle *[mushroom]*
Chantilly (with) whipped cream
chapelure breadcrumbs
chapon capon
charbon de bois charcoal
chariot trolley
charlotte charlotte
   charlotte aux pommes apple charlotte
chasseur, sauce red wine boiled with shallots, garlic, mushrooms, tomatoes and demi-glace sauce
châtaigne sweet chestnut
   châtaigne d'eau water chestnut
chateaubriand, chateaubriant Chateaubriand *[thick piece of grilled fillet of beef]*
chaud(e) hot *[not cold]*
chaud-froid jelly, aspic *[savoury]*
   chaud-froid de poulet chicken in jelly; aspic of chicken
chaudrée chowder
(faire) chauffer to heat up
chausson turnover
   chausson aux pommes apple turnover
chef chef, cook
cher/chère expensive
cherry brandy *[liqueur de cerise]* cherry brandy
cheval horsemeat
cheveux d'ange angel hair *[pasta]*
chèvre goat
chèvres en papillote goats cheese filo parcels
chevreuil venison *[deer]*
   chevreuil *[à la scandinave]* reindeer
chicorée frisée endive, frisée salad
chien de mer dogfish

chili con carne *[plat mexicain]*   chilli con carne
   chili végétarien   vegetable chilli
chinchard   horse mackerel
chips   (potato) crisps; *[US]* chips
chocolat   chocolate, cocoa
   chocolat au lait   milk chocolate
   chocolat blanc   white chocolate
   chocolat glacé   chocolate-covered ice lolly
   chocolat noir   dark, plain chocolate
   un chocolat *[bonbon]*   a chocolate *[sweet]*
   un chocolat *[une tasse]*   a cup of cocoa/hot chocolate
choisir   to choose
choix   choice
   au choix, choix de   choice of
   choix de légumes   assorted vegetables
chou   cabbage
   chou blanc   white cabbage
   chou de Chine   Chinese cabbage
   chou rouge   red cabbage
   chou vert *[pommé]*   green cabbage
   chou vert frisé *[non pommé]*   kale
   chou vert frisé *[pommé]*   savoy cabbage
chou à la crème   cream puff
choucroute   pickled cabbage
chou-fleur   cauliflower
   chou-fleur sauce Mornay, au gratin   cauliflower cheese
chou-navet   swede
chou-rave   kohlrabi
choux de Bruxelles   Brussels sprouts
ciboule   spring onion; *[US]* scallion
ciboulette   chives
cidre (de pomme)   cider
   cidre de poire   perry *[pear cider]*
cigare   cigar
cigarettes   cigarettes
   cigarettes russes   sweet rolled crisp wafer filled with hazelnut cream
citron   lemon
   citron pressé   freshly squeezed lemon juice drunk diluted with water and
   sugar
   citron vert *[lime]*   lime
citronnelle   lemon grass
cive   spring onion; *[US]* scallion
civet   stew of rabbit, hare or other game
   civet de lièvre   jugged hare
civette   chives
clafoutis aux cérises   cherries baked in a thick batter
clafoutis de la Foret-Noire   Black Forest gateaux
claire   type of oyster
clémentine   clementine
climatisé(e)   air-conditioned
clou de girofle   clove
clovisse   clam
club sandwich   club sandwich
Coca   coke
cochon de lait   suckling pig
cocktail   cocktail
coeur   heart
   coeur à la crème   curd cheese dessert made in heart-shaped mould

coeur d'artichaut artichoke heart
cognac brandy
coing quince
Cointreau orange liqueur
colin *[merlu]* hake
colin *[lieu noir]* saithe
colvert mallard
compagnon(s) de table dining companion(s)
complet full (restaurant)
complet wholemeal, brown
compote de fruits stewed fruit
compris(e) included
compte account
concombre cucumber
condiment condiment
confiserie shop selling handmade chocolates, sweets and cakes
confit de canard/d'oie duck/goose preserved in own fat
confit(e) *[fruit, etc.]* candied
confiture jam
   confiture de fraises strawberry jam
   confiture d'oranges orange marmalade
congelés frozen foods
congre *[anguille de mer]* conger eel
conserves preserves
consommé clear soup, consommé
   consommé en tasse/en gelée jellied consommé
contrefilet sirloin steak
coq au vin chicken cooked in red wine
coque, à la soft-boiled *[egg]*
coques cockles
coquetier egg cup
coquillages shellfish
coquille shell
   coquille St Jacques scallop
coriandre coriander
cornet (de glace) *[ice cream]* cone, cornet
corn flakes cornflakes
cornichon gherkin
   cornichon saumuré/au vinaigre pickled gherkin
corsé(e) full-bodied *[wine]*
côte chop
   côte de porc pork chop
côtelette cutlet, chop
   côtelette d'agneau lamb chop
   côtelette de chevreuil venison cutlet
côtes ribs
   côtes de boeuf ribs of beef
cotriade Breton fish stew with onions, potato and cream
coulibiac fish pie stuffed with rice and hard-boiled egg
coulis coulis *[sauce of sieved puréed fruit]*
coupe glacée dish of ice cream; sundae
couper to cut
courge squash, marrow *[vegetable]*
courgette courgette; *[US]* zucchini
   courgettes farcies stuffed courgettes
court-bouillon fish stock
couscous couscous

couteau knife
couvert cover charge
crabe *[tourteau]* crab
   crabe décortiqué prepared crab
   crabe froid à l'anglaise/à la russe dressed crab
crème cream
   crème légère/épaisse single/double cream
   à la crème with cream; with cream sauce
   crème aigre sour cream
   crème (à l') anglaise thick egg custard made from egg yolks and milk
   crème au beurre butter cream *[filling for cake]*
   crème caramel crème caramel *[baked custard with caramel sauce]*
   crème Chantilly, crème fouettée whipped cream
   crème fleurette top of the milk; single cream
   crème fraîche crème fraîche *[soured double cream]*
   crème pâtissière confectioner's custard
   un crème, un café crème a (large) coffee with cream or milk
crème (de) *[velouté]* cream of
   crème d'asperges cream of asparagus soup
   crème de tomates cream of tomato soup
   crème de volaille cream of chicken soup
crémeux (-euse) creamy
créole *[savoury]* with rice, tomatoes, pepper; *[sweet]* with orange peel
crêpe pancake
   crêpes gratinées stuffed pancakes with cheese topping
   crêpes Suzette pancakes with orange brandy
cresson cress
   cresson de fontaine watercress
crevette (grise) shrimp
   crevette rose king prawn
   crevettes mayonnaise shrimp cocktail
croissant croissant
   croissant au beurre croissant made with butter
croque-madame fried cheese and ham sandwich topped with a fried egg
croquembouche pyramid of profiteroles with caramel, served at weddings
croque-monsieur fried cheese and ham sandwich
croquette de poisson fish cake
   croquettes de pommes de terre potato croquettes
crottin de chèvre small round goat's cheese
croustade bread or pastry case
croustillant crisp
croûte fried or toasted bread base
croûtons croutons
crudités raw sliced vegetables as an hors d-oeuvre
cru(e) raw, uncooked
crumble crumble
crustacés shellfish
cube: en cubes diced *[cubed]*
cuillère, cuiller spoon
   cuillère à café coffee spoon
   cuillère à dessert tablespoon
   cuillère à soupe soup spoon
   cuillère à thé teaspoon
cuisine cookery, cooking, kitchen
   cuisine bourgeoise plain home cooking
   cuisine maigre, minceur low-fat cooking
   cuisine régionale regional cooking
   cuisine végétarienne vegetarian cooking

nouvelle cuisine   nouvelle cuisine
cuisinière   stove
cuisses de grenouilles   frog's legs
cuissot   haunch
cuit(e)   cooked, done
 cuit(e) au four   baked
 cuit(e) à grande friture   deep-fried
 cuit(e) à la vapeur   steamed
 pas assez cuit(e)   underdone
 trop cuit(e)   overdone
cumin   cumin (seed)
 cumin des prés   caraway (seeds)
curcuma   turmeric
cure-dent(s)   toothpick
curry   curry, curry powder
dacquoise   meringue filled with cream and soft fruit
dame blanche   chocolate sundae with Chantilly
darne de saumon   salmon steak
date de péremption   expiry date
datte   date
daube   rich casserole of meat, vegetables, garlic, herbs, and red wine
daurade   bream
dé: en dés   diced, cubed, chopped
déca   decaf
 un déca   a decaf coffee
décaféiné   decaffeinated
 café décaféiné   decaffeinated coffee
découper   to carve
défense de fumer   no smoking
dégeler   to thaw
déglacer   to deglaze *[mix meat juices at bottom of pan with stock or wine]*
dégustation   tasting
déguster   to taste, to savour
dehors   outdoors
déjeuner *[lunch]*   lunch; to have lunch
délicieux (-euse)   delicious
demi   half
demi-bouteille   half bottle
demi-glace, sauce   a mixture of equal parts of espagnole sauce and brown
 stock reduced, used as a basis for other sauces
demi-litre   half a litre
demi-sec   semi-dry
désossé(e) *[en filets]*   filleted
désossé(e) *[sans os, sans arête]*   boned
désosser *[lever les filets]*   to fillet; *[enlever les os, les arêtes]* to debone
dessert   dessert
desservir (la table)   to clear up
diable (à la)   devilled
 rognons à la (sauce) diable   devilled kidneys
 diable, sauce   a sauce of chopped shallots, white wine, vinegar, cayenne
 pepper and coarsely ground white pepper. Served with fried or grilled fish or
 meat
dijonnaise, à la   with mustard, or blackcurrants
dinde   turkey
 dinde rôtie   roast turkey
dîner *[midi]*   lunch
dîner *[soir]*   dinner, supper

dîner dinner party
dorade (aux sourcils d'or) gilthead bream
dorée *[poisson]* John Dory
dorer, faire dorer to brown
dormeur *[tourteau]* crab
double double (shot of spirits)
doux *[douce]* soft
dragées sugared almonds
du pays/local(e) local
Dubarry, à la with cauliflower
duchesse piped potato mixed with egg yolk
dur(e) hard; hard-boiled; tough *[meat]*
duxelles, sauce white wine, mushrooms and shallots mixed with demi-glace
    sauce and tomato purée
eau water
    eau bouillie boiling water
    eau chaude hot water
    eau froide cold water
    eau potable drinking water
    eau du robinet tap water
    eau de seltz soda water
    eau de source spring water
    eau en bouteille bottled water
    eau gazeuse sparkling water, fizzy water
    eau glacée/très froide iced water
    eau minérale mineral water
    eau plate still (mineral) water
    eau tonique/tonic tonic water
    sans eau ni glace neat; *[US]* straight *[whisky, etc.]*
eau de vie brandy
ébréché(e) *[verre, assiette]* chipped (glass, plate)
échalote shallot
échanger to change
éclair éclair
    éclair au chocolat chocolate eclair
écorce (de citron, etc.) (lemon, etc.) peel
    écorce confite candied peel
    écorce râpée *[zeste]* grated peel, zest
écrevisse crayfish
édulcorant sweetener
églefin haddock
émincés de veau/volaille thinly sliced cooked veal/chicken, served in a sauce
en beignets in batter
en daube meat stewed with red wine, onions, garlic, vegetables and herbs
en gelée jellied
endive chicory
enrobé de coated with
entrecôte rib steak of beef
    entrecôte à la bordelaise rib steak cooked in sauce made of Bordeaux
    wine, butter, herbs, shallots, bone marrow
entrée starter
entremets salé savoury
épais thick
épaule *[palette]* shoulder
éperlan smelt
épice spice
épicé(e) spicy

épicerie   general store/grocer's
   épicerie fine   delicatessen
épinard   spinach
   épinards en purée   creamed spinach
éplucher   to peel
escalope   escalope
   escalope de dinde   turkey escalope
   escalope de veau   veal escalope
escargot   snail
espagnole, sauce   sauce made from browned flour and butter mixed with
   tomato purée and brown stock flavoured with browned vegetables
espadon   swordfish
espresso   espresso
estragon   tarragon
esturgeon   sturgeon
étiquette   label
excellent(e)   excellent
express   espresso
faînes   beech nuts
faisan   pheasant
faisselle   curd cheese
fait à moitié   half done
falafel   falafel
far breton   Breton speciality of prune shortcake
farce   stuffing
farci(e)   stuffed (with)
farine   flour
   farine d'avoine   oatmeal
   farine de blé   wheat flour
   farine de blé complet   wholewheat flour
   farine de châtaigne   chestnut flour
   farine de maïs   cornmeal, polenta
faux filet   sirloin steak
fécule de maïs   cornflour
felafel   falafel
fenouil   fennel
fermé   shut, closed
fermier *[oeuf, poulet]*   free range, farm *[egg, chicken]*
fermière   with carrots, turnip, onion, celery
fête   party
feuille de laurier   bay leaf
feuilles de vigne   vine leaves
feuilleté   sweet or savoury puff pasty
   feuilleté au fromage   puff pastry with cheese filling
fève   bean
   fève des marais, grosse fève   broad bean
fiadone   Corsican lemon-flavoured cheesecake
ficelle   French bread *[very long thin loaf]*
ficelle picarde   ham rolled in pancake served with white sauce
figue   fig
filet   fillet; tenderloin
   filet de porc   pork tenderloin
   filet de boeuf   fillet of beef; *[US]* beef tenderloin
   filet de boeuf en croûte   beef Wellington
   filet mignon   steak cut from end of fillet
   filet de volaille   breast of chicken or turkey
fines herbes   mixed herbs

flageolet   flageolet (beans)
flambé(e)   flambé
flamiche   northern French sweet or savoury pastry tart
flan   baked custard
flet   flounder
flétan   halibut
   flétan noir   black halibut, Greenland halibut
flocons   flakes
   flocons d'avoine   rolled oats
florentine   with spinach
foie   liver
   foies de poulets/de volaille   chicken livers
   foie de veau   calf's liver
   foie d'oie, foie gras   goose liver pâté
fondant *[sweet]*   fondant
   fondant au chocolat   chocolate fudge (icing)
fondant *[meat, vegetables]*   tender
fondue   fondue
   fondue bourguignonne   meat fondue
   fondue savoyarde   cheese fondue
forestière   with mushrooms, bacon, sauté potatoes
forêt-noire   Black Forest gateau
forfait boissons   drinks included
formule   menu option
fort(e)   strong
fougasse   Provençal flat bread
fougazi   aniseed biscuits
four   oven
   cuit(e) au four   baked
   pommes au four   baked apples
fourchette   fork
fourré(e) (à/au/aux)   filled (with), stuffed (with)
frais (fraîche)   fresh
fraise   strawberry
   fraise des bois, fraise sauvage   wild strawberry
   glace à la fraise   strawberry ice cream
framboise   raspberry
frangipane   rich pastry cream filling made with ground almonds
friand   puffed pastry filled with meat
   friand à la saucisse   sausage roll
   friand au jambon   ham roll *[in puff pastry]*
fricandeau   braised veal
fricassée   stew
   fricassée de boeuf   stewed steak, beef stew
frisée aux noix   curly endive salad with walnuts
frire   to fry
frit(e)   fried
frites   (potato) chips; *[US]* French fries
friture   fried food
   friture de poissons   mixed fried fish
froid(e)   cold
fromage   cheese
   fromage 'cottage'   cottage cheese
   fromage à la crème   cream cheese
   fromage à pâte dure   hard cheese
   fromage à pâte molle   soft cheese
   fromage blanc   creamy low-fat cow's milk cheese
   fromage bleu   blue cheese

    fromage de (lait de) brebis sheep's milk cheese
    fromage de chèvre goat's cheese
    fromage de lait entier full-fat cheese
    fromage de pays local cheese
    fromage frais soft cow's milk cheese, often with added cream
fromage de tête brawn
froment wheat
fruit fruit
    fruits confits crystallised fruit
    fruits frais fresh fruit
    fruits de mer seafood, shellfish
fumé(e) smoked, cured
fumée smoke [*noun*]
fumer to smoke [*a cigarette*]
fumeur/fumeuse smoker
fumer to smoke [*food*]
galantine galantine
galette pancake
    galette de pommes de terre potato pancake
    galette de sarrasin buckwheat pancake
galette des Rois Twelfth Night cake [*round puff pastry cake with almond paste filling*]
gambas prawns
garbure thick vegetable soup of cabbage, beans, potatoes, leeks, ham, herbs, etc.
garçon waiter
garni with vegetables
garnis (de) garnished
garniture filling; garnish; serving of vegetables
gaspacho gazpacho
gastronomique gourmet
gâteau cake, gateau
    gâteau à la crème cream cake
    gâteau au chocolat chocolate cake
    gâteau au fromage blanc cheesecake
    gâteau au gingembre ginger cake
    gâteau aux carottes carrot cake
    gâteau breton rich cake, often made with nuts and dried fruit
    gâteau d'anniversaire birthday cake
    gâteau de mariage wedding cake
    gâteau de Noël [*anglais*] Christmas cake
    gâteau de Pithiviers round puff or flaky pastry tart filled with almond paste
    gâteau de Savoie madeira cake
    gâteau mousseline sponge cake
    gâteau quatre-quarts pound cake
    gâteau renversé upside-down cake
    gâteau roulé Swiss roll
    gâteaux secs biscuits; [*US*] cookies
gaufre de miel honeycomb
gaufres waffles
gaufrette wafer
gazeux/gazeuse carbonated, gassy
gélatine gelatine
gelée jelly
    gelée à la menthe mint jelly
    gelée de groseilles redcurrant jelly
genièvre [*eau-de-vie*] gin

baie de genièvre juniper berry
génoise sponge cake
    génoise au citron madeira cake
germe de blé wheatgerm
germes de luzerne alfafa sprouts
germes de soja bean sprouts
gésiers gizzards
gibier (à plume/à poil) game
gigot d'agneau leg of lamb
    gigot brayaude leg of lamb cooked with garlic
gin-tonic gin and tonic
gingembre ginger
gîte à la noix silverside
glaçage icing
glace ice
    avec glace with ice; *[whisky, etc.]* with ice, on the rocks
    sans eau ni glace neat; *[US]* straight *[whisky, etc.]*
glace *[crème glacée]* ice cream
    glace à la vanille vanilla ice cream
glace *[pour gâteaux]* icing
glacé(e) *[very cold]* icy cold
glacé(e) *[de sucre, etc.]* glazed
glaçon ice cube
glouteron burdock
glucides *[hydrates de carbone]* carbohydrate
glutamate monosodique/de sodium monosodium glutamate (MSG)
gluten gluten
    sans gluten gluten free
gnocchi Parmentier potato dumplings
gombo gumbo, okra, ladies finger
gougère choux pastry ring with added cheese
goujon *[poisson]* gudgeon
    goujons de poulet goujons, strips of fried fish or chicken
goulash, goulasch goulash
gourmet gourmet
gousse d'ail garlic clove
gousse de vanille vanilla pod/bean
goût taste
goyave guava
grain grain
    grains de genièvre juniper berries
    grains de raisin grapes
graine seed
    graines de pavot poppy seeds
    graines de sésame sesame seeds
    graines de tournesol sunflower seeds
graisse de rognon de bœuf suet
graisse de rôti dripping
grand(e) big
granité sorbet; granita
gras fat *[noun]*
    qui contient peu de gras low in fat
gras (grasse) fat *[adj]*
gras-double tripe
gratin dauphinois scalloped potatoes cooked with cream
gratiné(e) browned; *[US]* au gratin
gratuit(e) complimentary, free *[of charge]*

grecque, à la with olive oil and spices
grenade pomegranate
grenadine grenadine
gribiche, sauce mashed hard-boiled egg yolks blended with oil and vinegar, flavoured with capers and gherkins, tarragon, chervil and parsley
gril grill *[noun]*
grillade grilled piece of meat
   grillade de veau grilled veal chop
grillé(e) grilled, toasted
   grillé(e) au barbecue barbecued
   grillé(e) au charbon de bois charcoal-grilled
griller to grill
grive thrush
grondin gurnard
groseille à maquereau gooseberry
   groseille rouge redcurrant
gros sel rock salt
grosse fève broad bean
grouse grouse
guacamole guacamole
gueule de bois hangover
guimauve marshmallow
hachis *[viande hachée]* minced meat
   hachis de boeuf minced beef; *[US]* ground beef
   hachis Parmentier shepherd's pie
haddock *[aiglefin fumé]* smoked haddock
hamburger hamburger
   hamburger végétal vegetarian burger
hareng herring
   hareng mariné pickled herring
   hareng saur/fumé kipper
   hareng roulé (mariné) rollmop (herring)
harenguet sprat
haricot bean
   haricots blancs haricot beans
   haricots blancs aux tomates baked beans
   haricots grimpants runner beans
   haricots noirs black beans
   haricots pinto pinto beans
   haricots rouges kidney beans, red beans
   haricots verts green beans, French beans
harissa hot chilli paste served with couscous
herbes aromatiques mixed herbs
heure du thé tea-time
hochepot Belgian thick soup of pork, beef, mutton, cabbage and other vegetables
hollandaise, sauce thick sauce made from egg yolks, a little pepper and vinegar, whisked over a gentle heat
homard lobster
hongroise, à la with paprika and fresh cream
houmous hummus
hors d'oeuvre hors d'oeuvre; *[US]* appetizer
hot dog *[saucisse de Francfort dans un petit pain]* hot dog
houmous hummus
huile oil
   à l'huile with oil
   huile d'arachide peanut oil, groundnut oil
   huile de maïs corn oil

29

huile de noix walnut oil
huile de pépins de raisin grapeseed oil
huile de tournesol sunflower oil
huile d'olive olive oil
huile d'olive vierge virgin olive oil
huile d'olive extra vierge extra virgin olive oil
huile végétale vegetable oil
huître oyster
hydromel mead
hyposodé(e) low-salt
igname yam
îles flottantes floating islands *[dessert of poached egg whites in custard]*
incorporer to blend; to mix
indienne, à l' curried
infusion herbal tea
ingrédients ingredients
intoxication alimentaire food poisoning
jambon ham
jambon de Bayonne smoked cured ham
jambon blanc (slice of boiled) ham
jambon de Parme Parma ham
jambon fumé (désossé) gammon
jambon poché boiled ham
jambon de York York ham (British-style)
jardinière garnished with spring vegetables
jarret knuckle, shank
jaune d'oeuf egg yolk
jellied en gelée
jeûne fast (not eat)
julienne julienne *[cut into fine strips]*
jus juice *[of meat, fruit]*
au jus served in its own juices
jus (de fruits) (fruit) juice
jus de citron lemon juice
jus de fruits fruit juice
jus d'orange orange juice
jus de pomme apple juice
jus de tomate tomato juice
kaki date plum, kaki
kasher *[casher]* kosher
kébab *[brochette]* kebab
ketchup *[sauce tomate]* ketchup
kirsch cherry liqueur
kiwi kiwi fruit
kouign amman Breton rich puff pastry butter cake
koulibiac *see* **coulibiac**
kumquat kumquat
lactose lactose
lait milk
au lait entier full fat, whole milk
avec (du) lait, au lait with milk
sans lait without milk
lait caillé curd
lait condensé condensed milk
lait de beurre *[babeurre]* buttermilk
lait de brebis ewe's milk
lait de chèvre goat's milk
lait de coco coconut milk

    lait de soja soya milk
    lait de vache cow's milk
    lait demi-écrémé semi-skimmed milk
    lait écrémé skimmed milk
    lait entier full-cream milk
laitance soft roe
laitier dairy
    produits laitiers dairy products
laitue *[salade]* lettuce
    laitue iceberg iceberg lettuce
    laitue romaine cos lettuce
langouste crawfish, spiny lobster
langoustine Dublin bay prawn
langue tongue
    langue de boeuf ox tongue
lapereau young rabbit
lapin rabbit
lard de poitrine streaky bacon
    lard fumé smoked bacon
lardons cubed pieces of bacon
lasagne lasagne
    lasagne végétarienne/aux légumes vegetarian lasagne
lavabo toilet
lavande lavender
leberwurst liver sausage
léger, légère mild
légume vegetable
    légumes à vapeur steamed vegetables
    légumes bouillis boiled vegetables
    légumes braisés braised vegetables
    légumes verts green vegetables, greens
    légumes variés assorted vegetables
    petits légumes baby vegetables
légumineuses pulses
lentille lentil
    lentilles de Puy Puy lentils *[green or brown]*
letchi lychee
levure yeast
l'heure du déjeuner lunchtime
l'heure du dîner dinner time
lieu jaune pollack
lieu noir saithe, coley
lièvre hare
limande dab
limande-sole lemon sole
lime *[citron vert]* lime
limonade *[citron pressé]* lemonade
lingue ling
liqueur liqueur
lisette small mackerel
litchi lychee
litre litre
loganberry loganberry
longe (de veau/porc/chevreuil) loin (of veal/pork/venison)
lotte (d'eau douce) burbot
    lotte de mer *[baudroie]* monkfish
louche ladle

loup bass
    loup de mer sea bass
lyonnaise with sautéed onions
lyonnaise, sauce sauce of onion, vinegar and brown stock
macaron macaroon
macaroni macaroni
    macaroni au gratin macaroni cheese
macédoine de fruits fruit salad; fruit cocktail
macédoine de légumes mixed vegetables
mâche lamb's lettuce
macis mace
macrobiotique macrobiotic
madeleine small scallop-shaped sponge cake
madère *[vin]* Madeira
madère, sauce a demi-glace sauce with added Madeira and butter, served
    with ox tongue
magasin de produits diététiques health shop
magasin de fruits et légumes greengrocer
maïs *[plant]* maize; *[US]* corn
    maïs (en épis/en grains) sweetcorn
    épi de maïs, maïs en épi corn on the cob *[sweetcorn]*
    farine de maïs cornmeal
    maïs soufflé popcorn
    semoule de maïs *[polenta]* polenta
maison *[fait à la]* home-made, of the house
    pâté maison home-made pâté
maître d'hôtel, beurre butter mixed with lemon juice and chopped parsley,
    served with grilled meat or fish
malt malt
mandarine mandarin
manger to eat
mange-touts mangetout, sugar snap peas
mangouste, mangoustan mangosteen
mangue mango
maquereau mackerel
    maquereau mariné au vin blanc mackerel marinated in white wine
marc grape brandy
marcassin young boar
marchand de vin, sauce a sauce of red wine, shallots and stock
marché market
margarine margarine
marinade marinade
mariné(e) marinated
marjolaine marjoram
marmelade (orange) marmalade
marmite thick stew or soup; pot
marquise rich frozen dessert of fruit or chocolate
marron sweet chestnut
    marrons glacés candied chestnuts
    purée de marrons chestnut purée
marsala Marsala wine
massepain marzipan
matelote fish stew
mauvais(e) bad, off *[food, wine]*
mayonnaise mayonnaise
    mayonnaise à l'ail garlic mayonnaise
méchoui North African spit-roasted lamb

méchouia   North African mixed vegetable salad
médaillon   medallion *[round piece of meat or fish]*
mélanger   to blend; to mix
mélasse   treacle
mélisse   lemon balm
melon   melon
menthe   mint
   menthe poivrée   peppermint
   menthe verte   garden mint
menu   menu
   menu à prix fixe   set menu
   menu de Noël   Christmas menu
   menu du jour   today's menu
   menu enfants   children's menu
   menu gastronomique   gourmet menu
   menu touristique   mid-price set menu
merguez   North African spicy beef or lamb sausage
meringue   meringue
merlan   whiting
merlu *[colin]*   hake
mérou   grouper
mesclun   Provençal salad of rocket, lamb's lettuce, endive
meunière, à la   coated in flour and fried in butter
meurette   Burgundy fish stew in red wine
mi-cuit(e)   parboiled
miel   honey
   rayon de miel   honeycomb
mijoter   to simmer
milanaise   *[pasta]* with parmesan, tomato sauce; *[escalope]* breaded
milk-shake   milkshake
millefeuille   millefeuille, cream slice made with puff pastry
millésime   vintage
minestrone   minestrone *[soup]*
mirabelle   small yellow plum
mode, à la   with ice cream
moelle   bone marrow
moitié cuit, à   half-cooked
mollusque   mollusc
monnaie   change *[coins]*
Mont Blanc   dessert of chestnut puree with whipped cream
morceau   piece
morilles   morels *[mushrooms]*
Mornay   with white sauce and cheese
morue   cod
mouclade   mussel stew with white wine, onion, cream and egg yolks
moudre   to grind
moule   mussel
   moules marinière   moules marinière *[cooked with white wine, onions, parsley]*
moulin à poivre   pepper mill
moulu(e)   ground *[pepper, etc.]*
moussaka   moussaka
mousse *[de poisson, etc.]*   mousse *[fish, etc.]*
   mousse au chocolat   chocolate mousse
mousseline   mousse; purée
mousseline, sauce   hollandaise sauce mixed with whipped double cream
moutarde   mustard

    moutarde de Meaux whole grain mustard
mouton mutton
muffin muffin
mulet gris grey mullet
mûr(e) ripe
mûre *[de ronce]* blackberry
mûre *[du mûrier]* mulberry
myrtille blueberry, billberry, whortleberry
nage, à la *[fish]* served in its stock
Nantua with crayfish
Nantua, sauce béchamel sauce with cream and crayfish butter
nappe tablecloth
nappé de coated with *[sauce etc.]*
nature *[yoghurt, etc.]* plain; *[tea, coffee]* without milk
navarin lamb stew
navet turnip
navet swede
nèfle medlar
nem spring roll
niçoise, à la with olive oil, garlic, tomatoes, black olives
noisette hazelnut, cobnut
noisette *[de viande]* noisette *[small round piece of fillet or loin]*
noix nut; walnut
    noix d'acajou, noix de cajou cashew nut
    noix de coco coconut
    noix de coco séchée desiccated coconut
    noix muscade nutmeg
    noix de pécan, noix de pacane pecan nut
    noix du Brésil Brazil nut
    noix du noyer blanc d'Amérique hickory nut
    noix du noyer de Queensland macadamia nuts
noix de veau tender cut of veal
non fumeurs *[section]* non-smoking *[area]*
nonnette spiced bun
normande, à la with cream, Calvados or cider
normande, sauce a fish sauce with cream, egg yolks and butter
nougat blanc de Montélimar white nougat made with honey and roasted
    almonds
nougatine brittle
nouilles noodles
nourriture food
odeur smell
oeuf egg
    oeuf à la coque soft-boiled egg
    oeuf dur hard-boiled egg
    oeuf mollet soft-boiled egg
    oeuf poché poached egg
    oeuf pourri bad egg
    oeuf sur le plat fried egg
    œufs à la Florentine eggs florentine
    oeufs à la neige *[île flottante]* floating islands *[dessert of poached egg*
    whites in custard]
    œufs Bénédictine eggs Benedict
    oeufs brouillés scrambled eggs
    oeufs de cailles quail's eggs
    oeufs de poisson hard roe
    oeufs et bacon, oeufs au bacon bacon and eggs
oie goose

oignon onion
olive olive
  olives farcies stuffed olives
  olives noires black olives
  olives vertes green olives
omble chevalier char *[fish]*
omelette omelette
  omelette au fromage cheese omelette
  omelette au jambon ham omelette
  omelette aux épinards spinach omelette
  omelette aux fines herbs herb omelette
  omelette aux truffes truffle omelette
  omelette baveuse omelette which is runny on top
  omelette nature plain omelette
  omelette norvégienne baked Alaska
onglet flank of beef
orange orange
  à l'orange with orange
orge barley
  orge perlée pearl barley
origan oregano
ormeau abalone
ortie nettle
os bone
  os à moelle marrow bone
  avec l'os *[viande]* meat on the bone
oseille sorrel
oursin sea urchin
ouvrir open *[verb]*
ouvre-bouteille bottle opener
paillasson de pommes de terre grated sautéed potato
paille au fromage cheese straw
paillettes de son bran flakes
pain bread
  pain à la farine de maïs corn bread
  pain à l'ail garlic bread
  pain au chocolat rectangular croissant-style pastry with chocolate filling
  pain aux fuits fruit bread/loaf
  pain aux noix walnut bread
  pain aux raisins round croissant-style pastry with raisins
  pain blanc white loaf, white bread
  pain bis brown bread
  pain complet wholemeal bread
  pain croustillant crisp bread
  pain de campagne farmhouse loaf
  pain d'épice(s) gingerbread
  pain de mie white sandwich loaf
  pain de seigle rye bread
  pain de son wholemeal bread
  pain de viande meat loaf
  pain grillé *[rôtie]* toast
  pain moulé pan loaf
  pain noir de Westphalie pumpernickel bread
  pain perdu French toast
  pain pita pitta bread
palmier large crisp biscuit of flaky pastry
palourde clam

pamplemousse grapefruit
   jus de pamplemousse grapefruit juice
panaché *[boisson]* shandy
panaché de mixed plate of
   panaché de légumes selection of vegetables, mixed vegetables
panais parsnip
pan bagnat Provençal hollowed-out roll filled with tomatoes, green peppers,
   olives, onions, anchovies
pané(e) breaded
papaye papaya, pawpaw
papier hygiénique toilet paper
paprika paprika
parfait parfait
   parfait au café coffee parfait
Paris-Brest cake of chou pastry with praline filling
Parmentier with potatoes
parmesan Parmesan cheese
parve milk-free bread/pastry
pas trop cuit medium rare *[steak]*
pastèque watermelon
pastis aniseed-flavoured aperitif mixed with water, particularly popular in the
   South
patate douce sweet potato; *[US]* yam
pâte dough, pastry
   pâte à choux choux pastry
   pâte à frire batter
   pâte brisée shortcrust pastry
   pâte feuilletée puff pastry
pâte *[on cheese]* rind
pâte d'amandes almond paste
pâté pâté
   pâté de campagne coarse pork pâté
   pâté de canard duck paté
   pâté de foie gras liver pâté
   pâté de soja tofu
   pâté de gibier en croûte game pie
pâtes *[alimentaires]* pasta
   pâtes aux coquillages seafood pasta
   pâtes fraîches fresh pasta
paté en croûte meat pie
pâté végétal vegetable pie
pâtisserie French pastry; cake; cake shop
patte leg
   pattes de dinde/de poulet turkey/chicken drumsticks
paupiette thin rolled stuffed piece of meat
   paupiette de boeuf beef olive
   paupiette de veau veal olive
pavé square or rectangular piece of steak, cheese, etc.
payer to pay
paysanne served with carrots, turnips, onions, celery, potatoes, bacon
peau skin, peel
   sans peau peeled
pêche peach
peler to peel
pelure peel
   sans pelure peeled
perche d'eau douce perch

French-English

perdreau   young partridge
perdrix   partridge
périgourdine, à la   with truffles, liver pâté
persil   parsley
   persil frisé   curly parsley
   persil plat   flat parsley
persillé(e)   garnished with chopped parsley
pétillant(e)   sparkling, fizzy
petit beurre   butter biscuit
petit déjeuner   breakfast
petit pain   bread roll, bap
   petit pain au lait   bun
   petit pain au seigle   rye bread roll
   petit pain chapelet   brown roll
petits fours   petits fours *[small dessert or cake]*
petits pois   green peas, garden peas
   petits pois gourmands, pois mange-tout   mangetout, sugar snap peas
petit-suisse   cream cheese in a pot, eaten with sugar
petits gris   small dark brown snails
pets de nonne   deep-fried fritters often served hot with sugar
pibales   baby eels
pichet   carafe
   un pichet de rouge   a carafe of red wine
pickles   pickles
pieds   feet, trotters
   pieds de porc   pig's trotters
pieds et paquets   Provençal stuffed parcels of sheep's tripe cooked with
   trotters, wine, herbs and tomatoes
pigeon   pigeon
pigeonneau   squab
pignon   pine nut
pilaf aux champignons   mushroom pilaff
pilchard *[grosse sardine]*   pilchard
piment doux *[poivron]*   pepper, capsicum
   piment fort, piment rouge   chilli, red chilli, chilli pepper
   piment *[fort]* **en poudre**   chilli powder
   piment de la Jamaïque   allspice
pimprenelle   burnet
pintade   guinea fowl
piperade   peppers, onions, garlic and tomatoes with beaten eggs and sometimes
   ham
piquant(e)   hot *[strong]*
pique-nique   picnic
piqûre d'abeille   beesting
pissaladière   Provençal tart with onions, olives, tomatoes, anchovies
pistache   pistachio nut
pistou   pesto
pizza   pizza
place   seat
plaquemine *[kaki]*   persimmon
plat   dish
   plat du jour   dish of the day
   plat principal   main course; *[US]* entree
plateau à fromage, plateau de fromages   cheese board
pleurote   oyster mushroom
plie   plaice

poché(e) poached
   poché dans du lait poached in milk
pocher to poach
pochouse Burgundian stew of freshwater fish in white wine
poêlé(e) pan-fried
point, à *[rose]* medium-rare
pointes d'asperges asparagus tips
poire pear
   poires au vin de Bourgogne pears poached in red wine
poireau leek
   petits poireaux baby leeks
pois pea
   petits pois green peas, garden peas
   pois cassés split peas
   pois chiche chickpea
   pois gourmands, pois mange-tout mangetout
poisson fish
   poisson d'eau douce freshwater fish, river fish
   poisson de mer sea fish
   poisson frit fried fish
   poisson fumé smoked fish
   poisson plat flat fish
   poisson volant flying fish
poisson-chat *[silure]* catfish
poissonnerie fishmonger
poitrine breast
   poitrine d'agneau/de veau breast of lamb/veal
   poitrine de boeuf brisket of beef
poivrade, sauce a mix of vegetables cooked with wine, vinegar, pepper, and demi-glace sauce
poivre pepper *[spice]*
   moulin à poivre pepper mill
   poivre de cayenne cayenne pepper
   poivre en grains whole pepper
   poivre moulu ground pepper
   poivre noir/vert/blanc black/green/white pepper
poivrière pepper pot
poivron pepper *[vegetable]*
   poivron farci stuffed pepper
   poivron rouge *[piment doux]* red pepper
   poivron vert green pepper
polenta *[semoule de maïs]* polenta
pomme *[fruit]* apple
   pomme au four baked apple
   purée de pommes apple puree
pomme de terre potato
   pommes allumettes matchstick potatoes
   pommes chips potato crisps; *[US]* potato chips
   pommes de terre à l'ail au four baked garlic potatoes
   pommes de terre à l'anglaise/à l'eau boiled potatoes
   pommes de terre au four baked potatoes
   pommes de terre aux amandes amandine potatoes
   pommes de terre duchesse duchesse potatoes *[mashed and mixed with egg yolk, baked]*
   pommes de terre dauphine croquettes of mashed potatoes mixed with choux pastry
   pommes de terre dauphinoises sliced potatoes baked with milk, cream, eggs and seasoning

pommes de terre nouvelles   new potatoes
pommes de terre sautées   fried potoatoes
pommes frites   potato chips; *[US]* French fries
pommes mousseline   puréed potatoes
pommes purée   mashed potatoes; *[US]* creamed potatoes
porc   pork
porcelet   suckling pig
pot   jug
pot au chocolat   chocolate pot
pot au feu   braised meat or poultry and vegetables, with the broth served separately
potable   drinkable
potage   soup
   potage au cari   mulligatawny *[soup]*
   potage au vermicelle   noodle soup
   potage aux légumes   vegetable soup
   potage bonne femme   leek and potato soup
   potage St Germain   green pea soup
potée   thick soup or stew of pork, ham, cabbage, beans and other vegetables
potiron *[citrouille]*   pumpkin
pouding   fruit or milk pudding
   pouding au riz *[cuit au four]*   rice pudding
   pouding cabinet   cabinet pudding
   pouding de Noël *[anglais]*   Christmas pudding
poularde   fattened chicken
poule   boiling fowl
poulet   chicken
   poulet à la Kiev   chicken kiev
   poulet frit   fried chicken
   poulet rôti   roast chicken
poulpe   octopus
pourboire   tip, gratuity
pourpier   purslane
pousses de bambou   bamboo shoots
poussin   poussin
poutassou   blue whiting
pré-cuit(e)   par-boiled
premier plat/entrée   first course
presse-fruits   juicer
présure   rennet
   sans présure   rennet-free
primeurs   new season's fruit/vegetables
prix   price
   à prix fixe   set, fixed-price
profiteroles   profiteroles
propre   clean
protéines   protein
provençale, à la   with tomatoes, garlic, olive oil, olives
prune   plum
   prune de Damas   damson
pruneau *[sec]*   prune
prunelle   sloe
   eau de vie de prunelle   sloe gin
pur(e)   pure
purée   puree
   en purée   mashed *[potatoes]*; stewed *[fruit]*
   purée de pois   mushy peas
   purée de pois cassés   pease-pudding

purée de pommes apple puree, apple sauce
purée de pommes de terre mashed potatoes; *[US]* creamed potatoes
purée de tomates tomato purée
qualité quality
quark *[fromage blanc]* quark
quart quarter
quatre-épices allspice
quenelles *[de brochet, de poulet ou veau]* quenelles *[oval dumplings of pike, chicken or veal, poached]*
quetsche dark red plum
queue de boeuf oxtail
soupe à la queue de boeuf oxtail soup
queues de langoustine *[scampi]* scampi
quiche quiche
quiche lorraine quiche lorraine
quiche au saumon fumé smoked salmon quiche
râble *[de lapin/lièvre]* saddle *[of rabbit/of hare]*
racine root
radis radish, radishes
rafraîchi(e) chilled
rafraîchisseur *[à vin]* wine cooler
ragoût *[fricassée]* stew
ragoût de boeuf *[potée]* hotpot
ragoût de mouton à l'irlandaise Irish stew
raie skate
raifort horseradish
raifort, sauce a mixture of grated horseradish, vinegar and whipped cream. Served with roast beef and smoked fish
raisin(s) *[de table]* grape(s)
raisins de Corinthe currants
raisins de Smyrne sultanas
raisins sec raisins
ramequin ramekin
rance rancid
râpé(e) grated
rascasse scorpion fish
rassis(e) stale
ratatouille ratatouille
ravigote, sauce a vinaigrette made with oil and vinegar, egg yolk, capers, parsley, tarragon, chervil, chives, and onion
ravioli ravioli
recette recipe
recommander to recommend
reçu receipt
réglisse liquorice
reine-claude greengage *[plum]*
relever to spice up
remise discount
rémoulade, sauce mayonnaise with capers, gherkins, anchovy. Served with fried fish
repas meal
repas de Noël Christmas dinner
requin shark
réservation reservation
réserver reserve, to book
restaurant restaurant
rhubarbe rhubarb

rhum rum
riche en fibres high-fibre
rillettes shredded potted pork or goose
rillons fried pieces of crispy pork or goose
ris de veau sweetbreads
rissole rissole
rissoler *[faire]* to shallow-fry
riz rice
    riz au blanc, riz à la chinoise boiled rice
    riz au lait au four baked rice, rice pudding
    riz Caroline long-grained rice
    riz complet brown rice
    riz indien basmati rice
    riz pour risotto risotto rice
    riz rond pudding rice
    riz sauvage wild rice
Robert, sauce fried onion with stock, mustard, and castor sugar added. Served with fried pork chop
rognon kidney
    rognons à la sauce diable devilled kidneys
romaine *[laitue]* romaine lettuce, cos lettuce
romarin rosemary
romsteck rump steak
roquette rocket
rosbif roast beef
rosette de Lyon pork salami sausage
rôti roast
    rôti de boeuf *[rosbif]* roast beef
    rôti de porc roast pork
rôti(e) roasted
rôtie *[pain grillé]* toast
rôtir to roast
rouget barbet red mullet
rouille mayonnaise made of chillies, garlic, and olive oil
roulade stuffed rolled *[meat etc.]*
roux a mixture of fat and flour cooked together, used as the base for sauces
russe, à la served with sour cream, hard-boiled egg and beetroot
rutabaga swede
rye *[whisky de seigle]* rye whisky
sabayon zabaglione
sablé shortbread
saccharine saccharin
safran saffron
sagou sago
saignant(e) *[viande]* rare *[meat, steak]*
sain healthy
saindoux lard
Saint Germain with green peas
Saint-Pierre dory, John Dory
saisir to sear
saisonnier(-ière) seasonal
salade salad; lettuce
    salade au poulet chicken salad
    salade César Caesar salad
    salade composée mixed salad *[containing vegetables, meat or eggs, fish etc.]*
    salade de fruits fruit salad

salade de pommes de terre   potato salad
salade de tomate   tomato salad
salade mixte   lettuce and tomato salad
salade niçoise   salad of tomatoes, hard-boiled eggs, olives, anchovies, green beans, capers, potatoes, lettuce, green pepper, cucumber and/or tuna
salade panachée   mixed salad
salade tiède   warm salad
salade verte   green salad
salade Waldorf *[pommes, céleri, noix, avec mayonnaise]*   Waldorf salad
saladier   salad bowl
sale   dirty *[plate, tablecloth, etc.]*
salé(e)   salted; salty
salière   salt cellar, salt mill
salir   to dirty
salle à manger/salle de restaurant *[hotel]*   dining room
salmis   game bird served in rich wine sauce made with remains of bird
salsifis   salsify
sandre   pike-perch
sandwich   sandwich
  club sandwich   club sandwich
  sandwich au fromage   cheese sandwich
  sandwich au jambon   ham sandwich
sang   blood
sanglier   wild boar
Santé!   Cheers! health
sardine   sardine
sarrasin *[blé noir]*   buckwheat
sarriette   savoury *[herb]*
sauce *[jus de viande]*   sauce; gravy
sauce *[mayonnaise; vinaigrette]*   dressing
sauce   sauce
  sauce à l'aneth   dill sauce
  sauce à la crème   cream sauce
  sauce à la menthe *[fraîche]*   mint sauce
  sauce au beurre   butter sauce
  sauce au chocolat   chocolate sauce
  sauce au pain   bread sauce
  sauce aux canneberges   cranberry sauce
  sauce bigarade   *[bitter]* orange sauce
  sauce blanche *[béchamel]*   white sauce
  sauce béarnaise   *see* **béarnaise**
  sauce bordelaise   bordelaise *[red wine]* sauce
  sauce diable   devilled sauce
  sauce espagnole   brown sauce
  sauce hollandaise   hollandaise sauce
  sauce madère   Madeira sauce
  sauce Mornay   cheese sauce
  sauce soja   soy sauce, soya sauce
  sauce tartare   tartare sauce
  sauce tomate   tomato sauce
  sauce végétarienne   vegetarian gravy
  sauce Worcestershire   Worcestershire sauce
saucisse   sausage
  saucisse de Strasbourg   frankfurter
  saucisse de Toulouse   fat pork sausage
  saucisse de soja   vegetarian sausage
saucisson   French sausage
  saucisson italien   salami

sauge sage
saumon salmon
   saumon fumé smoked salmon
   darne de saumon salmon steak
sauté(e) sautéed
sauter à la chinoise to stir-fry
sautoir sauté pan
   au sautoir sautéd
sauvage wild
savoureux (savoureuse) tasty
saxifrage saxifrage
scampi scampi
seau de glace bucket of ice
s'ébouillanter to scald
sec *[sèche]* dry
   très sec very dry *[wine]*
séché(e) dried
   séché(e) au soleil sun-dried
seiche cuttlefish
seigle rye
sel salt
   qui contient peu de sel low-salt *[dish]*
   sel gemme rock salt
   sel marin sea salt
sélection selection
selle *[d'agneau]* saddle *[of lamb]*
semoule semolina
serpolet wild thyme
serveur waiter
serveuse waitress
service service charge
   service sitting *[first, second etc.]*
   service compris service included
   service non compris service not included
   service à la discrétion du client service discretionary
serviette *[de table]* napkin, serviette
sésame sesame seed
silure *[poisson-chat]* catfish
sirop syrup
   sirop d'érable maple syrup
   sirop de maïs corn syrup
socca chickpea flour pancake
soirée party
soja *[fève de]* soy bean, soya bean
   sauce soja soy sauce, soya sauce
sole Dover sole; sand sole
sommelier wine waiter
son *[de blé]* bran
sorbet sorbet
sorgho sorghum
soubise, sauce béchamel sauce with onion purée, flavoured with nutmeg.
   Used for roast meats
soucoupe saucer
soufflé soufflé
   soufflé au fromage cheese soufflé
   soufflé aux fraises strawberry soufflé

soupe soup
   soupe à la queue de boeuf oxtail soup
   soupe à l'oignon onion soup
   soupe au pistou Provençal soup of vegetables, noodles, beans, basil
   soupe aux légumes vegetable soup
   soupe aux pois *[cassés]* pea soup *[with split peas]*
   soupe de poisson(s) fish soup
   soupe de poulet chicken soup
   soupe/potage du jour soup of the day
souris d'agneau knuckle-end of leg of lamb *[on the bone]*
spaghetti spaghetti
   spaghetti à la bolognaise spaghetti bolognese
   spaghetti végétariens à la bolognaise vegetarian bolognaise
spécialité speciality
   spécialités de la maison house specialities
   spécialités du pays local specialities
spiritueux spirits *[alcohol]*
sprat *[harenguet]* sprat
steak steak
   steak au poivre pepper steak
   steak (et) frites steak and chips
   steak tartare raw minced fillet steak served with raw egg yolk, capers, onions
stoemp Belgian dish of mashed potato and chopped vegetables
stout *[bière brune]* stout
stroganoff de champignons mushroom stroganoff
strudel aux pommes apple strudel
stufatu mutton stew
succédané de lait *[en poudre]* coffee whitener
sucre sugar
   sucre de canne cane sugar
   sucre d'érable maple sugar
   sucre d'orge barley sugar
   sucre glace, sucre en poudre icing sugar
   sucre roux *[cassonade]* soft brown sugar
   sucre semoule caster sugar
   sucre vanillé vanilla sugar
sucré(e) sweet
sucreries confectionery
suif *[de boeuf]* suet
supermarché supermarket
supplément supplement
   supplément légumes €3 vegetables €3 extra
suprême de poulet *[blanc, filet]* chicken breast, breast of chicken
surgelé(e) frozen
syllabub *[sabayon]* syllabub
table table
   une table près de la fenêtre window table, a table by the window
taboulé tabouleh
tagliatelle tagliatelle
   tagliatelles aux champignons et à la crème creamy mushroom tagliatelle
tajine North African stew simmered in conical earthenware dish
tamiser to sift
tanche tench
tangerine tangerine
tapenade paste made of black olives, capers, lemon, anchovies, olive oil
tapioca tapioca
tarif price list

tartare *see* **steak tartare**
tarte pie
    part de tarte slice of pie
    tarte à la crème cream tart
    tarte à l'oignon onion tart
    tarte aux abricots apricot pie
    tarte aux fruits fruit tart
    tarte aux noix de pécan pecan pie
    tarte aux pommes apple pie
    tarte normande apple tart
    tarte Tatin upside down apple pie *[apples covered with pastry served upside down]*
tartelette small tart
    tartelette à la crème custard tart
    tartelette aux pommes apple tart
tartiflette baked potatoes, Reblochon cheese and bacon
tartine slice of bread and butter
tasse cup
    tasse à café coffee cup
    tasse à thé tea cup
    tasse de café cup of coffee
    tasse de chocolat cup of cocoa/hot chocolate
    tasse de thé cup of tea
    tasse et soucoupe cup and saucer
tempeh tempeh
tendre *[viande]* tender
terrine terrine *[chopped fish, meat or vegetable loaf]*
thé tea
    thé (au) citron lemon tea
    thé au lait tea with milk
    thé de Chine China tea
    thé glacé iced tea
    thé Japonais Japanese tea
    thé nature tea without milk or sugar
    thé vert green tea
théière teapot
thon tuna, tunny
    thon blanc albacore *[tuna]*
thym thyme
tian Provençal gratin of fish or vegetables cooked in a shallow dish
tiède warm, not hot or cold *[salad etc.]*
tilleul lime
timbale cup-shaped mould
    timbale de poisson fisherman's pie
tire-bouchon corkscrew
tisane herbal tea
toast toast *[tribute]*
tofu *[pâté de soja]* tofu
toilettes lavatory, toilet
    toilettes des dames ladies' toilets
    toilettes des hommes gents' toilets
tomate tomato
    tomate-cerise cherry tomato
    tomate oblongue/italienne plum tomato
    tomates farcis stuffed tomatoes
    tomates séchées *[au soleil]* sun-dried tomatoes
topinambour Jerusalem artichoke
torsade twisted plait

tourin   cream of onion soup
tournedos   fillet steak
tournesol   sunflower
   graines de tournesol   sunflower seeds
   huile de tournesol   sunflower oil
tourte   tart or flan with puff pastry
tourteau *[crabe]*   crab
tranche   slice
   tranche de jambon   slice of ham
   tranche de pain   slice of bread
   tranche napolitaine   Neapolitan ice cream
tranché(e)   sliced *[bread, etc.]*
travers de porc   spare ribs
très sucré(e)   very sweet
tremper   to dip
trévise *[chicorée rouge]*   radicchio
tripes   tripe
   tripes à la mode de Caen   tripe cooked with vegetables and white wine, for 7 to 8 hours
trou normand   glass of Calvados or other spirits between courses to clear the palate
truffade   Auvergne dish of potatoes, bacon, cheese and garlic, eaten with sausages
truffe   truffle
   truffé   garnished with truffle
   truffe au chocolat   chocolate truffle
   truffe blanche   white truffle
   truffe noire   black truffle
truite   trout
   truite arc-en-ciel   rainbow trout
   truite de mer   sea trout
   truite saumonée   salmon trout
tuile aux amandes   thin almond biscuit similar to brandy snap
turbot   turbot
vacherin   meringue filled with ice cream or cream
vaisselle *[service de porcelaine]*   china *[service]*
vanille   vanilla
   extrait de vanille   vanilla essence
   glace à la vanille   vanilla ice cream
vapeur   steamed
veau *[animal]*   calf
veau *[viande]*   veal
   escalope de veau   veal escalope
   foie de veau   calf's liver
   noix de veau   tender cut of veal
végétalien (-ienne)   vegan
végétarien (-ienne)   vegetarian
velouté (de)   cream (of) *[soup]*
   velouté de champignons   cream of mushroom soup
velouté, sauce   a white sauce made from fat and flour cooked till lightly coloured, with added white stock
venaison   venison
vermicelle   vermicelli
verre   glass
   verre à eau   glass for water
   verre à vin   wine glass
   verre d'eau   glass of water
   verre de vin   glass of wine

verre propre   clean glass
verte, sauce   mayonnaise mixed with tarragon or chervil, chives and
   watercress
verveine   lemon verbena
viande   meat
   viande de cheval   horse meat
   viande en cocotte   pot roast
   viande froide   cold meat
   viande fumé   smoked meat
   viandes rôties   roast meats
vichyssoise   vichyssoise *[leek and cream soup]*
vieilli(e)   aged
viennoiserie   croissants, brioches, pains aux raisins, etc
vigneronne, à la   served with grapes and a wine sauce
vin   wine
   vin blanc   white wine
   vin corsé   full-bodied wine
   vin de Bordeaux   Bordeaux wine
   vin de Bourgogne   Burgundy wine
   vin de pays   local wine of a particular grape variety and area
   vin de Porto   port
   vin de table   table wine
   vin doux, vin de dessert   dessert wine, sweet wine
   vin léger   light-bodied wine
   vin local   local wine
   vin (de la) maison   house wine
   vin mousseux; vin pétillant   sparkling wine
   vin pas trop corsé   medium wine
   vin rosé   rosé wine
   vin rouge   red wine
   vin sec   dry wine
vinaigre   vinegar
   vinaigre balsamique   balsamic vinegar
   vinaigre de cidre   cider vinegar
   vinaigre de vin *[rouge/blanc]*   *[red/white]* wine vinegar
vinaigrette   French dressing, vinaigrette
vivaneau   red snapper
volaille   fowl; chicken
vol-au-vent   *[bouchée feuilletée; timbale]* vol au vent
vue sur la mer   sea view *[i.e. table with]*
wagon-restaurant   dining car
waterzooi   Belgian dish of chicken cooked in stock, white wine and cream
   with vegetables
WC   toilet, lavatory
whiskey irlandais   Irish whiskey
whisky écossais   whisky
xérès   sherry
yaourt   yoghurt
   yaourt à la grecque   Greek yoghurt
   yaourt nature   plain yoghurt
   yaourt aux myrtilles   blueberry yoghurt
yoghourt   yoghurt
zabaglione   zabaglione
zeste *[écorce râpée]*   zest
   zeste de citron   lemon zest, grated lemon peel

English-French

abalone   ormeau
absinthe   absinthe
account   compte
aged   vieilli(e)
aïloli sauce   ailloli, aïoli
air-conditioned   climatisé(e)
albacore *[tuna]*   thon blanc, germon
alcohol   alcool
ale   bière (anglaise) blonde
alfalfa sprouts   germes de luzerne
allergic   allergique (à/au/aux...)
allergy   allergie (à/au/aux...)
allspice   piment de la Jamaïque
almond   amande douce
   almond paste   pâte d'amandes
   almond tart   amandine
   with almonds   aux amandes
amandine potatoes   pommes de terre aux amandes
anchovy   anchois
   anchovy butter   beurre d'anchois
   anchovy paste   purée, pâte d'anchois
angel food cake   angel cake *[génoise sans jaune d'oeufs]*
angel fish   ange de mer
angel hair pasta   cheveux d'ange
angels on horseback   angels on horseback *[huîtres entourées de bacon, grillées, sur toast]*
angelica   angélique
angler   baudroie, lotte *[de mer]*
anise   anis
aniseed   anis
aperitif   apéritif
appetizer *[US]* *[drink]* apéritif; *[food]* amuse-gueule; hors-d'oeuvres
apple   pomme *[fruit]*
   apple fritter   beignet de pommes
   apple juice   jus de pomme
   apple pie   tarte aux pommes
   apple puree   purée de pommes
   apple sauce   purée de pommes *[peu sucrée]*
   apple strudel   strudel aux pommes
   apple turnover   chausson aux pommes
   apple tart   tartelette aux pommes
apricot   abricot
aroma   arôme; bouquet *[of wine]*
arrowroot   arrow-root
artichoke   artichaut
ashtray   cendrier
asparagus   asperge
   asparagus tips   pointes d'asperges
aspic   aspic

assorted vegetables choix de légumes, légumes variés
aubergine aubergine
au gratin *[US]* gratiné(e), au gratin
avocado avocat
baby petit
   baby corn *[cob]* tout petit épi de maïs
   baby eels pibales
   baby food aliments pour bébés
   baby leeks petits poireaux
   baby vegetables petits légumes
   baby's bottle biberon
bacon bacon, lard fumé
   bacon and eggs oeufs au bacon
bad mauvais(e)
   bad egg oeuf pourri
bake (faire) cuire au four
baked cuit(e) au four
   baked Alaska omelette norvégienne
   baked apple pomme au four
   baked beans haricots blancs aux tomates; fèves au lard
   baked custard flan
   baked potato pomme de terre au four
   baked rice riz au lait au four, pouding au riz
bakery boulangerie; *[for cakes]* patisserie
balsamic vinegar vinaigre balsamique
bamboo shoots pousses de bambou
banana banane
   banana fritter beignet de bananes
   banana split banana split *[banane, glace à la vanille, Chantilly, amandes]*
   banana flambé banane flambée
bar *[pub]* bar, pub
Barbary duck canard de Barbarie
barbecue barbecue
barbecued grillé(e) au barbecue
barbel rouget barbet
barley orge
   barley sugar sucre d'orge
   barley water sirop d'orgeat *[fait avec de l'orge]*
basil basilic
   basil pesto pistou
basmati rice riz indien, riz Caroline
bass loup *[de mer]*, bar
baste arroser
bathroom WC/toilettes
batons *[of carrots, etc.]* bâtonnets
batter pâte à frire
   in batter en beignets
Bavarian cream bavarois
bay leaf feuille de laurier
bean haricot
   bean sprouts germes de soja
   broad beans grosses fèves; fèves des marais
   French beans, green beans haricot verts
   kidney beans haricots rouges
   runner beans haricots grimpants
   soya beans fèves de soja
   string beans haricots verts
béarnaise *[sauce]* sauce béarnaise

béchamel *[sauce]*   sauce béchamel
beech nuts   faînes
beef   boeuf
   beefsteak *[US]*   bifteck, steak
   beef stock   bouillon de boeuf
   beef stroganoff   bœuf stroganoff
   beef Wellington   filet de boeuf en croûte
   roast beef   rosbif
beer   bière
   draught beer   bière (à la) pression
beetroot   betterave
bergamot   bergamote
berries   baies
bib *[child's]*   bavette, bavoir
big   grand(e)
bilberry   airelle, myrtille
bill   addition
birthday cake   gâteau d'anniversaire
biscuits   biscuits, gâteaux secs
bitter   amer, amère
bitter   bière anglaise pression
black butter   beurre noir
black beans   haricots noirs
blackberry   mûre *[de ronce]*
black cherry   cerise noire
black coffee   café noir
blackcurrant   cassis *[groseille noire]*
Black Forest cake/gateau   forêt-noire
black halibut   flétan noir
black pepper   poivre noir
black pudding   boudin noir
black truffle   truffe noire
blaeberry   airelle, myrtille
blanch   blanchir
   blanched   blanchi(e)
blancmange   blanc-manger
blend   mélanger, incorporer
blinis   blinis
blood   sang
blueberry   myrtille, bleuet
blue cheese   fromage bleu
blue whiting   poutassou
boar   sanglier; *[young]* marcassin
boil   *[faire]* bouillir
boiled   bouilli(e), cuit(e) à l'eau, à l'anglaise
   boiled egg   oeuf à la coque
   boiled ham   jambon poché
   boiled potatoes   pommes de terre à l'anglaise/à l'eau
   boiled rice   riz au blanc, riz à la chinoise
   boiled vegetables   légumes bouillis
   hard-boiled egg   oeuf dur
boiling water   eau bouillie
bombe   bombe
bone   os
   boned   désossé(e) *[viande, poisson]*
   on the bone   *[meat]* avec l'os; *[fish]* dont les arêtes n'ont pas été retirées
   bones *[of fish]*   arêtes (de poisson)

bonito bonite
book [a table] réserver
borage bourrache
bordelaise sauce sauce bordelaise
borlotti beans haricots italiens
bouquet garni bouquet garni
bottle bouteille
    bottle opener ouvre-bouteille
bowl bol
brains cervelle [de veau]
braise braiser
braised braisé(e)
bran son [de blé]
    bran flakes paillettes de son
brandy cognac
    cherry brandy cherry brandy, liqueur de cerise
brawn fromage de tête
Brazil nut noix du Brésil
bread pain
    breadcrumbs chapelure
    bread knife petit couteau [pour beurrer son pain]
    bread roll petit pain
    bread sauce sauce au pain
    breadstick gressin
breaded pané(e)
breakfast petit déjeuner
    breakfast cereal céréales
bream brème [de mer]
breast poitrine
    breast of lamb/veal poitrine d'agneau/de veau
    chicken breast suprême de poulet
brill barbue
brioche brioche
brisket [of beef] poitrine [de boeuf]
brittle nougatine
broad bean grosse fève; fève des marais
broccoli [chou] brocoli
broth bouillon
brown [verb] [faire] brunir; [faire] dorer
brown bread pain complet
brown butter beurre noisette
brown rice riz complet
brown roll petit pain chapelet
brown sugar sucre roux, cassonade
brown sauce sauce espagnole
Brussels sprouts choux de Bruxelles
bubble and squeak choux et pommes de terre frits
buckwheat sarrasin, blé noir
buffalo buffle
buffet buffet
bulgar wheat, bulgur wheat blé concassé
bun petit pain au lait
burbot lotte [d'eau douce]
burdock glouteron, bardane
burgundy [wine] [vin de] bourgogne
burn [verb] brûler
burnet pimprenelle

burnt brûlé(e)
butcher's shop boucherie
butter beurre
    butter sauce sauce au beurre
    with butter avec beurre, au beurre
    without butter sans beurre
butterfish blennie
buttermilk lait de beurre, babeurre
cabbage chou
cabinet pudding pouding cabinet
Caesar salad salade César
café café
caffeine caféine
    caffeine-free sans caféine, décaféiné(e)
cake gâteau
    cake shop pâtisserie
    carrot cake gâteau aux carottes
    cream cake gâteau à la crème
    fruit cake cake *[aux fruits confits]*
    sponge cake génoise
calamari calamars
calf veau
    calf's brains cervelle de veau
    calf's liver foie de veau
camomile camomille
canapés canapés
candied confit(e)
    candied peel zeste confit, écorce confite
candle chandelle
candlestick chandelier
candy *[US]* bonbon
cane sugar sucre de canne
canned en boîte *[de conserve]*
cantaloup *[melon]* cantaloup
capers câpres
capon chapon
capsicum piment doux, poivron
carafe carafe
caramel caramel
caraway *[seeds]* cumin des prés, carvi
carbohydrate glucides *[hydrates de carbone]*
carbonara carbonara
carbonated gazeux/gazeuse
cardamom cardamome
carp carpe
carrot carotte
    carrot cake gâteau aux carottes
carve découper
cashier caissier
cassata cassate
cashew nut noix d'acajou/noix de cajou
casserole casserole
caster sugar sucre semoule
catfish poisson-chat, silure
catsup *[US]* ketchup, sauce tomate
cauliflower chou-fleur
    cauliflower cheese chou-fleur sauce Mornay, au gratin

caviar caviar
cayenne pepper poivre de cayenne
celeriac céleri-rave
celery céleri
cereal *[breakfast]* céréales
chair chaise
champagne champagne
change changer (de), échanger
change *[coins]* monnaie
chantilly *[crème]* Chantilly
chanterelle chanterelle *[mushroom]*
char *[fish]* omble chevalier
charcoal charbon de bois
   charcoal-grilled grillé(e) au charbon de bois
chard bette, blette
charlotte charlotte
   apple charlotte charlotte aux pommes
cheap bon marché
check *[US] [bill]* addition
cheddar *[cheese]* *[fromage]* cheddar
Cheers! A la vôtre!; A la tienne!; Santé!
cheese fromage
   cheese board plateau à fromage; plateau de fromages
   cheesecake gâteau au fromage blanc
   cream cheese fromage à la crème
   cheese sauce sauce Mornay
   cheese soufflé soufflé au fromage
   cheese straw paille, allumette au fromage
chef chef
cherry cerise
   cherry brandy cherry brandy, liqueur de cerise
   cherry tomato tomate-cerise
chervil cerfeuil
chestnut *[sweet]* marron, châtaigne
   water chestnut châtaigne d'eau
chickpea pois chiche
chicken poulet
   roast chicken poulet rôti
   breast of chicken suprême de poulet
   chicken gumbo *[potage de]* poulet et gombo
   chicken Kiev poulet à la Kiev
   chicken livers foies de poulets
   chicken salad salade au poulet
   chicken soup soupe de poulet
chicory endive
children's menu menu des enfants
chilled rafraîchi(e)
chilli piment fort, piment rouge
   chilli con carne chili con carne
   chilli pepper piment fort, piment rouge
   chilli powder piment en poudre
   chilli without meat chili végétarien
china *[service]* vaisselle; service de porcelaine
China tea thé de Chine
Chinese cabbage chou de Chine
chipped *[glass, plate]* *[verre, assiette]* ébréché(e)
chips pommes frites
chips *[US]* pommes chips

chitterling *[US]* friture de tripes *[découpées en morceaux]*
chives ciboulette, civette
chocolate chocolat
   chocolate cake gâteau au chocolat
   chocolate croissant pain au chocolat
   chocolate eclair éclair au chocolat
   chocolate mousse mousse au chocolat
   chocolate sauce sauce au chocolat
   chocolate truffle truffe au chocolat
   milk chocolate chocolat au lait
   plain chocolate chocolat amer; noir; à croquer
choose choisir
chop *[cutlet]* côte, côtelette
chop *[meat]* couper
chopped *[into pieces]* en dés; *[persil]* haché
chopsticks baguettes
choux pastry pâte à choux
chowder soupe de poissons à base de lait
Christmas cake gâteau de Noël *[anglais]*
Christmas Day le jour de Noël
Christmas dinner repas de Noël
Christmas Eve la veille de Noël
Christmas log bûche de Noël
Christmas menu menu de Noël
Christmas pudding pouding de Noël *[anglais]*
cider cidre
   cider vinegar vinaigre de cidre
cigar cigare
cigarettes cigarettes
cinnamon cannelle
citron cédrat
citrus agrumes
clam clam, palourde
   clam chowder chowder aux palourdes
claret bordeaux rouge
clean propre
clear up desservir *[la table]*
clear soup consommé
clementine clémentine
closed fermé
clove clou de girofle
   clove of garlic gousse d'ail
club sandwich club sandwich
cobnut noisette
cockles coques
cocktail cocktail
cocoa *[poudre de]* cacao
   cocoa butter beurre de cacao
   cup of cocoa une tasse de cacao; de chocolat
coconut noix de coco
   coconut milk lait de coco
   desiccated coconut noix de coco séchée
cod morue, cabillaud
coffee café
   cappuccino coffee cappuccino
   coffee whitener succédané de lait *[en poudre]*
   coffee with whipped cream café crème

coffee parfait   parfait au café
coffee pot   cafetière
coffee spoon   cuillère à café
decaffeinated coffee   café décaféiné, un déca
espresso / expresso coffee   café express
filter coffee   café filtre
instant coffee   café soluble
Coke   Coca
cold   froid(e)
    cold cuts *[US]*   assiette de viandes froides, assiette anglaise
    cold drink   boisson fraîche
    cold meat   viande froide
    cold water   eau froide
coley *[coalfish]*   lieu noir, colin
collared beef   rosbif roulé *[ficelé]*
complimentary   gratuit
condensed milk   lait condensé
condiment   condiment
confectionery   sucreries
confectioner's custard   crème pâtissière
conger eel   congre, anguille de mer
consommé *[soup]*   consommé
    cold consommé   consommé froid, consommé en gelée
continental breakfast   café complet
cook   chef
cookies *[US]*   biscuits, gâteaux secs
coriander   coriandre
corkscrew   tire-bouchon
corn   maïs
    corn bread   pain à la farine de maïs
    corn oil   huile de maïs
    corn on the cob   épi de maïs, maïs en épi
    corn syrup   sirop de maïs
    cornflakes   corn flakes
    cornflour   fécule de maïs
corned beef   boeuf de conserve
cornet *[ice cream]*   cornet *[de glace]*
cos lettuce   (laitue) romaine
cottage cheese   fromage 'cottage'
courgette   courgette
couscous   couscous
cover charge   couvert
crab   crabe, tourteau, dormeur
    dressed crab   crabe froid à l'anglaise/à la russe
    prepared crab   crabe décortiqué
crackling   couenne croquante *[du rôti de porc]*
cranberry   canneberge
    cranberry sauce   sauce de canneberges
crawfish   langouste
crayfish   écrevisse
cream   crème
    double cream   crème épaisse
    single cream   crème légère
    whipped cream   crème Chantilly, crème fouettée
    cream cheese   fromage à la crème
    cream cake   gâteau à la crème
    cream sauce   sauce à la crème *[béchamel]*

cream slice millefeuille *[où la crème Chantilly remplace la crème pâtissière]*
cream tea thé accompagné de scones avec confiture et crème fraîche
cream of crème (de), velouté (de)
  cream of asparagus soup crème d'asperges
  cream of chicken soup crème de volaille, velouté de volaille
  cream of tomato soup crème de tomates
creamed en purée, à la crème
  creamed potato *[US]* purée de pommes de terre
  creamed spinach purée d'épinards à la crème
creamy en crème, crémeux(-euse), velouté(e)
crème caramel *[baked custard]* crème caramel
crème fraîche crème fraîche
cress cresson
crispbread biscotte, biscuit scandinave
crisps pommes chips
croissant croissant
croquette potatoes croquettes de pommes de terre
croutons croûtons
crumble crumble
crumpet petite crêpe épaisse *[non sucrée]*
crystallised fruit fruits confits
cucumber concombre
  cucumber sandwich sandwich au concombre
cumin *[seed]* cumin
cup tasse
  cup and saucer tasse et soucoupe
  cup of coffee tasse de café; un café
  cup of tea tasse de thé; un thé
  coffee cup tasse à café
  tea cup tasse à thé
curd lait caillé
cured fumé(e), mariné(e), salé(e)
currants raisins de Corinthe
curry curry, cari
  curry powder curry
custard crème anglaise
  baked custard flan
  custard apple anone, pomme canelle
  custard sauce crème anglaise
  custard tart tartelette à la crème
cut couper
cutlery couvert
cutlet côtelette
cuttlefish seiche
dab limande
dairy products produits laitiers
damson prune de Damas
date datte
date plum kaki
debone désosser, lever les filets
decaffeinated, decaf *[café]* décaféine, un déca
deep-fried cuit(e) à grande friture
deer chevreuil
defrost dégeler
delicatessen épicerie fine
delicious délicieux (-euse)

demerara sugar   sucre roux cristallisé
dessert   dessert
   dessert spoon   cuiller à dessert
   dessert wine   vin doux, vin de dessert
devilled   (à la) diable
   devilled kidneys   rognons à la sauce diable
   devilled sauce   sauce (à la) diable
diced   en cube
dill   aneth
   dill sauce   sauce à l'aneth
dining car   wagon-restaurant
dining companion(s)   compagnon(s)/compagne(s) de table
dining room   salle à manger/salle de restaurant
dinner   dîner
   dinner party   dîner
   dinner time   l'heure du dîner
dip *[verb]*   tremper
dip *[noun]*   sauce froide *[pour crudités]*
dirty *[adj]*   sale
dirty *[verb]*   salir
discount   remise
dish   plat
   dish of the day   plat du jour
dogfish   aiguillat, chien de mer
done   cuit(e)
   under-done   pas assez cuit(e); *[viande]* saignant(e)
   well-done   bien cuit(e)
dory, John Dory   Saint-Pierre, dorée
double *[shot of spirits]*   double
double cream   crème épaisse
dough   pâte
doughnut   beignet
   jam doughnut   beignet fourré à la confiture
Dover sole   sole
draught beer   bière (à la) pression
dressing   vinaigrette
dried   séché(e), sec *[sèche]*
   sun-dried tomatoes   tomates séchées *[au soleil]*
drink   boisson
   drink *[verb]*   boire
   drinkable   potable
   drinking water   eau potable
   drinks included   forfait boissons
dripping   graisse de rôti
drumsticks   pattes de dinde ou de poulet
dry *[wine]* *[vin]*   sec
Dublin bay prawn   langoustine
duchesse potatoes   pommes *[de terre]* duchesse
duck *[domestic]*   canard *[domestique]*
duck *[wild]*   canard sauvage
   duck paté   pâté de canard
   duck with oranges   canard à l'orange
   duckling   caneton, canette *[female]*
dumpling   boulette de pâte
   potato dumpling   gnocchi Parmentier
eat   manger
eclair   éclair
eel   anguille

egg oeuf
    boiled egg oeuf à la coque
    egg and bacon oeuf et bacon
    egg cup coquetier
    egg white blanc d'oeuf
    egg yolk jaune d'oeuf
    eggs Benedict œufs Bénédictine
    eggs florentine œufs à la florentine
    fried egg oeuf sur le plat
    hard-boiled egg oeuf dur
    omelette omelette
    poached egg oeuf poché
    scrambled eggs oeufs brouillés
    soft-boiled egg oeuf mollet
eggplant *[US]* aubergine
elderberry baie de sureau
endive chicorée frisée
enough assez
entree *[starter]* entrée
entree *[US main course]* plat principal
escalope escalope
    turkey escalope escalope de dinde
    veal escalope escalope de veau
espresso espresso
essence extrait (de)
ewe's milk lait de brebis
    ewe's milk cheese fromage de *[lait de]* brebis
excellent excellent(e)
expensive cher/chère
extra virgin olive oil huile d'olive extra vierge
faggot ballottine
falafel felafel
farm *[eggs, chickens]* *[oeufs, poulets]* fermiers
fast *[not eat]* jeûne
fat *[adj]* gras *[grasse]*
fat *[noun]* gras
    fat-free sans gras
feet pieds
fennel fenouil
feta cheese *[fromage]* feta, féta
fig figue
filbert aveline
fillet filet
    fillet steak tournedos, steak prélevé dans le filet
    fillet of beef filet de boeuf
filleted désossé(e), en filets
filo pastry pâte phyllo
filter coffee café filtre
fine beans haricots verts *[fins]*
first course premier plat/entrée
fish poisson
    fish and chips friture de poisson avec frites
    fish stew matelote, bouillabaisse
    fish soup soupe de poissons
    fish cake croquette de poisson
    fishmonger poissonnerie
    anchovy anchois
    angel fish ange de mer

English-French

bass loup *[de mer]*, bar
bream brème
brill barbue
burbot lotte *[d'eau douce]*
catfish poisson-chat, silure
cod morue, cabillaud
coley *[coalfish]* colin, lieu noir
conger eel congre, anguille de mer
crayfish écrevisse
cuttlefish seiche
dogfish aiguillat, chien de mer
dory, John Dory Saint-Pierre, dorée
Dover sole sole *[la vraie]*
eel anguille
flounder flet
flying fish poisson volant
grey mullet mulet gris
haddock aiglefin, églefin
hake merlu, colin
halibut flétan
herring hareng
kipper hareng saur/fumé
lemon sole limande-sole
mackerel maquereau
monkfish baudroie, lotte de mer
pike brochet
pike-perch sandre
pilchard pilchard, *[grosse]* sardine
red mullet rouget barbet
rockfish rascasse
roe oeufs de poisson, laitance
salmon saumon
scorpion fish rascasse
sea bass loup *[de mer]*, bar
sea bream brème de mer
sea trout truite de mer, truite saumonée
shark requin, aiguillat
skate raie
skipjack bonite
smelt éperlan
sole sole
sturgeon esturgeon
swordfish espadon
tench tanche
trout truite
tunny, tuna thon
turbot turbot
whitebait *[sprats]* blanchaille
whiting merlan
fisherman's pie timbale de poisson
fish shop poissonerie
fixed price prix fixe
  fixed price menu menu à prix fixe
fizzy pétillant(e), gazeux(-euse)
flageolet *[beans]* flageolets
flakes flocons
flambé flambé(e)
flan flan

English-French

flat fish poisson plat
flavour [of ice cream] parfum
flavoured aromatisé
floating island(s) oeufs à la neige, île(s) flottante(s)
flounder flet
flour farine
flying fish poisson volant
fondant fondant
fondue fondue
food nourriture
    food poisoning intoxication alimentaire
fool mousse faite de fruits, crème anglaise et Chantilly
fork fourchette
fowl volaille
    boiling fowl poule
frankfurter saucisse de Strasbourg
free [of charge] gratuit(e)
free-range [egg, chicken] [oeuf, poulet] fermier
French beans haricots verts
French dressing vinaigrette
French fries [US] pommes frites
French toast pain perdu, pain doré
fresh frais; fraîche
freshwater [fish] [poisson] d'eau douce
fried frit(e)
    fried chicken poulet frit
    fried egg oeuf sur le plat
    fried fish poisson frit
    fried food friture
    mixed fried fish friture de poissons
frisée [salad] chicorée frisée
fritter beignet
    apple fritter beignet de pommes
frog's legs cuisses de grenouilles
frozen surgelé(e)
fruit fruit
    fruit bread/loaf pain aux fuits
    fruit cocktail salade de fruits, macédoine de fruits
    fruit juice jus de fruits
    fruit salad salade de fruits, macédoine de fruits
fry frire
fudge fondant au chocolat
full [restaurant] complet
full [after eating] rassasié(e)
full-bodied wine vin corsé
full-cream milk lait entier
full-fat [cheese] [fromage] de lait entier
fungi champignons
galantine galantine
game gibier [à plume, à poil]; chevreuil
    game pie pâté de gibier en croûte
gammon jambon fumé [désossé]
garden mint menthe verte
garden peas petits pois frais
garlic ail
    garlic bread pain à l'ail
    garlic mayonnaise mayonnaise à l'ail

English-French

    garlic mushrooms champignons à l'ail
garlicky aillé(e)
garnished garni (de)
gateau gâteau
gazpacho gaspacho
gelatine gélatine
general store/grocer's épicerie
gents' toilets toilettes des hommes
ghee beurre clarifié *[cuisine indienne]*
gherkin cornichon
giblets abats
gin genièvre
    gin and tonic gin-tonic
ginger gingembre
    ginger beer bière au gingembre
    gingerbread pain d'épice(s)
    ginger cake gâteau au gingembre
glacé cherry cerise confite
glass verre
    clean glass verre propre
    glass of water verre d'eau
    wine glass verre à vin
glazed glacé(e)
gluten-free sans gluten
GM *[genetically modified]* génétiquement modifié
gnocchi gnocchi
goat chèvre
    goat's cheese fromage de chèvre
    goat's milk lait de chèvre
good bon(ne)
goose oie
    goose liver foie d'oie
gooseberry groseille à maquereau
goulash goulash, goulasch
gourmet gourmet; gastronome
granary loaf pain complet
granita granité
granulated sugar sucre granulé
grape(s) raisin(s) *[de table]*
grapefruit pamplemousse
grapeseed oil huile de pépins de raisin
grated râpé(e)
gratuity pourboire
gravy sauce, jus de viande
    gravy boat saucière
grease graisse
Greek yoghurt yaourt à la grecque *[au lait de brebis]*
green beans haricots verts
greengrocer magasin de fruits et légumes
green olives olives vertes
green peas petits pois
green pepper poivron vert
green salad salade verte
greengage *[plum]* reine-claude
Greenland halibut flétan noir
greens légumes verts
grenadine grenadine

grey mullet   mulet gris
grill *[verb]*   griller, cuire sur le gril
grill *[noun]*   gril
   mixed grill   assiette de viandes grillées *[assorties]*
grilled   grillé(e)
grind   moudre
gristle   cartilage, croquant
grits *[US]*   bouillie de maïs, gruau de maïs
groats   gruau d'avoine
grocery   épicerie; *[small]* alimentation
ground   *[coffee]* moulu(e), *[meat]* haché(e)
   ground beef   hachis, boeuf haché
   ground coffee   café moulu
groundnut oil   huile d'arachide
grouper   mérou
grouse   grouse
guacamole   guacamole
guava   goyave
gudgeon   goujon
guinea fowl   pintade
gumbo   gombo
gurnard   grondin
haddock   aiglefin, églefin
haggis   haggis *[estomac de mouton contenant un hachis d'abattis de mouton, oignons et avoine, le tout bouilli]*
hake   merlu, colin
half   demi(e)
   half bottle   demi-bouteille
   half a litre   demi-litre
   half done   fait à moitié
   half-cooked   à moitié cuit
halibut   flétan
ham   jambon
   boiled ham   jambon poché
   slice of ham   tranche de jambon
hamburger   hamburger
hangover   gueule de bois
hard   dur(e)
hard-boiled egg   oeuf dur
hard cheese   fromage à pâte dure
hard roe   oeufs de poisson
hare   lièvre
haricot beans   haricots blancs
hash browns *[US]*   pommes de terre en dés, avec oignons, sautées
haunch   cuissot
hazelnut   noisette, aveline
health   santé
   health shop   magasin de produits diététiques
   healthy   sain
heart   coeur
heat up   chauffer, réchauffer
herbs   fines herbes
herbal tea   tisane, infusion
herring   hareng
hickory nut   noix du noyer blanc d'Amérique
highchair   chaise haute
high-fibre   riche en fibres

hollandaise sauce   sauce hollandaise
home-made   *[fait à la]* maison
hominy grits *[US]*   bouillie de maïs
honey   miel
honeycomb   rayon de miel, gaufre de miel
honeydew melon   cavaillon
hors d'oeuvre   hors d'oeuvre
horse mackerel   chinchard
horsemeat   viande de cheval, cheval
horseradish   raifort
hot   *[not cold]* chaud(e); *[strong]* piquant(e)
hot dog   hot dog *[saucisse de Francfort dans un petit pain]*
hot drink   boisson chaude
hot water   eau chaude
hotpot   ragoût *[de boeuf]*, potée
house wine   vin de la maison
hummus   houmous
hungry *[to be hungry]*   avoir faim
ice   glace
   bucket of ice   seau de glace *[pour garder le vin frais]*
ice cream   glace, crème glacée
   ice cream cone   cornet de glace/de crème glacée
   ice cream scoop   boule de glace/de crème glacée
ice cube   glaçon
iceberg lettuce   laitue iceberg
icing   glace, glaçage
   icing sugar   sucre glace/en poudre
ingredients   ingrédients, éléments
inside   à l'intérieur/de dans
instant coffee   café soluble
Irish stew   ragoût de mouton à l'irlandaise
Irish whiskey   whiskey irlandais
jam   confiture
jellied   en gelée
jelly *[savoury]*   aspic, chaud-froid, galantine
jelly *[sweet/pudding]*   gelée
jelly *[US, jam]*   confiture
jello *[US]*   gelée *[parfumée à la fraise, etc.]*
Jerusalem artichoke   topinambour
John Dory   Saint-Pierre, dorée
jug   pot
jugged hare   civet de lièvre
juice   jus *[de fruits; de viande]*
   juicer   presse-fruits/centrifugeuse
julienne   julienne
kaki   kaki, plaquemine
kale   chou vert frisé *[non pommé]*
kebab   kébab, brochette *[de viande]*
kedgeree   riz au poisson fumé avec oeufs durs et cari
ketchup   ketchup
kettle   bouilloire
key lime pie   tarte à la crème de citron vert
kidney   rognon
kidney beans   haricots rouges
king prawn   crevette rose
kipper   hareng fumé, hareng saur
kitchen   cuisine

kiwi fruit kiwi
knife couteau
knuckle jarret
kohlrabi chou-rave
kosher casher, kasher
kumquat kumquat
label étiquette
lactose lactose
   lactose intolerance intolérance au lactose
ladies fingers gombos
ladies' toilets toilettes des dames
ladle louche
lager bière blonde
   a lager shandy un demi panaché
lamb agneau
   lamb chop côtelette d'agneau
lamb's lettuce mâche
langoustine langoustine
lard saindoux
lark alouette
lasagne lasagne
latte *[coffee]* café crème
lavatory toilettes, WC, lavabo
lavender lavande
leek poireau
leg patte
   leg of lamb gigot d'agneau
legumes légumineuses
lemon citron
   lemon balm mélisse
   lemon grass citronnelle
   lemon juice jus de citron
   lemon sole limande-sole
   lemon zest zeste, écorce de citron
   lemonade limonade; *[freshly squeezed]* citron pressé
lentil lentille
lettuce laitue, salade
lime citron vert, lime
ling lingue
light-bodied wine vin léger
liqueur liqueur
liquorice réglisse
litre litre
liver foie
   liver sausage leberwurst
loaf pain
   meat loaf pain de viande
   white loaf pain blanc, pain de mie
lobster homard
   lobster bisque bisque de homard
local du pays/local(e)
   local cheese fromage de pays
   local specialities spécialités du pays
loganberry loganberry
loin *[of veal/pork/venison]* longe *[de veau/porc/chevreuil]*
low-fat *[diet]* basses calories; *[yoghurt etc.]* allégé
low in fat qui contient peu de gras; basses calories

low-salt   qui contient peu de sel; hyposodé(e)
lunch   déjeuner, lunch
   lunchtime   l'heure du déjeuner
luncheon meat   viande froide pressée *[de conserve]*
lychee   litchi, letchi
macadamia nuts   noix du noyer de Queensland
macaroni   macaroni
   macaroni cheese   macaroni au gratin
macaroon   macaron
mace   macis
mackerel   maquereau
macrobiotic   macrobiotique
Madeira   madère
   Madeira cake   génoise au citron, gâteau de Savoie
   Madeira sauce   sauce madère
main course   plat principal
maize   maïs
mallard   colvert
malt   malt
mandarin   mandarine
mangetout   pois gourmands, pois mange-tout
mango   mangue
mangosteen   mangouste, mangoustan
maple syrup   sirop d'érable
maple sugar   sucre d'érable
margarine   margarine
marinade   marinade
marinated   mariné(e)
marjoram   marjolaine
market   marché
marmalade   marmelade d'oranges, confiture d'oranges
marrow *[vegetable]*   courge
marrow   moelle
   marrowbone   os à moelle
Marsala wine   marsala
marshmallow   guimauve
marzipan   massepain
mashed   en purée
mashed potatoes   pommes purée
matches   allumettes
matchstick potatoes   pommes allumettes
mature   mûr(e), fait *[cheese]*
mayonnaise   mayonnaise
mead   hydromel
meal   repas
meat   viande
   meat ball   boulette de viande
   meat loaf   terrine/pain de viande
   meat pie   tourte/pie de viande
medallion   médaillon
medium cooked   à point
medium rare *[steak]*   pas trop cuit
medium wine   vin pas trop corsé
medlar   nèfle
melon   melon
melted butter   beurre fondu

menu menu, carte
   set menu menu à prix fixe
meringue meringue
mild léger, légère
milk lait
   cow's milk lait de vache
   ewe's milk lait de brebis
   goat's milk lait de chèvre
   soya milk lait de soja
   milk chocolate chocolat au lait
   milkshake milk-shake
   poached in milk poché dans du lait
   with milk avec (du) lait; au lait
   without milk sans lait
minced meat hachis, viande hachée
mincemeat mincemeat *[préparation sucrée à base d'un mélange de fruits et raisins secs, et de suif]*
mince pie mince pie *[tarte(lette) avec mincemeat]*
mineral water eau minérale
   fizzy mineral water eau gazeuse
   still mineral water eau plate
minestrone *[soup]* *[soupe]* minestrone
mint menthe
   mint sauce sauce à la menthe *[fraîche]*
   mint jelly gelée à la menthe
mixed grill assiette de viandes grillées *[assorties]*
mixed herbs herbes arômatiques
mixed salad salade composée
mixed vegetables macédoine de légumes
mollusc mollusque
monkfish baudroie, lotte de mer
monosodium glutamate *[MSG]* glutamate monosodique *[MSG]*
morels morilles
moussaka moussaka
mousse mousse, mousseline
muesli müesli
muffin *[sweet, savoury]* muffin
mug mug, tasse *[sans soucoupe]*
mulberry mûre *[du mûrier]*
mullet rouget
mulligatawny *[soup]* potage au cari
mushroom champignon
   button mushrooms champignons de Paris
mushy peas purée de pois
mussel moule
mustard moutarde
mutton mouton
napkin serviette *[de table]*
natural nature
Neapolitan ice cream tranche napolitaine
neat sans eau ni glace
nectarine brugnon, nectarine
nettle ortie
no smoking défense de fumer
non-alcoholic drink boisson non alcoolisée; boisson sans alcool
non-smoking area section non fumeurs

noodles nouilles
    noodle soup potage au vermicelle
nut noix
    almond amande
    Brazil nut noix du Brésil
    cashew nut noix d'acajou, noix de cajou
    chestnut marron
    cobnut noisette
    coconut noix de coco
    hazelnut noisette, aveline
    peanut arachide, cacah(o)uète
    pecan nut noix de pécan, noix de pacane
    sweet chestnut châtaigne, marron
    walnut noix
nutmeg noix de muscade
oatcake biscuit à la farine d'avoine *[pour manger avec le fromage]*
oatmeal farine d'avoine
oats avoine
    porridge oats flocons d'avoine
octopus poulpe
off [*food, wine*] mauvais(e), pourri(e), tourné *[wine]*
offal abats
oil huile
okra gombo
olive olive
    black olives olives noires
    green olives olives vertes
olive oil huile d'olive
omelette omelette
on the rocks *[with ice]* avec glace, on the rocks
onion oignon
    onion soup soupe à l'oignon
open *[verb]* ouvrir
orange orange
    orange juice jus d'orange
    orange sauce sauce à l'orange; *[less sweet]* sauce bigarade
oregano origan
organic biologique
ostrich autruche
outdoors, outside dehors, à l'extérieur
oven four
overdone trop cuit(e)
oxtail queue de boeuf
    oxtail soup soupe à la queue de boeuf
ox tongue langue de boeuf
oyster huître
oyster mushroom pleurote
pancake crêpe, galette
pan-fried à la poêle, poêlé(e)
papaya papaye
paprika paprika
par-boiled pré-cuit(e), mi-cuit(e)
parfait parfait
Parma ham jambon de Parme
Parmesan *[cheese]* Parmesan
parsley persil
    curly parsley persil frisé

    flat parsley persil plat
    parsley sauce sauce au persil *[béchamel fortement persillée]*
parsnip panais
partridge perdrix; *[young]* perdreau
party fête, soirée
pasta pâtes *[alimentaires]*
    fresh pasta pâtes fraîches
pastry pâtisserie
    filo pastry pâte phyllo
    puff pastry pâte feuilletée
    shortcrust pastry pâte brisée
pasty chausson avec viande et pommes de terre
pâté pâté
    liver pâté pâté de foie gras
pawpaw papaye
pay *[verb]* payer
pea pois
    green peas petits pois
    green pea soup potage St Germain
    split peas pois cassés
    pea soup *[with split peas]* soupe aux pois *[cassés]*
peach pêche
peanut arachide
    peanut butter beurre de cacahouètes; d'arachides
pear poire
pearl barley orge perlée
pease-pudding purée de pois cassés
pecan nut noix de pécan, noix de pacane
    pecan pie tarte aux noix de pécan
peel *[verb]* peler, éplucher
peel *[noun]* pelure, peau, écorce
    grated peel zeste, écorce râpée
peeled sans pelure, sans peau
pepper *[spice]* poivre
    black/green/white pepper poivre noir/vert/blanc
    ground pepper poivre moulu
    whole pepper poivre en grains
    pepper mill moulin à poivre
    pepper pot poivrière
    pepper steak steak au poivre
pepper *[vegetable]* poivron
    green pepper poivron vert
    red pepper poivron rouge
    stuffed pepper poivron farci
peppermint menthe poivrée
perch perche *[d'eau douce]*
perry cidre de poire
persimmon plaquemine, kaki
pesto pistou
petits fours petits fours
pheasant faisan
pickled cabbage choucroute
pickled gherkin/cucumber cornichon *[saumuré/au vinaigre]*
pickled herring hareng mariné
pickled onion oignon au vinaigre
pickles pickles
picnic pique-nique
pie tarte, tourte

piece morceau
pig porc, cochon
   suckling pig cochon de lait, porcelet
pigeon pigeon
pig's trotters pieds de porc
pike brochet
pike-perch sandre
pilchard pilchard, *[grosse]* sardine
pine nuts pignons de pin
pineapple ananas
pinto bean haricot pinto
pistachio nut pistache
pitcher pichet, carafe
pitta bread pita
pizza pizza
plaice plie, carrelet
plain nature
   plain chocolate chocolat amer, noir, à croquer
plantain banane verte *[à cuire]*
plate assiette
plum prune
plum pudding plum pudding, pouding de Noël
plum tomato tomate oblongue, tomate allongée
poach pocher
poached poché(e)
poached egg oeuf poché
polenta polenta, semoule de maïs
pollack lieu
pomegranate grenade
popcorn *[sweet/salted]* maïs soufflé *[sucré/salé]*
porcini mushroom cèpe
pork porc
   pork chop côte de porc
   pork crackling couenne croquante *[du rôti de porc]*
porridge porridge, bouillie d'avoine
port *[vin de]* porto
pot roast viande en cocotte
potato pomme de terre
   baked potato pomme de terre au four
   boiled potatoes pommes de terre à l'anglaise
   fried potatoes pommes de terre sautées
   mashed potatoes purée de pommes de terre, pommes purée
   new potatoes pommes de terre nouvelles
   potato chips pommes frites
   potato crisps pommes chips
   potato dumpling gnocchi Parmentier
   potato salad salade de pommes de terre
potted shrimp petite terrine de crevettes au beurre
poultry volaille
pound cake gâteau quatre-quarts
poussin poussin
prawn bouquet, crevette rose
   Dublin bay prawn langoustine
preserves conserves
price prix
   price list tarif
prime rib côte de boeuf *[première qualité]*

profiteroles profiteroles
protein protéines
prune pruneau *[sec]*
pudding *[savoury]* pouding
pudding *[sweet]* dessert, pouding, pudding
pudding rice riz rond
pudding wine vin de dessert, vin doux
puff pastry pâte feuilletée
pulses légumineuses
pumpkin potiron, citrouille
pure pur(e)
purée purée
purslane pourpier
puy lentils lentilles de Puy
quail caille
   quails' eggs oeufs de cailles
quality qualité
quark quark, fromage blanc
quarter quart
quiche quiche
   quiche lorraine quiche lorraine
quince coing
rabbit lapin; *[young]* lapereau
rack carré
   rack of lamb carré d'agneau
   rack of ribs carré *[d'agneau, de porc]*
radicchio trévise, chicorée rouge
radish/radishes radis
ragout ragoût
rainbow trout truite arc-en-ciel
raisin raisin sec
ramekin ramequin
rancid rance
rare *[steak, meat]* saignant(e)
raspberry framboise
ravioli ravioli
raw cru(e)
receipt reçu
recommend recommander
recipe recette
red cabbage chou rouge
red chilli piment fort, piment rouge
redcurrant groseille rouge
   redcurrant jelly gelée de groseilles
redfish rascasse
red mullet rouget barbet
red pepper poivron rouge, piment doux rouge
red wine vin rouge
reindeer chevreuil
rennet présure
reservation réservation
reserve réserver
restaurant restaurant
rhubarb rhubarbe
ribs côtes
   rack of ribs carré *[d'agneau, de porc]*
   rib of beef côte de boeuf, entrecôte

    spare ribs   travers de porc, côtes levées
rice riz
    long-grained rice   riz Caroline
    rice paper   papier de riz
    rice pudding   pouding au riz; riz au lait *[cuit au four]*
    risotto rice   riz pour risotto *[riz rond du Piémont]*
    wild rice   riz sauvage
rind *[cheese]* pâte
ripe mûr(e)
rissole rissole
river rivière; *[fish]* d'eau douce
roast *[verb]* rôtir
roast *[noun]* rôti de boeuf/porc etc
    roast beef   rôti de boeuf, rosbif
    roast chicken   poulet rôti
    roast pork   rôti de porc
    roast meats   viandes rôties
roasted rôti(e)
rock salt sel gemme
rocket roquette
rockfish rascasse
roe oeufs de poisson
    hard roe   oeufs de poisson
    soft roe   laitance
roll *[bread]* petit pain
rolled oats flocons d'avoine
rollmop herring rollmop, hareng roulé *[mariné]*
romaine *[lettuce]* romaine
room temperature chambré(e)
root racine
rosé *[wine]* *[vin]* rosé
rosehip fruit de l'églantier
rosemary romarin
roulade roulade
rum rhum
    rum baba   baba au rhum
rump steak romsteak
runner bean haricot grimpant
rusk biscotte *[pour bébé]*
rye seigle
rye bread pain de seigle, pumpernickel
rye whisky rye *[whisky de seigle]*
saccharin saccharine
saddle *[of rabbit, lamb]* râble *[de lapin]*; selle *[d'agneau]*
safflower carthame
saffron safran
sage sauge
sago sagou
saithe lieu noir
salad salade
    green salad   salade verte
    mixed salad   salade composée, salade panachée
    salad bowl   saladier
    salad cream   crème mayonnaise
    salad dressing   vinaigrette
    side salad   salade verte *[en accompagnement]*
salami saucisson italien

salmon   saumon
   salmon steak   darne de saumon
   salmon trout   truite saumonée
salsify   salsifis
salt   sel
   low-salt   hyposodé(e)
   sea salt   sel marin
   salt cellar, salt mill   salière
salted   salé(e), avec sel
salty   salé(e)
sand sole   sole *[plus petite que la 'vraie sole']*
sandwich   sandwich
   cheese sandwich   sandwich au fromage
   club sandwich   club sandwich
   ham sandwich   sandwich au jambon
sardine   sardine
sauce   sauce
   white sauce   *[sauce]* béchamel, sauce blanche
saucer   soucoupe
saury   balaou
sausage   saucisse
   liver sausage   leberwurst
   sausage roll   friand
sauté   sauté
   sauté pan   sautoir
   sautéed   sauté(e), au sautoir
saveloy   cervelas
savoury   entremets salé
savoy cabbage   chou vert frisé *[pommé]*
scald   ébouillanter
scallion *[US]*   ciboule, cive
scallop   coquille St Jacques
scalloped chicken *[US]*   poulet en sauce blanche, au four
scalloped potatoes *[US]*   gratin dauphinois
scampi   queues de langoustine, scampi
scone *[UK]*   scone *[petit pain qu'on mange avec confiture et crème]*
scorpion fish   rascasse
Scotch   à l'ecossaise
   Scotch broth   potage de mouton, légumes et orge
   Scotch egg   oeuf en croquette *[oeuf (dur) enrobé de chair à saucisse, pané et frit]*
scrambled eggs   oeufs brouillés
sea bass   loup *[de mer]*, bar
sea bream   brème de mer
seafood   fruits de mer
sear   *[faire]* saisir
sea salt   sel marin
sea trout   truite de mer
sea view *[a table with]*   vue sur la mer
seasoning   assaisonnement
seasoned   assaisonné
seat   place
seaweed   algue
second course   plat principal, deuxième plat
selection   sélection, choix
sell-by date   date limite de vente
semi-dry   demi-sec

semi-skimmed milk lait demi-écrémé
semolina semoule
service service
    service charge service
    service discretionary service à la discrétion du client
    service included service compris
    service not included service non compris
serviette serviette *[de table]*
sesame seeds graines de sésame
shad alose
shallot échalote
shallow-fry *[faire]* rissoler
shandy panaché
    a half of shandy un demi panaché
shank jarret
shark requin, aiguillat
sharp fort(e), acide
shell coquille
shellfish crustacé, coquillage, fruits de mer
shepherd's pie hachis Parmentier
sherbet sorbet, granité
sherry xérès
shiitake mushrooms champignons chinois *[shiitake]*
shop magasin
shortbread sablé
shortcrust *[pastry]* pâte brisée
shoulder épaule, palette
shrimp crevette *[grise]*
    shrimp cocktail crevettes mayonnaise
shut fermé
side dish/es accompagnement(s)
sift tamiser
silverside gîte à la noix
simmer *[laisser]* mijoter
single cream crème *[légère]*
sirloin aloyau, faux-filet
skate raie
skewer brochette
skimmed milk lait écrémé
skin peau, pelure
skipjack bonite
slice tranche
    slice of bread tranche de pain
    slice of pie part de tarte
    slice of ham tranche de jambon
sliced tranché(e)
sloe prunelle
    sloe gin eau de vie de prunelle
smell arôme, odeur
smelt éperlan
smoke *[a cigarette]* fumer
smoke *[noun]* fumée
smoked fumé(e)
    smoked bacon lard fumé
    smoked cheese fromage fumé
    smoked eel anguille fumée
    smoked fish poisson fumé

smoked haddock aiglefin fumé
smoked kipper hareng saur, hareng fumé
smoked meat viande fumé
smoked salmon saumon fumé
smoker fumeur, fumeuse
snack *[light meal]* repas léger; *[between meals]* casse-croûte
snail escargot
snipe bécassine
soda bread pain au bicarbonate de soude
soda water eau de seltz
soft doux; douce
soft-boiled egg oeuf à la coque
soft cheese fromage à pâte molle
soft drink boisson *[gazeuse]* non alcoolisée
soft roe laitance
sole sole
sorbet sorbet
sorghum sorgho
sorrel oseille
soufflé soufflé
   cheese soufflé soufflé au fromage
soup soupe, potage
   broth bouillon
   chowder soupe de poissons et légumes à base de lait
   consommé consommé
   fish stock court-bouillon
   fish soup soupe de poisson(s)
   mulligatawny potage au cari
   onion soup soupe à l'oignon
   soup of the day soupe/potage du jour
   soup spoon cuillère à soupe
   vegetable soup soupe de légumes; minestrone
   vichyssoise vichyssoise
sour aigre
   sour cream crème aigre
   sweet and sour aigre-doux (-douce)
soya bean *[fève de]* soja
soya milk lait de soja
soya sauce sauce soja
spaghetti spaghetti
   spaghetti bolognese spaghetti à la bolognaise
spare ribs travers de porc, côtes levées
sparkling pétillant(e)
   sparkling water eau gazeuse
   sparkling wine vin mousseux, vin pétillant
speciality spécialité
spice épice
spicy épicé(e)
spinach épinard
spiny lobster langouste
spirits alcool *[fort]*, spiritueux
sponge biscuits biscuits à la cuillère
sponge cake gâteau mousseline; génoise
spoon cuillère, cuiller
   spoonful cuillerée
sprat sprat, harenguet, anchois de Norvège
spring greens jeunes feuilles de choux, brocolis, etc.
spring onion ciboule, cive

spring lamb agnelet
spring roll nem
spring water eau de source
sprouts *[Brussels]* choux de Bruxelles
squab pigeonneau
squash courge
squid calmar, encornet
starch amidon
stale rassis(e)
starter entrée
steak *[beef]* bifteck, steak
steak and kidney pie pie de bifteck et rognons
steak and kidney pudding pouding de bifteck et rognons
steam *[verb]* cuire à la vapeur
  steamed *[cuit]* à la vapeur
  steamed vegetables légumes à la vapeur
stew *[meat]* fricassée, ragoût
  lamb stew navarin
stewed *[meat]* (en) fricassée; *[fruit]* en compote
  stewed fruit compote de fruits, fruits en compote
  stewed steak fricassée/ragoût de boeuf
Stilton fromage stilton
stir-fry sauter à la chinoise
stock bouillon
  vegetable stock bouillon de légumes
stout stout *[bière brune]*
stove cuisinière, four
straight *[US]* sans eau ni glace
strawberry fraise
  strawberry jam confiture de fraises
  strawberry shortcake gâteau fourré aux fraises, recouvert de crème
  Chantilly
streaky bacon lard de poitrine, poitrine fumée
strip steak entrecôte
strong fort(e)
stuffed farci(e), fourré(e)
  stuffed olives olives farcies
stuffing farce
sturgeon esturgeon
suckling pig cochon de lait, porcelet
suet graisse de rognon de bœuf
sugar sucre
  caster sugar sucre semoule
  granulated sugar sucre granulé
  icing sugar sucre en poudre, sucre glace
  sugar-coated almonds dragées
sugar snap peas petit pois gourmands, pois mange-tout
sultanas raisins de Smyrne
sundae coupe glacée
sun-dried séché(e) au soleil
sunflower tournesol
  sunflower oil huile de tournesol
  sunflower seeds graines de tournesol
supermarket supermarché
supper dîner, souper
supplement supplément
swede navet *[de Suède]*, rutabaga

English-French

sweet   sucré(e), doux (douce)
   sweets *[candy]*   bonbons; friandises
   sweet *[wine]* *[vin]* doux, vin de dessert
   sweet chesnut   châtaigne, marron
   sweet potato   patate douce
   sweet trolley   desserts *[présentés sur une table roulante]*
sweet and sour   aigre-doux (-douce)
sweetbreads   ris de veau
sweetcorn   maïs (en épis, en grains)
sweetener *[artificial]*   édulcorant
Swiss roll   (gâteau) roulé
swordfish   espadon
syllabub   syllabub, sabayon
syrup   sirop
table   table
   tablecloth   nappe
   tablespoon   cuillère à dessert
   table by the window   table près de la fenêtre
   table wine   vin de table
tagliatelle   tagliatelle
take away   à emporter
tangerine   tangerine
tap water   eau du robinet
tapioca   tapioca
tarragon   estragon
tart   tartelette
tartar sauce   sauce tartare
tartare   tartare
taste   goût
tasty   savoureux, savoureuse
tea   thé
   afternoon tea   (le) thé de 5 heures
   beef tea   bouillon de boeuf
   cup of tea   tasse de thé
   green tea   thé vert
   herbal tea   tisane, infusion
   high tea   repas de 5 heures *[Ecosse et Nord de l'Angleterre]*
   iced tea   thé glacé
   lemon tea   thé (au) citron
   teacake   brioche *[coupée, grillée, avec beurre, servie avec du thé]*
   teaspoon   cuillère à thé
   tea with milk   thé au lait
   tea-time   heure du thé
   teapot   théière
tench   tanche
tender   tendre
tenderloin   filet *[de boeuf, de porc]*
terrine   terrine
thick   épais
thirsty *(to be thirsty)*   avoir soif
thrush   grive
thyme   thym
tin   boîte de conserve
tinned   en boîte *[de conserve]*
tip   pourboire
toad in the hole   saucisses couvertes de pâte *[au four]*
toast *[tribute]*   toast

toast   pain grillé
   French toast   pain perdu, pain doré
toasted   grillé(e)
toffee   caramel *[au beurre]*
tofu   tofu, pâté de soja
toilet(s)   WC; toilettes
   toilet paper   papier hygiénique
tomato   tomate
   tomato juice   jus de tomate
   tomato ketchup   ketchup, sauce tomate
   tomato purée   purée de tomates
   tomato salad   salade de tomate
   tomato sauce   sauce (à la) tomate
tongue   langue *[de boeuf]*
tonic water   eau tonique, tonic
toothpick   cure-dent(s)
tope   milandre
tough *[meat]*   dur(e)
treacle   mélasse
   treacle tart   tarte au sirop de maïs
trifle   trifle *[génoise, fruits, Chantilly]*
trimmings   accompagnement, garniture
tripe   tripes, gras-double
trolley   chariot
trout   truite
truffle   truffe
   chocolate truffle *[sweet]*   truffe *[au chocolat]*
   truffle butter   beurre de truffes
tuna, tunny   thon
turbot   turbot
turkey   dinde
   roast turkey   dinde rôtie
turmeric   curcuma
turnip   navet
   turnip tops   fanes de navet
turnover   chausson *[aux pommes, etc.]*
uncooked   cru(e); qui n'est pas cuit(e)
underdone   pas assez cuit(e)
unsalted butter   beurre sans sel
upside-down cake   gâteau renversé
use by   à consommer avant
vanilla   vanille
   vanilla essence   extrait de vanille *[liquide]*
   vanilla ice cream   glace à la vanille
   vanilla pod/bean   gousse de vanille
   vanilla sugar   sucre vanillé
veal   veau
   veal escalope   escalope de veau
vegan   végétalien (-ienne)
vegetable   légume
   vegetable chilli   chili végétarien
   vegetable oil   huile végétale
   vegetable soup   soupe de légumes; minestrone
vegetarian   végétarien (-ienne)
   vegetarian bolognaise   spaghetti végétariens à la bolognaise
   vegetarian burger   hamburger végétal
   vegetarian cooking   cuisine végétarienne
   vegetarian gravy   sauce végétarienne

vegetarian lasagne lasagne végétarienne
vegetarian sausage saucisses de soja
venison venaison, chevreuil
  venison cutlets côtelettes de chevreuil
vermicelli vermicelle
very dry *[wine]* très secretary
very rare *[meat]* bleu
very sweet très sucré(e)
Victoria sponge *[cake]* génoise
vinaigrette vinaigrette
vinegar vinaigre
vine vin
  vine leaves feuilles de vigne
vintage millésime
virgin olive oil huile d'olive vierge
vol au vent vol-au-vent, bouchée feuilletée
  chicken vol au vent bouchée à la reine
wafer gaufrette
waffles gaufres
waiter garçon, serveur
waitress serveuse
Waldorf salad salade Waldorf *[pommes, céleri, noix, avec mayonnaise]*
walnut noix; cerneau *[de la noix]*
warm *[salad etc.]* tiède
water eau
  bottled water eau en bouteille
  fizzy water eau gazeuse
  glass of water verre d'eau
  iced water eau glacée, très froide
  jug of water carafe d'eau
  mineral water eau minérale
  sparkling water eau gazeuse
  spring water eau de source
  still water eau plate, eau non gazeuse
watercress cresson de fontaine
watermelon pastèque
wedding cake gâteau de mariage
well done *[meat]* bien cuit(e)
Welsh rarebit/rabbit pain avec fromage grillé
whale baleine
wheat blé
  wheat flour farine de blé
  wheatgerm germe de blé
whelk buccin
whipped cream crème Chantilly, crème fouettée
whisky whisky écossais
whitebait *[sprats]* blanchaille
white blanc *[blanche]*
  white bread pain de mie, pain blanc
  white meat viande blanche
  white wine vin blanc
white truffle truffe blanche
whiting merlan
whole complet
whole grain mustard moutarde de Meaux
wholemeal bread pain complet
wholewheat blé complet
  wholewheat flour farine de blé complet

whortleberry   myrtille
wild   sauvage
    wild boar   sanglier
    wild rice   riz sauvage
    wild strawberry   fraise des bois, fraise sauvage
    wild mushrooms   champignons sauvages
window table   table près de la fenêtre
wine   vin
    bottle of wine   bouteille de vin
    glass of wine   verre de vin
    house wine   vin (de la) maison
    local wine   vin local, vin de pays
    red wine   vin rouge
    sparkling wine   vin mousseux, vin pétillant
    sweet/pudding wine   vin doux, vin de dessert
    wine cooler   rafraîchisseur *[à vin]*
    wine list   carte des vins
    wine vinegar *[red, white]*   vinaigre de vin *[rouge, blanc]*
    wine waiter   sommelier
    white wine   vin blanc
winkle   bigorneau
woodcock   bécasse
Worcestershire sauce   sauce Worcester(shire)
yam   igname; *[US]* patate douce
yeast   levure
yoghurt   yaourt, yogourt
    plain yoghurt   yaourt nature
Yorkshire pudding   Yorkshire pudding *[beignet de pâte frite, salé]*
zabaglione   zabaglione, sabayon
zest   zeste
zucchini *[US]*   courgette

Useful German Expressions

Restaurants

Biergarten	*beer garden: garden pub with little indoor service*
Brauhaus	*literally 'brewery': pub that brews its own beer*
Café	*place that chiefly sells coffee and cakes*
Cafeteria	*self-service restaurant*
Gasthof	*a country inn (with accommodation)*
Gaststätte	*pub, inn or restaurant*
Gastwirtschaft	*a simpler type of 'Gaststätte'*
Hof	*a superior type of hotel*
Hotel	*hotel*
Imbiss(-Bude)	*snack bar*
Kneipe	*pub or bar usually frequented by younger people*
Lokal	*simple restaurant, pub with food*
Pizzeria	*restaurant (chiefly selling pizzas)*
Restaurant	*restaurant*
Schankwirtschaft	*pub with little or no food*
Schnellimbiss	*fast-food restaurant*
Stehcafé	*stand-up café*
Weinstube	*wine bar*

Menus

In Germany, menus are usually only split into:

Vorspeisen	*starters*
Hauptgerichte	*main courses*
Desserts	*desserts*

Meals

06:30 - 09:00	Frühstück *breakfast*
12:00 - 14:00	Mittagessen *lunch*
18:30 - 22:00	Abendessen *dinner*

Tipping

Restaurants in Germany automatically add their service (*Bedienung)* charge to the bill (around 15%) and, although it isn't compulsory, a small tip is appreciated as an indication of how good the service was — simply rounding up the bill is acceptable. Always hand the tip to the waiter/waitress, as leaving money on the table is considered extremely poor etiquette.

Restaurant rating scheme

Star scheme

Getting to a restaurant

Can you recommend a good restaurant?	*Können Sie ein gutes Restaurant empfehlen?*
I would like to reserve a table for evening	*Ich möchte für heute abend einen* this *Tisch reservieren*
Do you have a table for three/four people?	*Haben Sie einen Tisch für drei/vier Personen?*
We would like the table for 8 o'clock	*Wir hätten gern den Tisch für acht Uhr*
Could we have a table ....?	*Könnten wir einen Tisch .... haben?*
by the window	*am Fenster*
outside	*draußen*
on the terrace	*auf der Terrasse*
in the non-smoking area	*für Nichtraucher*
What time do you open?	*Um wieviel Uhr öffnen Sie?*
Could you order a taxi for me?	*Könnten Sie mir bitte ein Taxi bestellen?*

Ordering

Waiter/waitress!	*Ober/Hallo!*
What do you recommend?	*Was empfehlen Sie?*
What are the specials of the day?	*Welche Tagesgerichte haben Sie?*
Is this the fixed-price menu?	*Ist das die Tageskarte?*
Can we see the à-la-carte menu?	*Können wir bitte die Speisekarte haben?*
Is this fresh?	*Ist dies hier frisch?*
Is this local?	*Kommt dies aus der Umgebung hier?*
I would like a/an ...	*Ich hätte gern ein/eine/einen ...*
Could we have ... please?	*Könnten wir bitte ... haben?*
an ashtray	*einen Aschenbecher*
the bill	*die Rechnung*
our coats	*unsere Mäntel*
a cup	*eine Tasse*
a fork	*eine Gabel*
a glass	*ein Glas*
a knife	*ein Messer*
the menu	*die Speisekarte/das Menü*
a napkin	*eine Serviette*
a plate	*einen Teller*
a spoon	*einen Löffel*
a toothpick	*einen Zahnstocher*
the wine menu	*die Weinkarte*
May I have some ...?	*Könnte ich bitte ... haben?*

bread		*etwas Brot*
butter		*etwas Butter*
ice		*ein paar Eiswürfel*
lemon		*ein Stück/Scheibe Zitrone*
milk		*(ein wenig) Milch*
pepper		*den Pfeffer*
salt		*das Salz*
sugar		*etwas Zucker*
water		*ein Glas/eine Flasche/*
		einen Krug/etwas Wasser
I would like it ...		*Ich hätte es gern ...*
baked		*gebacken*
boiled		*gekocht*
fried		*(in der Pfanne) gebraten*
grilled		*gegrillt*
poached		*pochiert*
roast		*(im Ofen) gebraten*
smoked		*geräuchert*
steamed		*gedünstet*
very rare		*sehr blutig*
rare		*blutig*
medium		*rosa, englisch*
well-done		*durchgebraten*

Useful phrases for vegetarians

I am ...		*Ich bin...*
vegetarian		*Vegetarier*
lacto-ovo-vegetarian		*Lacto-Ovo-Vegetarier*
lacto-vegetarian		*Lacto-Vegetarier*
vegan		*Veganer*
I don't eat ...		*Ich esse kein(e)...*
I don't eat meat/pork/chicken		*Ich esse kein Fleisch/*
		Schweinefleisch/Hühnchen
I don't eat fish		*Ich esse keinen Fisch*
I eat eggs/milk/cheese		*Ich esse Eier/Milch/Käse*
I don't eat eggs/milk/cheese		*Ich esse keine Eier/Milch/Käse*
I don't eat suet/lard/dripping		*Ich esse keinen Rindertalg/*
		Schweineschmalz/Bratenfett
Do you have anything without meat?		*Haben Sie etwas ohne Fleisch?*
Do you have any vegetarian dishes?		*Haben Sie vegetarische Gerichte?*
Is there a vegetarian restaurant near here?		*Ist hier ein vegetarisches Restaurant in der Nähe?*
Is this cheese made with rennet?		*Ist dieser Käse mit Lab gemacht?*
Do you have a rennet-free cheese?		*Haben Sie einen labfreien Käse?*
Do you serve this dish without meat/eggs/cheese?		*Servieren Sie dieses Essen ohne Fleisch/Eier/Käse?*
Does this sauce/soup contain beef/chicken/fish/meat stock?		*Enthält diese Soße/Suppe Rindfleisch/Hühnchen/Fisch/ Fleischbrühe?*

Does this dish contain gelatine/aspic?	*Enthält dieses Gericht Gelatine/Aspik?*
Does this contain organic ingredients?	*Enthält das biologisch angebaute Zutaten?*
Do you use GM foods/MSG?	*Verwenden Sie Genprodukte/Natriumglutamat?*

Useful phrases for people on special diets etc.

I am diabetic	*Ich bin Diabetiker*
Does this dish contain nuts?	*Enthält dieses Gericht Nüsse?*
I am allergic to …	*Ich bin allergisch gegen...*
I have a peanut/seafood/wheat allergy	*Ich habe eine Erdnuss-/Meeresfrüchte-/Weizenallergie*
I don't eat wheat/gluten	*Ich esse keinen Weizen/kein Gluten*

Drinks

Can I see the wine menu, please?	*Kann ich bitte die Weinkarte haben?*
I would like a/an …	*Ich hätte gern …*
aperitif	*einen Aperitif*
another	*das Gleiche nochmal*
I would like a glass of ...	*Ich hätte gern ein Glas ...*
red wine	*Rotwein*
white wine	*Weißwein*
rosé (wine)	*Rosé*
sparkling wine	*Sekt/Schaumwein*
still water	*(Mineral)wasser ohne Kohlensäure*
sparkling water	*Mineralwasser (mit Kohlensäure)*
tap water	*Leitungswasser*
with lemon	*mit Zitrone*
with ice	*mit Eis*
with water	*mit Wasser*
neat	*pur*
I would like a bottle of....	*Ich hätte gern eine Flasche ...*
this wine	*von diesem Wein*
house red	*roten Hauswein*
house white	*weißen Hauswein*
Is this wine ...?	*Ist dieser Wein ...?*
very dry	*sehr trocken*
dry	*trocken*
sweet	*süß*
local	*aus örtlichem Anbau*
This wine is	*Dieser Wein ist ...*
not very good	*nicht sehr gut*
not very cold	*nicht sehr kalt*
corked	*verkorkt*
I would like a …	*Ich hätte gerne...*
fruit juice	*Fruchtsaft*
lemonade	*Limonade*
non-alcoholic beer	*alkoholfreies Bier*

non-alcoholic wine	*alkoholfreier Wein*
low-alcohol beer	*Bier mit wenig Alkoholgehalt*
low-alcohol wine	*Wein mit wenig Alkoholgehalt*
non-alcoholic beverage	*alkoholfreies Getränk*
decaffeinated	*entkoffeiniert*
soft drink	*Erfrischungsgetränk*

Complaints

This is not what I ordered	*Das habe ich nicht bestellt*
I asked for ...	*Ich wollte ...*
Could I change this?	*Kann ich es umtauschen?*
The meat is ...	*Das Fleisch ist ...*
overdone	*verbraten*
underdone	*nicht durchgebraten; blutig*
tough	*zäh*
I don't like this	*Das schmeckt mir nicht*
The food is cold	*Das Essen ist kalt*
This is not fresh	*Das ist nicht frisch*
What is taking so long?	*Warum dauert es so lang?*
This is not clean	*Das ist nicht sauber*

Paying

Could I have the bill?	*Die Rechnung, bitte*
I would like to pay	*Ich möchte gern zahlen*
Can I charge it to my room?	*Können Sie es auf meine Rechnung setzen?*
We would like to pay separately	*Wir möchten getrennt bezahlen*
There's a mistake in the bill	*Die Rechnung stimmt nicht*
What's this amount for?	*Was wurde hier berechnet?*
Is service included?	*Ist die Bedienung eingeschlossen?*
Do you accept traveller's cheques?	*Nehmen Sie auch Reiseschecks?*
Can I pay by credit card?	*Kann ich mit Kreditkarte bezahlen?*

Numbers

0	*null*	15	*fünfzehn*
1	*eins*	16	*sechszehn*
2	*zwei*	17	*siebzehn*
3	*drei*	18	*achtzehn*
4	*vier*	19	*neunzehn*
5	*fünf*	20	*zwanzig*
6	*sechs*	30	*dreißig*
7	*sieben*	40	*vierzig*
8	*acht*	50	*fünfzig*
9	*neun*	60	*sechszig*
10	*zehn*	70	*siebzig*
11	*elf*	80	*achtzig*
12	*zwölf*	90	*neunzig*
13	*dreizehn*	100	*einhundert*
14	*vierzehn*	200 etc.	*zweihundert*

German-English

Aachener Printen   spicy honey biscuits
Aal   eel
Aalraupe   burbot
Abendbrot   supper
Abendessen   dinner *[evening]*, supper
abräumen   clear up
Ahornsirup   maple syrup
Ahornzucker   maple sugar
Aland   ide *[fish]*
Alfalfasprossen   alfalfa sprouts
Alge   seaweed
Alkohol   alcohol
alkoholfreies Getränk   soft drink
Allergie   allergy
allergisch *[gegen]*   allergic *[to]*
Allgewürz   allspice
Alpenklüber   dried Swiss pork and beef sausage, eaten raw
Alse   shad
Alsterwasser   shandy
alt, altbacken   aged, old, stale
an der Sonne getrocknet   sun-dried
Ananas   pineapple
anbräunen, anbraten   brown *[verb]*
ändern   change
angebrannt   burnt
Angelika   angelica
angeschlagen   chipped *[glass, plate]*
Anis   aniseed
ankochen   par-boil
Anschovis   anchovy
Aperitif   aperitif
Apfel   apple
    Äpfel mit Haube   baked apples and custard
Apfel-Beignet   apple fritter
Apfelbettelmann   apple crumble
Apfelcharlotte   apple charlotte
Apfelessig   cider vinegar
Apfelkompott   apple sauce
Apfelkren   apple and horseradish sauce
Apfelkuchen   apple tart
Apfelmus   apple purée
Apfelsaft   apple juice
Apfelschnitze   apple fritter
Apfelsine   orange
Apfelstrudel   apple strudel
Apfeltasche   apple turnover
Apfeltorte   apple tart
Apfelwein, Appelwoi   cider
Apostelkuchen   brioche

Appetithappen   canapé(s)
Aprikose   apricot
arme Ritter   French toast
Aroma   aroma; flavour, taste
Arrowrootstärke   arrowroot
Artischocke   artichoke
Artischockenböden   artichoke bottoms
Aschenbecher   ashtray
Aspik   aspic
Aubergine   aubergine, eggplant
auf Holzkohle gegrillt   charcoal grilled
aufgeschnitten   carved, sliced
Auflauf   bake *[noun]*
Auflaufförmchen   ramekin *[small container]*
aufschneiden   carve
Aufschnitt   cold meat
auftauen   defrost
aufwärmen   heat up
ausgezeichnet   excellent
Auslese   selection
Auslese   German wine from selected grapes
Auster   oyster
Austernpilz   oyster mushroom
Auswahl   selection
Avocado   avocado
Baby-Aale   baby eels
Babyflasche   baby's bottle
Baby-Gemüse   baby vegetables
Baby-Lauch *[stangen]*   baby leeks
Baby-Mais *[kolben]*   baby corn *[cob]*
Babynahrung   baby food
Bachforelle   river trout
backen   bake
Bäckerei   bakery
Backfisch mit Pommes frites   fish and chips
Backhähnchen, Backhuhn, Backhendl   fried chicken
Backobst   dried fruit
Backofen   oven
Backpflaume   prune
Backwerk   cakes, pastries
Baiser   meringue
ballaststoffreich   high-fibre
Balsamessig   balsamic vinegar
Bambser   potato and apple fritters
Bambusprosse   bamboo shoot
Banane   banana
   Banane-Beignet   banana fritter
   Bananensplit   banana split
Bandnudeln   ribbon pasta
Bar   bar *[pub]*
Barbecue   barbecue
Bärenfang   honey liqueur
Basilikum   basil
   Basilikum-Pesto   basil pesto
Basmatireis   basmati rice
Batate   sweet potato
Bauernbrot   round brown crusty *[rye]* loaf

German-English

87

Bauernfrühstück   mixture of fried potatoes, eggs and bacon
Bauernomelett   bacon and onion omelette
Bauernschmalz   dripping made from pork fat, apples and herbs
Bauernschmaus   sauerkraut, pork sausages and dumplings
Bauernsuppe   bean, bacon and vegetable soup
Baumkuchen   tree-shaped Christmas cake, iced with chocolate
Bay(e)rische Creme   Bavarian cream
Bearner Soße   béarnaise *[sauce]*
Béchamelsoße   béchamel *[sauce]*
Becher   mug
Bedienung   service
  Bedienungskosten   service charge
  Bedienung *[nicht]* **inbegriffen**   service *[not]* included
Beefsteak   beef steak, *[US]* strip steak
Beere   berry
Beerenauslese   German wine made from fully or overripe grapes
Beetensuppe   borscht *[beetroot soup]*
Beignet   fritter
Beilage   side dish
Beilagen   accompaniments, garnishes, trimmings
Beinfleisch   boiled beef *[on the bone]*
Beize   marinade
Beleg   receipt
belegtes Brot   sandwich
Bergamotte   bergamot
Berliner   doughnut
Berliner Riesen Bratwurst   large bratwurst
Berliner Rotwurst   black pudding made with pig's blood
Berliner Weiße mit Schuss   low-alcohol beer with fruit juice
beschmutzen   dirty *[verb]*
Besteck   cutlery
betagt   aged
Bethmännchen   marzipan biscuits decorated with almonds
Beugel   filled croissant
Beutelmelone   cantaloup *[melon]*
bezahlen   pay *[verb]*
Bickbeere   bilberry, whortleberry
Bienenstich   cream-filled cake coated with sugar and almonds
Bier   beer
Biergarten   beer garden
Bierschinken   lean pork slicing sausage
Bierwurst   coarse dried pork or beef and garlic slicing sausage
billig   cheap
biologisch   organic
Birkhuhn   grouse
Birne   pear
Birnenmost   perry
Biskotten   sponge biscuits
Biskuitkuchen   sponge cake, angel food cake
Biskuitrolle   Swiss roll
Bismarckheringe   marinated herring fillets with sliced onion
bitter   bitter
Bitterschokolade   plain chocolate
blanchieren   blanch
  blanchiert   blanched
Blätterteig   puff pastry
Blätterteigpastete   vol-au-vent

Blätterteigschnitte mit Sahnefüllung   cream slice
Blaubeere   blueberry, blaeberry
blauer Wittling   blue whiting
Blaufelchen   pollan, whitefish
Blauschimmelkäse   blue cheese
Blauschimmelsteak   steak cooked with blue cheese, mushrooms and bacon
Blieschen   dab
Blindhuhn   green bean and bacon casserole with apples and pears
Blinis   blinis
Blumenkohl   cauliflower
Blut   blood
blutig   rare *[meat]*
Blutwurst   similar to black pudding
Blutwurstroulade   rolled white cabbage leaf stuffed with Blutwurst
Bockbier   strong dark beer
Bockwurst   smoked Frankfurter, made with minced veal or beef and pork;
  served hot
Bohne   bean
Bohnenfleisch   beef fillet cooked with green beans
Bohnenkraut   savory
Bohnentopf   bean stew
Bonbon   sweet, candy *[US]*
Bonito   bonito
Bordelaise, Bordeauxsoße   bordelaise sauce
Borlotti-Bohnen   borlotti beans
Borretsch   borage
Bouillon   broth, stock
Bouletten   hamburger
Bowle   fruit cup
Brachse(n), Brassen   bream
Brandteig   choux pastry
Branntwein   brandy
Bratapfel   baked apple
braten   roast *[verb]*
braten: in der Pfanne braten   fry
Braten   roast *[noun]*
Bratenfett   dripping
Bratensoße   gravy
Bratfisch   fried fish
Brathähnchen, Brathendl   roasting chicken, poussin
Brateringe: eingelegte Bratheringe   marinated fried herrings
Brathuhn   roast chicken
Bratkartoffeln   fried potoatoes
Bratpfanne   sauté pan
Bratwurst   fine pale pork or veal sausage
Brauhaus   brewery
braune Butter   brown butter
braune Soße   brown sauce
brauner Zucker   brown sugar, demerara sugar
Braunschweiger Kohl   cabbage
Brechbohnen   French beans
Breitling   brisling, sprats, whitebait
Brezel   pretzel
Bries   sweetbreads
Brioche   brioche
Brokkoli   broccoli
Brombeere   blackberry

German-English

Bröschen sweetbreads
Brot bread; loaf
Brotlaib loaf
Brötchen roll *[bread]*
Brotkock bread pudding
Brotmesser bread knife
Bratkartoffeln fried potoatoes
Brühe broth, gravy
Brühwurst lightly smoked sausage scalded to seal in flavour
Brunnenkresse watercress
Brust, Bruststück breast
Bruzzelfleisch fried pork with onions
Bucheckern beech nuts
Büchse tin
Büchsen-, in Büchsen tinned, canned *[US]*
Buchweizen buckwheat
Bückling kipper
Büfett buffet
Büffel buffalo
Bug shoulder
Bulette rissole
Bulgur bulgar wheat, bulgur wheat
Bündner Fleisch cured air-dried beef
bunt colourful
bunter Kartoffelsalat mixed potato salad
Burgunder *[wein]* Burgundy *[wine]*
Buschbohnen French beans
Butter butter
Butterfisch butterfish
Buttermilch buttermilk
Buttersalat butterhead lettuce, round lettuce
Butterschmalz melted butter
Buttersoße butter sauce
Cafe café
Cappuccino cappucino *[coffee]*
Caramelcreme crème caramel
Carbonara carbonara
Cäsar-Salat *[mit mit knoblauch Salatsoße, Croûtons und Parmesankäse]* Caesar salad
Cashewnuss cashew nut
Cassata cassata
Cayennepfeffer cayenne pepper
Cerealien *[breakfast]* cereal(s)
Champagner champagne
Champignon mushroom
Chantilly-Soße chantilly
Charlotte charlotte
Cheddar *[-Käse]* cheddar *[cheese]*
Cherry Brandy cherry brandy
Chicorée chicory
Chili chilli
Chili con carne chilli con carne
Chilipfeffer chilli pepper
Chilipulver chilli powder
Chinakohl Chinese cabbage
Chinatee China tea
Club Sandwich club sandwich

German-English

Cocktail cocktail
   Cocktail-Kirsche glacé cherry
Cornflakes cornflakes
Crème fraîche crème fraîche
Cremetorte cream cake
cremig creamy
Croissant croissant
Croûtons croutons
Curry curry
Currysuppe mulligatawny *[soup]*
Currywurst spicy sausage *[with curry sauce]*
Custard custard *[sauce]*
Damaszenerpflaume damson
Damentoiletten ladies' toilets
Dampfbraten beef stew
Dampfnudeln sweet steamed dumplings with stewed fruit and custard
Dattel date
Dattelpflaume date plum
Delikatessbohnen fine beans
Delikatessen delicatessen
Dessert dessert
Dessertlöffel dessert spoon
Dessertwagen sweet trolley
Dessertwein dessert wine, pudding wine
dick thick
dicke Bohne broad bean
Dill dill
Dillsoße dill sauce
Dip dip *[noun]*
Dobosch Torte, Dobostorte layered chocolate-cream sponge cake
Doppelbock very strong dark beer
Doppelter double *[shot of spirits]*
Dornhai dogfish
Dörrfleisch *[diced]* salted smoked pig's belly
Dörrpflaume prune
Dorsch cod
Dose tin
Dosen-, in Dosen tinned, canned *[US]*
draußen outside
Dresdner Stollen Christmas cake
Dressing dressing
Duchesse-Kartoffeln duchesse potatoes
Duft aroma
dünsten stew *[fruit]*
durch done
durchgebraten well-done *[steak]*
durchsieben sift
durchwachsener Speck streaky bacon
durstig thirsty
echter Bonito skipjack tuna
Éclair éclair
Edelkastanie *[sweet]* chestnut
Ei egg
Eichblattsalat oak leaf lettuce
Eidotter egg yolk
Eierbecher egg cup
Eierfrucht eggplant, aubergine

German-English

Eierhaber type of pancake broken up with a fork
Eierkuchen omelette
Eierpfannkuchen pancake
Eierpflanze aubergine
Eierstich cubes of cooked seasoned egg, served in soups *[royale]*
Eierteigwaren egg noodles, egg baked pasta
Eigelb egg yolk
ein halbes Radler a half of shandy
einfach plain
einfache Sahne single cream
eingelegt pickled
Eingemachtes preserves
einrühren blend
Eintopf stew *[noun]*
eintunken dip *[verb]*
Eis ice
   Eis am Stiel ice lolly
Eisbecher sundae
Eisbein boiled pickled knuckle of pork
Eisbergsalat iceberg lettuce
Eisbombe bombe
eisgekühlt chilled
eisgekühlter Tee iced tea
eisgekühltes Wasser iced water
Eiskrem ice cream
Eiskübel, Eiskühler bucket of ice
Eiskugel ice cream scoop
Eistüte ice cream cone, cornet
Eiswaffel wafer
Eiswein sweet German wine made from grapes frozen on the vine
Eiswürfel ice cube
Eiweiß egg white
Elefantenlaus cashew nut
empfehlen recommend
Endivie endive
Engelhai angel fish
Engelwurz angelica
englisch medium-rare
Ente duck
Entenbrüstechen duck breast
Entenleberpastete duck pâté
entkoffeiniert decaffeinated
   entkoffeinierter Kaffee decaffeinated coffee
entrahmte Milch skimmed milk
Entsafter juicer
Eppich celery
Erbse pea
Erbsenbrei, Erbspüree mushy peas; pease-pudding
Erdapfel potato
Erdartischocke Jerusalem artichoke
Erdbeere strawberry
Erdbeermarmelade strawberry jam
Erdnuss peanut
Erdnussbutter peanut butter
Erdnussöl groundnut oil
erhitzen scald
erster Weihnachtsfeiertag Christmas Day

German-English

Espresso espresso, expresso *[coffee]*
essen eat
Essen dinner party; food
Essenszeit dinner time
Essenz essence
Essig vinegar
Essiggurke gherkin
Essigkren horseradish sauce
Esskastanie *[sweet]* chestnut
Essstäbchen chopsticks
Estragon tarragon
Etikett label
Fadennudeln vermicelli, angel hair pasta
Falafel falafel
falscher Hase meat loaf
Färberdistel safflower
Farce stuffing
farcierter Krebs dressed/prepared crab
Fasan pheasant
Faschierte minced meat
faschierter Braten meat loaf
Fassbier draught beer
fasten fast *[not eat]*
faul bad, rotten
Feige fig
Feldsalat lamb's lettuce
Fenchel fennel
festen Preisen, zu fixed price *[meal]*
festgelegtes Menü set menu
Festpreismenü fixed price menu
Fetakäse feta cheese
Fett fat *[noun]*
fett fat *[adj]*
fettarm low in fat, low-fat
fettfrei fat-free
Fettgebackenes fritter
Filet fillet
filetieren debone/fillet
filetiert filleted
Filetsteak fillet steak
Filo-Teig filo pastry
Filterkaffee filter coffee
Fisch fish
Fischauflauf fisherman's pie
Fischbestand fish stock
Fischfrikadelle fish cake
Fischgeschäft fish shop
Fischhackbraten baked fish loaf
Fischhändler fishmonger
Fischlaich *[hard]* roe
Fischragout fish stew
Fischschüssel fish and bacon terrine
Fischsud fish broth
Fischsuppe fish soup, chowder
Fischtopf fish stew
Fladen round flat oatcake
Flädlesuppe thin strips of pancake in broth

Flageolettbohnen flageolet *[beans]*
flambiert flambéed
flambierte Banane banana flambé
Flammeri blancmange
Flasche bottle
Flasche Wein bottle of wine
Flaschenöffner bottle opener
Flaschentomate plum tomato
Flaschenwasser bottled water
Flecke tripe
Fleisch meat
Fleischbrühe broth
Fleischgerichte meat dishes
Fleischkäse meat loaf
Fleischkloß, Fleischklößchen meat ball
fleischlos meat-free
fleischloses Chili chilli without meat
Fleischpastete meat pie
Fleischsalat strips or cubes of beef, pork or veal and gherkins in mayonnaise
Fleischschnitte slice of meat
Fleischwurst ring-shaped pork and beef sausage
fliegender Fisch flying fish
Flocken flakes
Flügel wing
Flunder flounder
Fluss river
Flussbarsch perch
Flusskrebs crayfish
Fogas(ch) pike-perch
Folienkartoffel baked potato in foil
Fondant fondant
Fondue fondue
Forelle trout
    Forelle Blau fresh trout cooked in a court bouillon
    Forelle Müllerin fried trout with almonds
Frankfurter Kranz rich rum-flavoured cake with two layers of butter cream filling, coated in crushed almonds
Frankfurter Soße 7 herbs *[parsley, chervil, salad burnet, tarragon, borage, sorrel, lovage]* with chopped eggs in a yoghurt dressing
Frankfurter Würstchen fine pale boiled pork sausage
Frankische Butterplatzchen butter biscuits
Freiland free-range
Frikadelle rissole
frisch fresh
frische Leberwurst fresh pork sausage
frischer Hering fresh herring
frisches Obst fresh fruit
frischgemachte freshly cooked, cooked to order
frischgemachte Nudeln fresh pasta
Frischkäse cream cheese, quark
Frischling young wild boar
Friséesalat frisée *[salad]*
fritiert deep-fried
Froschschenkel frog's legs
Frucht fruit
Fruchtcocktail fruit cocktail
Früchtebecher sundae

Früchteis   water ice
Früchtekuchen   fruit cake
Früchtpastete   fruit pie, fruit tart
Fruchtsaft   fruit juice
Fruchtsalat   fruit salad
Frühkohl   spring greens
Frühlingsrolle   spring roll
Frühlingszwiebel   spring onion, scallion *[US]*
Frühstück   breakfast
Frühstücksfleisch   luncheon meat
Füße   feet, trotters
Füllung, Füllsel, Fülle   stuffing
Fürst-Pückler-Eis   Neapolitan ice-cream
Gabel   fork
Gaisburger Marsch   beef stew with Spätzle noodles
Galantine   galantine
Gallert   jelly
Gamskeule   roast marinated leg of chamois *[mountain goat]*
Gans   goose
Gänseleber   goose liver
Gänsebraten   roast goose
ganz   whole
gar   done, cooked
Garnele   prawn
garniert   garnished
Gartenbohnen   French beans
Gartenerbsen   garden peas
Gartenkresse   cress
Gartenkürbis   pumpkin
Gartenminze   garden mint
Gartensalat   lettuce
Gasthof   inn
Gaststätte, Gastwirtschaft   restaurant; pub
Gazpacho   gazpacho
Gebäck   biscuits, cakes or pastries
Gebäck aus Mürbeteig   shortcrust pastry
gebacken   baked
gebackene Bodenseefelchen   fried breaded pollan *[whitefish]* with a white
   caper and anchovy sauce
gebackene Bohnen   baked beans
gebackene Kartoffel   baked potato
gebeizt   marinated
Geburtstagskuchen   birthday cake
gebraten   fried; roasted
gebratene Leber mit Zwiebeln, Apfelringen und Kartoffelbrei   fried liver
   and onions with apple rings and mashed potato
gebratener Fisch   fried fish
gebunden   thickened
gedämpft   steamed
   gedämpfte Ente   steamed duck
Gedeck   place/table setting; cover *[charge]*
gedeckter Apfelkuchen   apple pie
gedünstet   steamed, stewed
   gedünstete Ochsenschlepp   braised oxtail
   gedünstetes Gemüse   steamed vegetables
Geflügel   fowl, poultry
Geflügelinnereien, Geflügelklein   giblets

95

Geflügelleber chicken livers
Geflügelsalat chicken salad
Geflügelunterschenkel drumstick
gefroren frozen
gefüllt stuffed
  gefüllte Oliven stuffed olives
  gefüllte Rinderbraten roast and stuffed rib of beef
  gefüllte Schöpsenrücken roast and stuffed saddle of mutton
  gefüllte Paprika stuffed pepper
gegrillt grilled, barbecued
Gehackte(s) minced meat
Gehirn brains
Geiß goat
gekocht boiled
  gekochte Kartoffeln boiled potatoes
  gekochter Reis boiled rice
  gekochter Schinken boiled ham
  gekochtes Ei boiled egg
  gekochte Gemüse boiled vegetables
gekühlte Kraftbrühe cold consommé
Gelatine gelatine
gelbe Rübe carrot
Gelbwurst pale yellow fine pork, beef or veal sausage; often eaten cold in
  slices
Gelbwurzel turmeric
Gelee jelly *[savoury]*
gemahlen ground
  gemahlener Pfeffer ground pepper
gemeiner Dornhai rock salmon
gemeiner Krake octopus
gemeiner Kürbis marrow *[vegetable]*
gemeiner Meerengel angel fish
gemeiner Tintenfisch cuttlefish
gemischte Kräuter mixed herbs
gemischter Salat mixed salad
Gemüse vegetable
Gemüsebrühe vegetable stock
Gemüsehändler greengrocer
Gemüseladen grocery
Gemüsesuppe vegetable soup
genetisch modifiziert genetically modified *[GM]*
Genever gin
genug enough
gepökelt salted, cured
geraspelt grated
geräuchert smoked
  geräucherter Schellfisch smoked haddock
Gericht course, dish
gerieben grated
  geriebene Schale grated peel
  geriebene Zitronenschale lemon zest
  geriebene Zitrusschale zest
geröstet *[shallow]* fried
  geröstete Kartoffeln fried potatoes
Gerste barley
Gerstengraupen pearl barley
Gerstenschleim barley water

Gerstenzucker barley sugar
Geruch smell, aroma
gesalzen salted
Geschäft shop
geschält peeled
geschlossen closed
Geschmack flavour, taste
geschmort braised, stewed
   geschmorter Rindfleisch stewed steak
Geschnetzelte(s) small thin strips of meat cooked in a sauce
Gesottenes Lämmernes stewed rolled joint of lamb served with strips of
   potato, carrot, parsnip, celeriac in a marjoram sauce
gespickt spiked with fatty bacon
gestürzt turned out
gesund healthy
Gesundheit health
Gesundheitsladen health shop
getoastet toasted
Getränk drink
   Getränke inclusive drinks included
Getreide corn
getrocknet dried
   getrocknete *[halbe]* Erbsen split peas
Gewürz seasoning, spice, condiment
Gewürzgurke gherkin
Gewürznelke clove
gewürzt flavoured
Gin gin
   Gin Tonic gin and tonic
Glas glass
   Glas Wasser/Wein glass of water/wine
glasiert glazed
Glasur glaze; icing
Glattbutt brill
glatte Petersilie flat parsley
Glatthai dogfish
Glattrochen skate
Glühwein mulled wine
Glumse quark
glutenfrei gluten-free
Gnocchi gnocchi
Goldbutt plaice
Götterspeise jelly *[sweet/ pudding]*, jello *[US]*
Gourmet gourmet
Granat shrimp
Granatapfel pomegranate
Grapefruit grapefruit
Gräten bones *[of fish]*
Gratifikation gratuity
gratiniert au gratin
Gratis-; frei complimentary
Graubrot brown bread
Graupensuppe barley soup
Graute broad bean
Grenadine grenadine
Griechischer Jogurt Greek yoghurt
Grieß semolina

Grießbrei semolina pudding
Grießklöße, -nockerl semolina dumplings
Grill grill *[noun]*
grillen grill *[verb]*
Grillfest barbecue
Grillplatte, Grillteller mixed grill
Grillsteak grilled steak *[beef, pork or turkey]*
grobkörniger Senf whole-grain mustard
groß big
grosse Bohne broad bean
Gründling gudgeon
grüne Bohne French bean, green bean, string bean
grüne Erbsen green peas
grüne Erbsensuppe green pea soup
grüne Gurke cucumber
grüne Oliven green olives
grüne Reneklode greengage *[plum]*
grüner Paprika green pepper
grüner Salat green salad; round lettuce
grüne Soße green sauce: *[herbs, leek, onion and chopped egg in a white sauce]*; see also **Frankfurter Soße**
grüner Tee green tea
Grüngemüse greens
Grünkohl kale
Grütze groats, grits *[US]*
Guacamole guacamole
Guave, Guajave guava
Gugelhopf, Gugelhupf fatless sponge cake with raisins, chopped almonds, orange or lemon zest
Gulasch, Gulyas goulash
Gumbo gumbo
Gurke cucumber
Gurkenbrot cucumber sandwich
Gurkenroulade pork olive with a gherkin filling
gut good
gut durchgebraten well done *[steak]*
Hachse knuckle
Hackbraten meat loaf
Hackfleisch minced meat
Hackfleischauflauf similar to cottage/shepherd's pie
Hafer oats
Haferbrei porridge
Haferflocken bran flakes
Hafergrütze groats
Haferkeks oatcake
Hafermehl, Haferschrot oatmeal
Haferwurz salsify
Hagebutte rosehip
Hähnchen chicken
Hai shark
halb- half
   halb durchgebraten medium rare *[steak]*
   halb roh rare *[steak]*
   halbe Flasche half bottle
Halbfettmilch semi-skimmed milk
halbgekocht half done, half-cooked, medium cooked
halbharter Käse semi-hard cheese

Halbliter half a litre
halbtrocken semi-dry
halbtrockener Wein medium wine
halbweicher semi-soft cheese
Hamburger hamburger
Hammelfleisch mutton
Handkäs mit Musik soft cheese on bread with onions in dressing
hart hard
hartgekochtes Ei hard-boiled egg
Hartkäse hard cheese
Harzer Käse small round hard cheese
Hase hare
Haselnuss hazelnut, cobnut, filbert
Haselnussgefrorenes home-made hazelnut ice cream
Hasenpfeffer, Hasenklein jugged hare
Häuptelsalat salad
Hauptgericht main course
Hauptspeise/ Hauptgang main course
Hauptspeise; zweiter Gang second course
Hausente domestic duck
Hausfrauenart family-style
hausgemacht home-made
Hausspezialitäten house specialities
Hauswein house wine
Haut skin
Haxe knuckle
Hecht pike
Hechtdorsch hake
Hefe yeast
Hefekloß rich steamed yeast dumpling
Hefeteig yeast dough
Heidelbeere bilberry, blueberry, whortleberry
Heidehonig heather honey
Heidesand vanilla butter biscuits
Heilbutt halibut
heiß hot *[not cold]*
    heiß machen heat up
    heißes Getränk hot drink
    heißes Wasser hot water
helle Soße white sauce
herb medium dry *[wine]*
Herd stove
Hering herring
Heringskönig dory, John Dory
Herrentoiletten gents' toilets
Herz heart
Herzmuscheln cockles
Hickorynuss hickory nut
Himbeere raspberry
Himmel und Erde potato and apple purée with fried onions and bacon *[topped with fried liver or black pudding]*
Hirn brains
Hirsch *[fleisch]* deer, venison
Hirschbraten roast venison
Hirse millet
Hochrippe prime rib
Hochstuhl highchair

Hochwild game
Hochzeitssuppe consommé with bone-marrow dumplings and chives
Hochzeitstorte wedding cake
Hof hotel
holländische Soße hollandaise sauce
Holsteinschnitzel breaded veal escalope topped with a fried egg and anchovies
Holsteinwurst beef and pork sausage
Holunderbeere elderberry
Holundersuppe dessert with elderberry juice and pears
Holzkohle charcoal
Honig honey
Honigkuchen honey cake topped with almond flakes
Honigmelone honeydew melon
Honigwabe honeycomb
Honigwein mead
Hopfen hops
Hoppelpoppel fried potatoes, scrambled eggs and bacon
Horsd'oeuvre hors d'oeuvre
Huhn chicken
Hühnerbein chicken leg
Hühnerbrühe chicken broth
Hühnerbrust chicken breast, breast of chicken
Hühnercremesuppe cream of chicken soup
Hühnerfrikassee chicken fricassée
Hühnerklein chicken giblets
Hühnerleber chicken liver
Hühnersalat chicken salad
Hühnersuppe chicken soup
Hühnertopf chicken stew
Hülsenfrüchte pulses
Humus hummus
Hummer lobster
Hummerkrabbe king prawn
Hummersuppe lobster bisque
Hundshai tope
hungrig hungry
Hüttenkäse cottage cheese
Hutzelbrot fruit bread
Imbiss *[-Bude]* hot dog etc. stand
im Freien outdoors/outside
Indianerkrapfen small chocolate-covered cream puffs
indisches Ragoutpulver curry powder
Ingwer ginger
Ingwerbier, Ingwerlimonade ginger beer
Ingwerkuchen ginger cake
Ingwerlebkuchen gingerbread
innen inside
Innereien offal
Irischer Whiskey Irish whiskey
Ischler Törtchen almond butter biscuits filled with raspberry jam
Jägerschnitzel pork or veal escalope in a spicy mushroom sauce
jägert sautéed with onions
Jagdwurst large coarse beef and pork sausage *[served sliced]*
Jahrgang vintage
Jakobsmuschel scallop
Jamswurzel yam

Japanischer Tee Japanese tea
Jerez *[wein]* sherry
Jogurt yoghurt
Johannisbeere: rote/schwarze Johannisbeere redcurrant/blackcurrant
   rote Johannisbeergelee redcurrant jelly
Julblock Christmas log
Julienne julienne *[cut in fine strips]*
junge Ente duckling
junge Zuchtchampignons button mushrooms
junges Hammefleisch lamb
junges Huhn spring chicken
Jungtaube squab
Kabeljau cod
Kabinett first category of German quality wine
Kaffee coffee
   Kaffeekanne coffee pot
   Kaffeelöffel coffee spoon
   Kaffee mit Sahne coffee with whipped cream
   Kaffeetasse coffee cup
   Kaffeeweißer coffee whitener
Kaffee-Parfait coffee parfait
Kaiserfleisch smoked pork belly
Kaisergranat Dublin bay prawn
Kaisergranatschwänze scampi
Kaiserschmarr(e)n rum and raisin pancake, served with fruit
Kakao cocoa
Kakaobutter cocoa butter
Kakaopulver cocoa powder
Kaki *[frucht]* kaki
Kalb calf
Kalbfleisch veal
Kalbsbraten roast veal
Kalbsbries calf's sweetbreads
Kalbsbrust breast of veal
Kalbsgehirn calf's brains
Kalbshaxe knuckle of veal
Kalbsleber calf's liver
Kalbslende fillet of veal
Kalbsmilch calf's sweetbreads
Kalbsnierenbraten roast boned loin of veal with kidneys
Kalbsrippchen veal chop
Kalbsschnitzel veal escalope
Kalbsvögerl braised veal olives stuffed with veal sausagemeat, with a caper
   and anchovy sauce
Kaldaunen tripe
Kalmar squid
kalt cold
   kalter Aufschnitt cold cuts
   kalte Weichselsuppe chilled sour cherry dessert with red wine and cream
   kaltes Wasser cold water
kaltgepresstes Olivenöl virgin olive oil
Kaltgetränk cold drink
Kaltschale cold sweet soup
Kamille camomile
Kammmuschel scallop
kandiert candied
   kandierte Früchte crystallised fruit

kandierte Fruchtschalen candied peel
Kaneel cinnamon
Kaninchen rabbit
Kanne, Kännchen jug
Kantalupe cantaloup *[melon]*
Kapaun capon
Kapern capers
Kapselheber bottle-opener
Kapuzinerkresse nasturtium
Karaffe carafe
Karamell caramel
Kardamom cardamom
Karfiol cauliflower
Karotte carrot
Karottenkuchen carrot cake
Karpfen carp
Karthäuser Klöße dumplings covered with sugar and cinnamon
Kartoffel potato
Kartoffel im Silberfrack baked potato in foil
Kartoffelauflauf scalloped potatoes
Kartoffelbrei mashed potato(es), creamed potato *[US]*
Kartoffelchips potato crisps, chips *[US]*
Kartoffelkloß potato dumpling
Kartoffelpuffer potato fritter(s), hash browns *[US]*
Kartofelpüree mashed potato(es), creamed potato *[US]*
Kartoffelsalat potato salad
Käse cheese
Käse der Region local cheese
Käseboden *[cheese]* flan
Käsebrett, Käseplatte, Käseteller cheese board
Käsebrötchen cheese sandwich
Käsefladen cheese omelette
Käsekuchen cheesecake
Käserösti cheese potato cakes topped with Gruyère cheese
Käsesoße cheese sauce
Käsesoufflé cheese soufflé
Käsespätzle Emmentaler cheese and spätzle bake
Käsestange cheese straw
Käsetoast cheese on toast
Käsetorte cheesecake
Kasseler Rippchen/Rippenspeer roasted smoked loin and spare rib of pork
Kasserolle casserole
Kassler lightly salted smoked loin of pork
Kastorzucker caster sugar
Katenschinken smoked ham
Katen(rauch)wurst large coarse smoked pork sausage
Kater hangover
Katfisch catfish, rockfish
Katzenhai dogfish
Kaviar caviar
Kebab kebab
Keks biscuit, cookie *[US]*
Kellner waiter
Kellnerin waitress
Kerbel chervil
Kerscheplotzer bread and butter pudding with cherries
Kerze candle

Kerzenhalter candlestick
Ketchup ketchup, catsup *[US]*
Keule leg
Kichererbse chickpea
Kidneybohne kidney bean, red bean
Kindermenü children's menu
Kinderteller children's menu
Kipper kipper
Kirsche cherry
Kirschenmichel bread and butter cherry pudding
Kirschlikör cherry brandy
Kirschtomaten cherry tomato
Kirschwasser Kirsch, cherry liqueur
Kiwi kiwi fruit
klare Brühe clear soup
Kleie bran
Kleiner Wiesenknopf burnet
Kleingeld change *[coins]*
Klementine clementine
Klette burdock
Kliesche dab
Kleist brill
klimatisiert air-conditioned
Klops meat ball
Kloß dumpling
Knäckebrot crispbread
Knackwurst short fat type of Frankfurter
knapp very rare *[of meat]*
Kneipe pub
Knoblauch garlic
Knoblauch-, knoblauchhaltig garlicky
Knoblauchbrot garlic bread
Knoblauchmayonnaise garlic mayonnaise
Knoblauchpilze garlic mushrooms
Knoblauchwurst pork and garlic sausage
Knoblauchzehe clove of garlic
Knochen bone
    am/mit Knochen on the bone
    vom/ohne Knochen boned
Knochenmark bone marrow
Knödel, Knödl dumpling
Knollensellerie celeriac
Knöpfle, Knöpfli drop-shaped Spätzle noodles
Knorpel gristle
Knurrhahn gurnard
Koch cook, chef *[male]*
Kochbanane plantain
köcheln simmer
kochen boil
kochendes Wasser boiling water
Köchin cook, chef *[female]*
Kochsalz cooking salt
Kochwurst steamed or boiled sausage
Koffein caffeine
koffeinfrei caffeine-free
Kohl cabbage
    Kohl und Pinkel kale, onions, Kassler and bacon with sausage

Kohlenhydrat   carbohydrate
kohlensäurehaltig   fizzy
Köhler   coley, coalfish, saithe
Kohlrabi   kohlrabi
Kohlrouladen   stuffed cabbage leaves
Kohlrübe   swede
Kokoscreme   coconut cream
Kokosmilch   coconut milk
Kokosnuss   coconut
Kokosraspeln   desiccated coconut
Kompott   stewed fruit
Kondensmilch   condensed milk
Konditorei   cake shop
Konfitüre   jam
Königinpastetchen   chicken vol-au-vent
Königinsuppe   rich chicken soup
Königsberger Klopse   boiled meatballs in a white caper sauce
kontinentales Frühstuck   continental breakfast
Kopfsalat   lettuce
Koriander   coriander
Korinthen   currants
Korkenzieher   corkscrew
Korn   corn, grain; clear grain schnapps
Körnerbrot   granary loaf
Körnersteinbrech   saxifrage
körperreich   full-bodied *[wine]*
koscher   kosher
kostenlos   free *[of charge]*
köstlich   delicious
Kotelett   chop, cutlet
Kotelettkrone   crown roast of pork
Krabbe   crab
Kraftbrühe   broth, consommé
kräftig   strong
Kraftsuppe   beef and vegetable soup
Krakauer   reddish coarse lean beef and pork sausage, eaten sliced
Krake   octopus
Krapfen   doughnut; fritter
Krapfensuppe   type of Maultaschen *[pasta parcels]* in broth
krause Endivien   frisée *[salad]*
krause Petersilie   curly parsley
Krauskohl   kale
Kraut   cabbage
    Kraut mit Eisbein und Erbsensuppe   pig's knuckles and cabbage with pea
    soup
Krautsalat   coleslaw
Kräuter   herbs
Kräuterklösse   herb dumplings
Kräuterlikör   herb liqueur
Kräutermischung   bouquet garni
Kräuterschmand   sour cream with herbs
Kräuterschnaps   herb schnapps
Kräutertee   herbal tea
Krautkräpfli   type of spinach-filled ravioli
Krebs   crab
Kren   horseradish
Krenfleisch   slices of hot boiled beef with horseradish

Kresse cress
Kreuzkümmel cumin (seed)
Kroketten croquette potatoes
Kronfleisch brisket (of beef)
Kronsbeere cranberry
Krug jug, pitcher; mug
   ein Krug Wasser a jug of water
Krustenbraten roast shoulder of pork with crackling
Küche kitchen
Kuchen cake, gâteau
Kugelhopf sponge cake or large choux pastry balls filled with whipped cream;
   see also **Gugelhopf**
Kuhmilch cow's milk
Kükenragout stewed chicken and vegetables in a cream sauce
Kümmel caraway
Kümmelstange bread roll sprinkled with salt and caraway seeds
Kumquat kumquat
Kürbis pumpkin
Kürbisgewächs squash
Kurkuma turmeric
Kuskus couscous
kurz anbraten to sauté
Labskaus salted beef, boiled potatoes and onions minced and served cold
   with pickled beetroot, matjes fillets and a fried egg
Lachs salmon
Lachsfilet salmon steak
Lachsforelle salmon trout, sea trout
Lachshering bloater
Lachsschinken smoked rolled loin of pork wrapped in bacon
Lactose lactose
Lactoseunverträglichkeit lactose intolerance
Lakritze liquorice
Lamm lamb
Lammbrust breast of lamb
Lammeintopf lamb stew
Lammkammbraten rack of lamb
Lammkeule leg of lamb
Lammkotelett lamb chop
Landeier farm eggs
Landjäger smoked beef and pork sausage
Langkornreis long-grained rice
Languste crawfish, spiny lobster
Langustine langoustine
Lasagne lasagne
Lattich lettuce
Latz, Lätzchen bib *[child's]*
Laubfrösche stuffed cabbage or spinach leaves
Lauch leek
Laugenbrezel pretzel
Lavendel lavender
Lebensmittelgeschäft general store/grocer's
Lebensmittelvergiftung food poisoning
Leber liver
Leberbraten roast calf's liver
Leberfrikadelle faggot
Leberkäse meat loaf of minced sausage meat, eggs and spices
Leberklöße, Leberknödel small bread and beef liver dumplings

105

Leberknödelsuppe   consommé with liver dumplings and herbs
Leberpastete   liver pâté
Leberspatzen   liver dumplings
Leberspiessli   bacon-wrapped liver kebabs
Leberwurst   pork and liver sausage
Lebkuchen   gingerbread
lecker   delicious, tasty
leichter Wein   light-bodied wine
leichtgebraten   rare *[meat]*
Leinsamen   linseed
Leipziger Allerlei   mixed spring vegetables in a white sauce
Leiterchen   spare ribs
Leitungswasser   tap water
Lende   loin
Lendenbraten   roast loin
Lendenfilet   sirloin
Lendenschnitte am Grill   grilled fillet of beef
Lendenstück   tenderloin
Leng   ling
Lerche   lark
Leuchter   candlestick
Liebesknochen   chocolate éclair
lieblich   medium sweet *[wine]*
Liebstöckel   lovage
Liegnitzer Bomben   chocolate-covered honey cakes filled with marzipan or nuts and currants
Likör   liqueur
Limande   lemon sole
Limette   lime
Limettepastete   key lime pie
Limone   lime
Linse   lentil
   Linsen du Puy   puy lentils
Linsensuppe   lentil soup with slices of Frankfurter *[sausage]*
Linsentopf   lentil stew
Linzertorte   almond pastry flan filled with raspberry jam
Liter   litre
Litschi   lychee
Löffel   spoon
   Löffel *[voll]*   spoonful
Löffelbiskuits   sponge biscuits
Lokal   pub; restaurant
Loganbeere   loganberry
Lorbeerblatt   bay leaf
Lübeck   marzipan
Lungen   lights *[lungs]*
Lüngerl   calf's lights
Macadamia-Nüsse   macadamia nuts
Maccaroni-Auflauf   macaroni cheese
Madeira *[wein]*   Madeira
Madeirakuchen   Madeira cake
Madeirasoße   Madeira sauce
Magen   stomach
Magenbitter   bitters
Magenbrot   cinnamon-flavoured cake
mager   lean
Magermilch   skimmed milk

mahlen grind
Mahlzeit Essen meal
Maibowle sweet woodruff cup
Maifisch shad
Mais corn, maize
Maisbrot corn bread
Maisgrütze hominy grits *[US]*
Maiskolben corn on the cob
Maissirup corn syrup
Mainzer Rippchen pork chops
Majonäse mayonnaise
Majoran marjoram
Makkaroni macaroni
Makrele mackerel
Makrelenhecht saury
makrobiotisch macrobiotic
Makrone macaroon
Malz malt
Mandarine mandarin
Mandel almond
Mandelkroketten amandine potatoes
Mandelplätzchen almond biscuits
Mandelroulade veal olive filled with almonds
Mandeltorte almond layer cake with a jam or crème patissière filling
Mango mango
Mangold chard, spinach beet
Mangostane mangosteen
Margarine margarine
Marinade marinade
mariniert marinated
Mark bone marrow
Markklößchen small dumplings made with bone marrow
Markknochen marrow bone
Markt market
Marmelade jam, jelly *[US]*
Marone (sweet) chestnut
Marsalawein Marsala wine
Marshmallow marshmallow
Martinsgans roast goose with apple and mince stuffing
Marzipan marzipan
Marzipanmasse almond paste
Mastgeflügel corn-fed poultry
Matjes(hering) lightly cured young herring
Matjesfilet matjes herring fillet
Maulbeere mulberry
Maultaschen small pasta parcels filled with mince and spinach
Mayonnaise mayonnaise
Mazis mace
Medaillon medallion
Meer bass
Meeraal conger eel
Meeräsche grey mullet
Meerbarbe barbel, red mullet
Meerbarsch sea bass
Meerblick *[ein Tisch mit Meerblick]* sea view *[i.e. table with]*
Meerbrassen sea bream
Meerengel: gemeiner Meerengel angel fish

Meeresfrüchte seafood; shellfish
Meerrettich horseradish
Meersalz sea salt
Mehl flour
Mehlbanane plantain
Mehlsoße white sauce
Mehlspeise dessert, sweet; pastry
Meiskeimöl corn oil
Melasse molasses, treacle
Melone melon
Meringe meringue
Merlan whiting
Messer knife
Met mead
Mettwurst pork, beef and bacon sausage, dried, cured and smoked
Metzger butchers shop
Miasmehl cornflour
Miesmuschel mussel
Milch milk; soft roe
Milchkaffee latte *[coffee]*
Milchmixgetränk, Milchgetränk milkshake
Milchprodukte dairy products
Milchreis baked rice, rice pudding; pudding rice
mild mild
Milz spleen
Milzwurst spicy Bavarian veal sausage with spleen
Mineralwasser mineral water
Minestrone minestrone *[soup]*
Minze mint
Minzgelee mint jelly
Minzsoße mint sauce
Minztee mint tea
Mispel medlar
mit *[Speise-]* **Eis** with ice cream
mit Gelee jellied
mit Kohlensäure carbonated, gassy
mit nach Hause nehmen take home
mit Zucker überzogene Mandeln sugar-coated almonds
Mittagessen lunch; dinner *[midday]*
Mixed Pickles pickles
Mohn poppy
Mohnbrötchen poppy seed covered bread roll
Mohnkuchen poppy seed cake
Möhre, Mohrrübe carrot
Mohrenkopf small chocolate-covered cream cake
Mokka mocha
Molluske mollusc
Mononatriumglutamat monosodium glutamate *[MSG]*
Moosbeere cranberry
Morcheln morels
Mostrich mustard
Moussaka moussaka
Mousse mousse
moussierend sparkling
Mulligatawnysuppe mulligatawny *[soup]*
Mürbeteig shortcrust *[pastry]*
Muskat *[nuss]* nutmeg

Muskatblüte mace
Müsli breakfast cereal, muesli
Muzen-Mandeln small pear-shaped almond doughnuts
Nachmittagstee afternoon tea
Nachlass discount
Nachspeise, Nachtisch dessert, pudding, sweet
Nagelrochen dessert
Napfkuchen Gugelhupf
Natur- natural
Naturjogurt plain yoghurt
Naturreis brown rice
Nektarine nectarine
Nelkenpfeffer allspice
Neptunspieß fish kebab
Nessel nettle
neue Kartoffeln new potatoes
nicht durchgebraten underdone
Nichtraucher *[zone]* non-smoking area
Niere kidney
   saure Nieren braised kidneys in a vinegar and white wine sauce
Nierentalg, Nierenfett suet
Nordseekrabbe shrimp
   eingekochte Nordseekrabben potted shrimps
Nordseekrabbencocktail shrimp cocktail
Nudeln noodles, pasta
Nudelsuppe noodle soup
Nugat nougat, brittle
Nürnberger *[Bratwurst]* small lean pork sausage, grilled or fried
Nürnberger Lebkuchen gingerbread
Nuss nut
   Nuss und Mohnstrudel walnut and poppy seed strudel
Ober waiter
Obers cream
Obertasse und Untertasse cup and saucer
Obst fruit
Obstboden *[fruit]* flan
Obstkompott stewed fruit
Obstkuchen fruit cake
Obstler apple and pear schnapps
Obstsaft fruit juice
Obstsalat fruit salad
Obsttorte glazed open mixed fruit tart
Obstwasser fruit schnapps
Ochsenauge fried egg
   Ochsenauge auf Schwarzbrot raw smoked ham and fried egg on toasted
   dark rye bread
Ochsenbraten roast beef
Ochsenlende fillet of beef
Ochsenmaulsalat thin strips of pickled ox lip and onions
Ochsenniere beef kidney
Ochsenschwanz oxtail
Ochsenschwanzsuppe oxtail soup
Ochsenzunge ox tongue
Ofen oven
Ofentori mashed potatoes mixed with fried finely diced bacon
öffnen open *[verb]*
ohne Milch without milk

Okra okra
Öl oil
Olive olive
Olivenöl olive oil
Omelett(e) omelette
Orange orange
Orangen-Ente duck with oranges
Orangenmarmelade marmalade
Orangensaft orange juice
Orangensoße orange sauce
organisch organic
Origano oregano
Palatschinken thin pancakes sprinkled with chopped nuts
Pampelmuse grapefruit
Paniermehl breadcrumbs
paniert breaded
   panierte Hühnerbrust mit Knoblauchfüllung chicken Kiev
Papaya papaya, pawpaw
Paprika paprika; pepper *[vegetable]*, capsicum
Paprikaschnitzel escalopes of veal in a paprika sauce
Paprikaschoten (red, green, yellow) pepper, capsicum
Paprikaskrumpli pepper and paprika goulash
Paradeiser tomato
Paradeissalat tomato salad
Paradeissuppe tomato soup
Paranuss brazil nut
Parfait parfait
Parmaschinken Parma ham
Parmesankäse Parmesan cheese
Party party
Pastete pâté; pie; vol-au-vent
Pastinak(e) parsnip
Pekannuss pecan nut
Pekannusstorte pecan pie
Pelamide bonito
Pellkartoffeln potatoes boiled in their skins
Peperoni chilli pepper
perlend sparkling
Perlgraupen pearl barley
Perlhuhn guinea fowl
Perlwein sparkling wine
Persimone persimmon
Pesto pesto
Petersfisch dory, John Dory
Petersilie parsley
Petersiliensoße parsley sauce
Petersilienwurzel parsnip
Petits Fours petits fours
Pfahlmuschel mussel
Pfannkuchen pancake
Pfeffer pepper *[spice]*
Pfefferkörner whole pepper
Pfefferkuchen spicy gingerbread biscuits
Pfefferminze peppermint
Pfefferminztee peppermint tea
Pfeffermühle pepper mill
Pfeffernüsse spiced ginger biscuits

Pfefferpotthast peppery beef stew
Pfeffersteak pepper steak
Pfefferstreuer pepper pot
Pfeilwurz *[mehl]* arrowroot
Pferdebohne broad bean
Pferdefleisch horse meat
Pfifferling chanterelle
Pfirsich peach
Pflanzenöl vegetable oil
Pflaume plum
Pflaumenmus plum jam/purée
Pfundkuchen pound cake
Pfnutli apple fritters
Pichelsteiner *[fleisch]* mixed meat and vegetable casserole
Pickert bread made from potato or wheat flour
Picknick picnic
pikant spicy
    pikante Nieren devilled kidneys
    pikante Soße devilled sauce
Pilchard pilchard
Pilgermuschel scallop
Pilz mushroom
Pilzroulade pork olive with mushroom filling
Pilzschnitzel vegetarian cutlet with mushrooms
Piment allspice
Pimpinelle salad burnet
Piniennuss pine nut
Pinkel *[wurst]* seasoned smoked sausage with oats
Pistazie pistachio nut
Pittabrot pitta bread
Pizza pizza
Plantain plantain
Plättchen pretzels
Platte plate
Plattfisch flat fish
Plätzchen biscuit, cookie *[US]*
Plinsen blinis
Plinz fritter, pancake
Plockwurst smoked beef and pork sausage eaten sliced
Plumpudding plum pudding
pochieren poach
    pochiertes Ei poached egg
Pokel pickle
Pökelfleisch salt meat
Pökelhering salt herring
Polenta polenta
Pollack pollack
Pommes *[frites]* *[potato]* chips, French fries *[US]*
Popcorn popcorn
Porree leek
Portulak purslane
Portwein port
Porzellan china *[service]*
Preis price
Preisliste price list
Preiselbeere cranberry
Preiselbeersoße cranberry sauce

Presskopf coarse spreading sausage
Prickelnde Hähnchenbrust fried breast of chicken in a lekt and brandy sauce
Printen chewy spicy honey biscuits *[with nuts]*
Profiterole profiterole
Prost! Cheers!
Pudding pudding; blancmange
Puddingmasse confectioner's cream
Puderzucker icing sugar
Puffbohne broad bean
Puffer fritter, potato pancake
Puffmais popcorn
Pulverkaffee instant coffee
Punsch punch
pur neat, straight *[US]*
Püree purée
puriert creamed
Pute(r) turkey
Putenroulade turkey olive/roulade
Putenschnitzel turkey escalope
Qualität quality
Qualitätswein *[mit Prädikat]* *[high]* quality wine
Qualm smoke *[noun]*
Quappe burbot
Quark quark
Quarkkuchen cheesecake
Quellwasser spring water
Quiche quiche
   Quiche Lorraine quiche Lorraine
Quitte quince
Quittengelee quince jelly
Raclette melted raclette cheese, eaten with boiled potatoes, ham and pickles
Radicchio radicchio
Radieschen radish
Radler shandy
   ein halbes Radler a half of shandy
Raffinade caster sugar, granulated sugar
Ragout ragout
Rahm cream
Rahmkäse cream cheese
Rahmschnitzel escalopes of veal in a cream sauce
Rahmsoße cream sauce
ranzig rancid
rasch anbraten sear
rauchen smoke *[a cigarette]*
Rauchen verboten no smoking
Raucher smoker
Räucheraal smoked eel
Räucherfisch smoked fish
Räucherhering smoked kipper, bloater
Räucherkäse smoked cheese
Räucherlachs smoked salmon
räuchern smoke *[food]*
Räucherspeck smoked bacon
Rauchfleisch smoked meat
Rauke, Raukenkohl rocket
Ravioli ravioli
Rebe, Rebstock vine

Rebhuhn   partridge
Rechnung   bill, check *[US]*; account
Regenbogenforelle   rainbow trout
regional, der Region   local
Reh *[fleisch]*   deer, venison
Rehbraten   roast venison
Rehragout   venison stew
Rehrücken   (1) saddle of venison; (2) long thin chocolate cake decorated with *[upright]* almonds
Reibekuchen   grated potato pancake
reif   ripe
Reineclaude   greengage
Reis   rice
Reispapier   rice paper
Remoulade   salad cream
Reneklode   greengage
Renette   rennet
Rentier   reindeer
reservieren   to book *[a table]*
   reserviert   reserve
   Reservierung   reservation
Restaurant   restaurant
Rettich   radish
Rezept   recipe
Rhabarber   rhubarb
Ribisel   redcurrant
Riesengarnele   king prawn
Rinde   rind *[cheese]*
Rinderbraten   roast beef
Rinderbrust   brisket *[of beef]*
Rinderfilet   fillet of beef
Rinderfilet-Wellington   beef Wellington
Rinderhackfleisch   minced beef, ground beef *[US]*
Rinderrippen   ribs of beef
Rindfleisch   beef
Rindfleisch Stroganoff   beef stroganoff
Rindfleischbrühe   beef tea
Rindsrouladen   beef olives
Rindertalg   suet
Rippchen mit Kraut   cured pork chop with sauerkraut
Rippen   ribs
Rippenbraten   rack of ribs
Risottoreis   risotto rice
Rissole   rissole
Ritscherle   lamb's leaf salad
Rochen   skate
Rogen *[hard]* roe
Roggen   rye
Roggenbrot   rye bread
Roggenwhiskey   rye whiskey
roh   raw
   roher Schinken   raw ham
Rohkostsalat   raw vegetable salad
Rohwurst   raw *[dried or smoked]* sausage
Rohrzucker   cane sugar
Rollbraten   rolled joint
Rollmops   rollmop herring

Romagna-Salat, römischer Salat   cos lettuce, romaine lettuce
rosa   medium-rare
Rosé *[wein]*   rosé *[wine]*
Rosenkohl   *[Brussels]* sprouts
Rosine   raisin
Rosinenbrötchen   teacake
Rosmarin   rosemary
Rostbraten   roast joint
rösten   roast *[verb]*
Rösti   fried potato cakes or patties made from grated potatoes, chopped onion
  and seasoning
Röstkartoffeln   fried potatoes
Rotbarsch   redfish
rote Bete   beetroot
rote Bohne   kidney bean
rote Grütze mit Vanillesoße   thickened red fruits with custard
rote Johannisbeere   redcurrant
roter Bordeauxwein   claret
roter Chili   red chilli
roter Paprika   red pepper
rote Rübe   beetroot
Rothbart   red mullet
Rotkohl, Rotkabis   red cabbage
Rotwein   red wine
Rotzunge   lemon sole
Roulade   roulade *[with various fillings]*
Rübe   turnip
   gelbe Rübe   carrot
Rübenblätter   turnip tops
Rübstiel   chard stems and white turnip leaves, with mashed potatoes
Rücken   saddle
Rucola   rocket
Rührei   scrambled eggs
Rum   rum
Rum-Baba   rum baba
Rumtopf   fruit marinated in rum
Rumpsteak   rump steak
Rundkornreis   pudding rice
Saccharin   saccharin
Sachertorte   chocolate sponge cake with a layer of apricot jam
Saflor   safflower
Safran   saffron
Saft   juice
Sago   sago
Sahne   cream
Sahnesoße   cream sauce
Sahnetorte   cream cake
sahnig   creamy
Sahnequark   cream cheese
Sahnekaramel   toffee
Saibling   char
saisonal   seasonal
Salami   salami
Salat   salad
   Salat als Beilage   side salad
Salatcreme   salad cream
Salatschüssel   salad bowl

Salatsoße salad dressing
Salatgurke cucumber
Salatrübe beetroot
Salbei sage
Salm salmon
Salz salt
salzarm low-salt
salzig salty
Salzmühle salt mill
Salzstreuer salt cellar
Salzburger Nockerln sugar-sprinkled soufflé omelette
Salzgebäck pretzels or crackers sprinkled with coarse salt
Salzwasser brine
Sandklaffmuschel clam
Sandtorte sponge cake
Sandwich sandwich
Sandzunge sand sole
Sardelle anchovy
Sardellenbutter anchovy butter
Sardellenpaste anchovy paste
Sardine sardine; pilchard
satt full *[after eating]*
sauber clean
Saubohne broad bean
Sauce sauce, gravy
Sauciere gravy boat
sauer sour
Sauerampfer sorrel
Sauerbraten beef marinated in vinegar with raisins *[Rheinland]*; beef in red wine with bacon *[Baden]*
Sauerkirsch sour cherry
Sauerkraut sauerkraut: salted pickled white cabbage
Sauerrahm sour cream
Sauerrahmcreme sour cream pudding *[served with puréed strawberries]*
Sauerteig sour dough
Saumagen pig's stomach filled with minced pork, breadcrumbs, onions, eggs, potatoes, chestnuts, herbs and spices
saure Gurke pickled cucumber
saure Nieren braised kidneys in a vinegar and white wine sauce
saure Sahne sour cream
sautiert sautéed
Schaf(s)käse ewe's milk cheese
Schafmilch ewe's milk
Schale peel, skin, shell
schälen peel *[verb]*
Schalotte shallot
Schälrippchen spare ribs
Schaltenoßes large quark- and sultana-filled noodle parcels
Schaltiere shellfish
Schankbier draught beer
Scharbe dab
scharf hot *[sharp, strong]*
Schaumrolle puff pastry roll filled with whipped cream
Schaumwein sparkling wine
Scheibe slice
   in Scheiben geschnitten sliced
    Scheibe Brot/Schinken slice of bread/ham

Schellfisch haddock
Schill pike-perch
Schillerlocke (1) cream horn; (2) curled strip of smoked dogfish
Schinken ham
Schinkenbrötchen ham sandwich
Schinkenfleckerln ham and pasta bake
Schinkenwurst smoked ham slicing sausage
Schlachtplatte plate of *[freshly made]* sliced cold meat and sausage
Schlackwurst cervalat sausage
Schlag with cream
Schlagsahne, Schlagobers whipped cream
Schlegel drumstick; haunch; leg
Schlehe sloe
Schlehenlikör sloe gin
Schleie tench
Schlesisches Himmelreich dried fruit and fresh or cured pork, with potato
    dumplings
Schmalz lard
Schmand fatty sour cream
Schmankerl cone-shaped sweet pastry
Schmarren thick pancake broken up with a fork after frying
Schmetterling-Steak butterfly *[pork]* chop
Schmorbraten pot roast
schmoren braise, stew
Schmortopf casserole
schmutzig dirty
Schnecken snails
Schneidebohnen sliced green beans
Schnellimbiss snack bar, fast-food restaurant
Schnepfe snipe
Schnippelbohnen finely sliced green beans
Schnittlauch chives
Schnitzel cutlet, escalope
Schokolade chocolate
Schokoladeneis chocolate ice cream
Schokoladenkuchen chocolate cake
Schokoladenmousse chocolate mousse
Schokoladensoße chocolate sauce
Schokoladentrüffel chocolate truffle
Scholle plaice
Schottischer Whisky Scotch *[whisky]*
Schöpsenbraten roast mutton
Schöpsenschlegel roast leg of lamb
Schottisches Moorschneehuhn grouse
Schrotbrot brown wholewheat bread
Schübling smoked beef and pork sausage
Schulter shoulder
Schupfnudele finger-shaped potato noodles
Schuppenannone custard apple
Schüssel bowl, dish
Schwammerl mushrooms
Schwanzstück silverside
Schwarte pork rind
Schwartemagen pig's stomach stuffed with pork rind, rib meat, pig's ears,
    onions, bay leaves, allspice, cloves and nutmeg
Schwarzbrot brown rye bread
schwarze Bohnen black beans

schwarze Butter   black butter
schwarze Johannisbeere   blackcurrant
schwarze Kirsche   black cherry
schwarze Oliven   black olives
schwarze Trüffel   black truffle
schwarzer Heilbutt   black halibut, Greenland halibut
schwarzer Kaffee   black coffee
schwarzer Pfeffer   black pepper
Schwarzwälder Kirschtorte   Black Forest gâteau
Schwarzwälder Schinken   Black Forest ham (smoked and air-dried)
Schwarzwurzeln   salsify
Schwein   pig
Schweinebauch   belly of pork
Schweinebraten   roast pork
Schweinebratenkruste   crackling
Schweinedünndarm   chitterlings
Schweinefleisch   pork
Schweinekotelett   pork chop
Schweinelende   loin of pork
Schweinerollbraten   rolled joint of roast pork
Schweinesaitling   chitterlings
Schweineschmalz   lard
Schweinsfüße   pig's trotters
Schweinshaxe   knuckle of pork
Schweinsrippchen   spare ribs
Schweinswurst, Schweinswürstl   Bavarian pork sausage
Schwertfisch   swordfish
Seebarsch   sea bass
Seebrassen   bogue
Seehecht   hake
Seelachs   coley, coalfish, saithe
Seeohr   abalone
Seeteufel   monkfish, angler fish *[US]*
Seewolf   catfish, rockfish
Seezunge   *[Dover]* sole
sehr trocken   very dry *[wine]*
Sekt   sekt *[sparkling wine]*
Selchfleisch   smoked pork
Sellerie   celeriac; celery
Sellerieschnitzel   breaded celeriac slices
Selterswasser   soda water
Semmel   roll *[bread]*
Semmelknödel   bread dumpling
Senf   mustard
Senfkohl   rocket
Seniorenteller   senior citizen's menu
Servierlöffel   serving spoon, tablespoon
Serviette   serviette, napkin
Serviettenkloß   large bread dumpling cooked in a cloth
Sesamkörner, Sesamsamen   sesame seeds
Sherry   sherry
Shiitakepilze   shiitake mushrooms
Shrimp   shrimp
Sirup   syrup
Sodawasser   soda water
Sojabohne   soy(a) bean, soja bean
Sojabohnensprossen   bean sprouts

German-English

Sojamilch soya milk
Sojasoße soy(a) sauce
Soleier hard-boiled eggs in brine
Sommelier wine waiter
Sonnenblume sunflower
Sonnenblumenöl sunflower oil
sonnengetrocknet sun-dried
Sorbet sorbet; sherbet
Sorghum sorghum
Soße sauce; gravy
Soßenschüssel gravy boat
Soufflé soufflé
Spaghetti spaghetti
   Spaghetti Bolognese spaghetti bolognese
Spanferkel suckling pig
spanischer Pfeffer capsicum
Spargel asparagus
Spargelcremesuppe cream of asparagus soup
Spargelspitzen asparagus tips
Spargelkohl broccoli
Spätlese German wine made from ripe late-harvested grapes
Spätzle wheat-flour *[egg]* noodles
Speck mildly cured and smoked pork fat; bacon
Speckknödel bread, onion and diced bacon dumpling
Speiseeis ice cream
Speisekarte menu
Speisepilz mushroom
Speisestärke cornflour
Spekulatius very thin butter almond biscuit
Spezi orangeade and cola
Spezialität speciality
   Spezialitäten der Region local specialities
Spickgans smoked breast of goose
Spiegelei fried egg
Spieß skewer; spit; kebab
Spinat spinach
Spinatpüree creamed spinach
Spirituosen spirits
Spitzkohl spring cabbage
Springerle aniseed-flavoured Christmas biscuits
Spritzgebäck specially shaped shortbread biscuits
Sprotten sprats, whitebait
sprudelnd fizzy
Sprudelwasser sparkling/fizzy *[mineral]* water
Stachelbeere gooseberry
Stangenbohne runner bean
Stangenbrot French bread
Stangensellerie celery
Stärkemehl cornflour
Steak steak *[beef, pork, turkey]*
Steckerlfisch barbecued fish on a stick
Steckrübe swede
Stehcafé stand-up café
Steinbutt turbot
Steinpilz cep, porcini mushroom
Steinsalz rock salt
Steirisches Schöpsernes/Schweinernes mutton/pork stew

Stielmus   chard stems and white turnip leaves, eaten with mashed potatoes
stilles Mineralwasser   still mineral water
Stilton *[käse]*   Stilton
Stint   smelt
stippen   dip *[verb]*
Stöcker   horse mackerel
Stollen   sweetened yeast dough, filled with dried vine fruits and nuts *[eaten at Christmas]*
Stör   sturgeon
Stoßsuppe   potato soup with sour milk, sour cream and caraway
Stout   stout
Strammer Max   smoked ham, fried egg and chives on brown or rye bread
Strandschnecke   winkle
Strauß   ostrich
Streichhölzer   matches
Streichholzkartoffeln   matchstick potatoes
Streichwurst   spreading sausage
Streifenbarbe   barbel, red mullet
Streuselkuchen   yeast cake with a crumble topping
Strudel   strudel
Stuhl   chair
Sturzkuchen   upside-down cake
Sultanine   sultana
Sülze   jelly *[savoury]*; brawn
Sülzkotelett   escalope of pork in aspic
Sülzplatte   galantine
Suppe   soup
Suppengemüse   julienne
Suppengrün   bundle of carrot, celery, leek and parsley, used to flavour soups
Suppenhuhn   boiling fowl
Suppenlöffel   soup spoon
süß   sweet
   süßer Wein   sweet wine
Süßholz   liquorice
Süßigkeiten   sweets, candy *[US]*
Süßkartoffel   sweet potato
Süßmais   sweetcorn
süßsauer   sweet and sour
Süßspeise   pudding *[sweet]*
Süßwasser *[fisch]*   freshwater *[fish]*
Tafel   table
Tafelsalz   table salt
Tafelspitz   boiled fillet of beef, served with apple and horseradish purée, and chive sauce
Tafelwein   table wine
Tageskarte   dish of the day
Tagesgericht   special *[dish of the day]*, plat du jour
Tagessuppe   soup of the day
Tagliatelle   tagliatelle
Tang   seaweed
Tangerine   tangerine
Tapioka   tapioca
Tartar   tartare
Tascherln   small pastries filled with jam or preserved fruit
Tasse   cup
   Tasse Kaffee/Tee   cup of coffee/tea
Tatarensoße   tartar sauce

Taube pigeon
Tee tea
Teekanne teapot
Teelöffel tea spoon
Teestunde tea-time, afternoon tea
Teetasse tea cup
Teewurst smoked pork and beef spreading sausage
Teig pastry
Teigpastete pasty
Teigwaren pasta
Teller plate
Teltower Rübchen glazed turnip
Terrine terrine
Thun, T(h)unfisch tunny, tuna
Thüringer *[Bratwurst]* long pork sausage, grilled or fried
Thymian thyme
tiefgekühlt frozen
Tiefseekrebs Dublin bay prawn
Tiefseekrebsschwänze scampi
Tintenfisch octopus
   gemeiner Tintenfisch cuttlefish
   zehnarmiger Tintenfisch squid
Tirolen Eierspeise casserole of hard boiled eggs, potatoes and anchovies
Tirolersuppe soup with dumplings
Tisch table
  Tisch am Fenster window table, table by the window
Tischdecke, Tischtuch tablecloth
Toast toast
Tofu tofu
Toilette lavatory, toilet
Toilettenpapier toilet paper
Tomate tomato
Tomatencremesuppe cream of tomato soup
Tomatenketchup tomato ketchup
Tomatensaft tomato juice
Tomatensalat tomato salad
Tomatensoße tomato sauce
Tonikwasser tonic water
Tontopf clay pot
Topfenknödel sweet dumpling flavoured with quark
Topfenpalatschinke quark-filled pancake
Topfenstrudel quark strudel
Topinambur Jerusalem artichoke
Törtchen tart
Torte cake, gâteau
tranchieren carve
Traube grapes
Traubensaft grape juice
Traubenkernöl grapeseed oil
Trifle trifle
trinkbar drinkable
trinken drink *[verb]*
Trinkgeld tip, gratuity
Trinkspruch toast *[tribute]*
Trinkwasser drinking water
trocken dry *[wine]*

Trockenbeerenauslese German wine made from selected grapes left to dry
   on the vine at the end of the season
Trüffel truffle
Trüffelbutter truffle butter
Truthahn turkey
Tunke sauce; gravy
ungekocht uncooked
ungesalzene Butter unsalted butter
Unterschale silverside
Untertasse saucer
Vanille vanilla
Vanilleeis vanilla ice cream
Vanille-Essenz vanilla essence
Vanillekipfel crescent-shaped vanilla biscuit
Vanillepudding vanilla custard
Vanilleschote vanilla pod/bean
Vanillesoße custard sauce
Vanillezucker vanilla sugar
Veganer vegan
vegetarisch vegetarian
   vegetarisches Chili vegetable chili
   vegetarische Brühe vegetarian gravy
   vegetarischer Hamburger vegetarian burger
   vegetarische Küche vegetarian cooking
   vegetarische Lasagne vegetarian lasagne
   vegetarische Spaghetti Bolognese vegetarian bolognaise
verbrennen burn *[verb]*
verdorben off *[food, wine]*
Venusmuschel clam
verbrannt burnt
verbraten; verkocht overdone
Verfallsdatum sell-by-date
verlorenes Ei poached egg
verschiedene Gemüse assorted/mixed vegetables
Viertel quarter
Vinaigrette vinaigrette, French dressing
voll full *[restaurant]*
vollfett full-fat *[cheese]*
Vollkorn wholewheat
Vollkornbrot wholemeal bread
Vollkornbrötchen brown roll
Vollkornmehl wholewheat flour
Vollmilch full-cream milk
Vollmilchschokolade milk chocolate
vollmundig full-bodied *[wine]*
Vorspeise starter, hors d'oeuvre, appetizer
Wabenhonig comb honey
Wachsbohne wax bean: yellowish-white French bean
Wachtel quail
Wachteleier quail's eggs
Wackelpeter, Wackelpudding jelly *[sweet/pudding]*, jello *[US]*
Waffel wafer; waffle
Wagen trolley
Walderdbeere wild strawberry
Waldmeister sweet woodruff
Waldorfsalat Waldorf salad
Waldpilze wild mushrooms

German-English

Waldschnepfe woodcock
Walfisch whale
Walnuss walnut
warm warm *[salad etc.]*
Waschraum lavatory
Wasser water
Wasserkastanie water chestnut
Wasserkresse watercress
Wassermelone water melon
weich soft
weich *[gekocht]* **es Ei** soft-boiled egg
Weichkäse soft cheese
Weichsel type of sour cherry
Weichtier mollusc
Weihnachtsblock Christmas log
Weihnachtsessen Christmas dinner
Weihnachtskuchen Christmas cake
Weihnachtsmenü Christmas menu
Wein wine
Weinbergschnecke snail
Weinblätter vine leaves
Weinbrand brandy
Weinessig wine vinegar
Weinglas wine glass
Weinkarte wine list
Weinkellner wine waiter
Weinkühler wine cooler
Weinraute rue
Weinschaumsoße sauce made from white wine and whipped eggs
Weinstube wine bar
Weintraube grape
weiß white
Weißbier wheat beer
Weißbrot white bread; white loaf
weiße Bohnen haricot beans
weiße Soße white sauce
weißer Thunfisch albacore *[tuna]*
Weißherbst German rosé wine
Weißwein white wine
Weißwurst mild white pork and veal sausage, eaten hot
Weizen wheat
Weizenbier wheat beer
Weizenbrot brown bread
Weizenkeim wheatgerm
Weizenmehl wheat flour
Wellhornschnecke whelk
Wels large freshwater catfish
Welschkohl savoy cabbage
Wermut absinthe
Wiener Schnitzel panéed veal escalope served with a wedge of lemon
Wienerwurst coarse beef, pork or veal sausage
Wiesensteinbrech saxifrage
Wild, Wildbret game
Wildente *[wild]* duck
Wildgeflügel game birds
Wildpastete game pie
Wildreis wild rice

Wildroulade   rolled red cabbage leaf filled with game meat
Wildschwein   *[wild]* boar
Windbeutel   profiterole
Wirsing *[kohl]*   savoy cabbage
Wirsingrouladen   stuffed savoy cabbage leaves
Wittling   whiting
Wollwurst   very fine white Bavarian veal sausage, fried in butter
Worcestershire Soße   Worcestershire sauce
Wurst, Würstchen   sausage
   Würstchen im Schlafrock   sausage roll
Würstel   Wienerwurst
Wurstsalat   strips of sausage, gherkins, carrots and onion in a piquant oil and
   vinegar dressing
Würze   condiment
Wurzel   root
würzig   spicy
Yamswurzel   yam
Zabaglione   zabaglione
Zackenbarsch   grouper
zäh   tough *[meat]*
Zahnstocher   toothpick
Zander   pike-perch
zart   tender
zehnarmiger Tintenfisch   squid
Ziegenpfeffer   sweet pepper
zerdrückt   mashed
zerhackt, zerkleinert   chopped *[into pieces]*
zerstampft   mashed
zerlassene Butter   melted butter
zerteilen   carve
Zervelatwurst   cervelat sausage
Zichorie   chicory
Ziege(nfleisch)   goat
Ziegenkäse   goat's cheese
Ziegenmilch   goat's milk
Zigaretten   cigarettes
Zigarre   cigar
Zigeunerschnitzel   veal or pork escalope in a spicy green/red pepper sauce
Zigeunerspieß   meat, pepper and onion kebab
Zimmertemperatur   room temperature
Zimt   cinnamon
Zimtplätzchen   cinnamon cakes
Zimtapfel   custard apple
Zitronat   candied peel, citron
Zitrone   lemon
Zitronengras   lemon grass
Zitronenlimonade   lemonade
Zitronenmelisse   lemon balm
Zitronensaft   lemon juice
Zitronentee   lemon tea
Zitrus   citrus
Znüni   mid-morning snack, second breakfast
zu   shut, closed
Zucchini   courgette, zucchini *[US]*
Zucker   sugar
Zuckerablaufsirup   treacle
Zuckererbse   mangetout, sugar snap pea

Zuckerguss   icing
Zuckermais   sweetcorn
Zuckerrübe   sugar beet
Zündhölzer   matches
Zunge   tongue
Zungenwurst   slicing sausage with cooked tongue
Zürchertopf   beef, macaroni and tomato sauce casserole
Zusatz   supplement
Zutaten   ingredients
Zwetsch(g)e   plum
Zwetschengrütze   stewed halved plums in red wine and plum brandy *[eg. Slivovitz]*
Zwetschenknödel   plum dumplings
Zwieback   rusk
Zwiebel   onion
Zwiebelfleisch   strips of fried beef and onions with gravy
Zwiebelkuchen   onion tart
Zwiebelringe   onion rings
Zwiebel Rostbraten   fried steak and onions in gravy
Zwiebelsoße   onion sauce
Zwiebelsuppe   onion soup
Zwiebelwurst   coarse spreading sausage with onions
Zwischengericht   entrée
Zwischenmahlzeit   snack *[between meals]*
Zwischenrippenstück   rib steak of beef

English-German

abalone Seeohr
absinthe Wermut
account Rechnung
aged betagt, alt
aïloli sauce Ailloli: *[pikante, kalte Soße]*
air-conditioned klimatisiert
albacore *[tuna]* weißer Thunfisch
alcohol Alkohol
ale englisches Bier, Ale
alfalfa sprouts Alfalfasprossen
allergic *[to]* allergisch *[gegen]*
allergy Allergie
allspice Nelkenpfeffer, Piment
almond Mandel
    almond biscuits Mandelplätzchen
    almond paste Marzipanmasse
    almond tart Mandeltorte
    with almonds mit Mandeln
amandine potatoes Mandelkroketten
anchovy Anschovis, Sardelle
    anchovy butter Sardellenbutter
    anchovy paste Sardellenpaste
angel food cake Biskuitkuchen
angel fish Engelhai, gemeiner Meerengel
angel hair pasta Fadennudeln
angels on horseback mit Austern gefüllte, gegrillte Frühstücksspeckröllchen
angelica Angelika, Engelwurz
angler Seeteufel
anise Anis
aniseed Anis
aperitif Aperitif
appetizer Vorspeise
apple Apfel
    apple fritter Apfel-Beignet
    apple juice Apfelsaft
    apple pie gedeckter Apfelkuchen
    apple purée Apfelmus
    apple sauce Apfelkompott
    apple strudel Apfelstrudel
    apple turnover Apfeltasche
    apple tart Apfelkuchen, Apfeltorte
    baked apple Bratapfel
apricot Aprikose
aroma Aroma, Duft, Würze
arrowroot Pfeilwurz *[mehl]*, Arrowrootstärke
artichoke Artischocke
ashtray Aschenbecher
asparagus Spargel
    asparagus tips Spargelspitzen

aspic Aspik
assorted vegetables verschiedene Gemüse
aubergine, eggplant Aubergine, Eierfrucht
au gratin *[US]* gratiniert
avocado Avocado
baby corn *[cob]* Baby-Mais *[kolben]*
baby eels Baby-Aale
baby food Babynahrung
baby leeks Baby-Lauch *[stangen]*
baby vegetables Baby-Gemüse
baby's bottle Babyflasche
bacon durchwachsener Speck, Frühstücksspeck, Bacon
   bacon and eggs Spiegeleier mit *[Frühstücks]* speck
bad faul
   bad egg faules Ei
bake backen
baked gebacken
   baked Alaska Eiscreme auf Biskuitboden mit Baiserhaube
   baked apple Bratapfel
   baked beans gebackene Bohnen
   baked custard Caramelcreme, karamelisierter Vanillepudding
   baked potato gebackene Kartoffel
   baked rice Milchreis
bakery Bäckerei
balsamic vinegar Balsamessig
bamboo shoots Bambussprossen
banana Banane
   banana fritter Banane-Beignet
   banana split Bananensplit
   banana flambé flambierte Banane
bar *[pub]* Bar, Lokal, Kneipe
barbecue Barbecue, Grillfest
barbecued gegrillt
barbel Meerbarbe, Streifenbarbe
barley Gerste
   barley sugar Gerstenzucker
   barley water Gerstenschleim
basil Basilikum
   basil pesto *[Basilikum-]* Pesto
basmati rice Basmatireis
bass, sea bass Seebarsch
bathroom Toiletten
batter geschlagener Teig
Bavarian cream Bay(e)rische Creme
bay leaf Lorbeerblatt
bean Bohne
   bean sprouts Sojabohnensprossen
   broad bean dicke Bohne, Puffbohne, Saubohne
   French bean, green bean, string bean grüne Bohne
   kidney bean, red bean Gartenbohne, Kidneybohne
   runner bean Stangenbohne
   soya bean Sojabohne
béarnaise sauce Bearner Soße
béchamel sauce Béchamelsoße
beech nuts Bucheckern
beef Rindfleisch
   beef stroganoff Rindfleisch Stroganoff

beefsteak *[US]* Beefsteak
beef tea Rindfleischbrühe
beef Wellington Rinderfilet-Wellington
roast beef Rinderbraten, Roastbeef
beer Bier
draught beer Fassbier
beetroot rote Rübe, rote Bete
bergamot Bergamotte
berries Beeren
bib *[child's]* Latz, Lätzchen
big groß
bilberry Heidelbeere, Bickbeere, Blaubeere
bill Rechnung
birthday cake Geburtstagskuchen
biscuit Zwieback, Plätzchen, Keks
bitter bitter
bitter *[beer]* halbdunkles, obergäriges Bier
black beans schwarze Bohnen
blackberry Brombeere
black butter schwarze Butter
black cherry schwarze Kirsche
black coffee schwarzer Kaffee
blackcurrant schwarze Johannisbeere
Black Forest cake/gâteau Schwarzwälder Kirschtorte
black halibut schwarzer Heilbutt
black pepper schwarzer Pfeffer
black pudding Blutwurst
black truffle schwarze Trüffel
blaeberry Blaubeere, Heidelbeere, Bickbeere
blanch blanchieren
blanched blanchiert
blancmange Flammeri, Pudding
blend einrühren, mixen
blinis Plinsen, Blinis
bloater Lachshering, Räucherhering
blood Blut
blueberry Blaubeere, Heidelbeere, Bickbeere
blue cheese Blauschimmelkäse
blue whiting blauer Wittling
boar Wildschwein; Frischling
bogue *[fish]* Seebrassen
boil kochen
boiled gekocht
boiled egg gekochtes Ei
boiled ham gekochter Schinken
boiled potatoes gekochte Kartoffeln
boiled rice gekochter Reis
boiled vegetables gekochtes Gemüse
hard-boiled egg hartgekochtes Ei
boiling water kochendes Wasser
bombe Eisbombe
bone Knochen
bone marrow Knochenmark
boned vom/ohne Knochen
on the bone am/mit Knochen
bones *[of fish]* Gräten
bonito Bonito, Pelamide

English-German

book *[a table]* reservieren
borage Borretsch
bordelaise sauce Bordelaise, Bordeauxsoße
borlotti beans Borlotti-Bohnen
bouquet garni Kräutermischung
bottle Flasche
    bottle opener Flaschenöffner
bowl Schüssel
brains Gehirn, Hirn
braise schmoren
braised geschmort
bran Kleie
    bran flakes Haferflocken
brandy Weinbrand, Kognak, Branntwein
    cherry brandy Cherry Brandy, Kirschlikör
brawn Sülze, Presskopf
brazil nut Paranuss
bread Brot
    breadcrumbs Paniermehl
    bread knife Brotmesser
    brown bread Graubrot, Schwarzbrot, Schrotbrot
    brown roll Vollkornbrötchen
    bread roll Brötchen
    bread sauce Brottunke
breaded paniert
breakfast Frühstück
    breakfast cereal Müsli
bream, sea bream Brachse(n), Brassen
breast Brust, Bruststück
    breast of lamb/veal Lamm/Kalbsbrust
    chicken breast Hühnerbrust
brill Glattbutt
brioche Brioche, Apostelkuchen
brisket *[of beef]* Bruststück, Rinderbrust
brittle Nugat
broad bean dicke Bohne, Puffbohne, Saubohne
broccoli Brokkoli, Spargelkohl
broth Fleischbrühe, Kraftbrühe, Bouillon
brown *[verb]* (an)bräunen; anbraten
brown bread Graubrot, Schwarzbrot, Schrotbrot
brown butter braune gebräunte Butter
brown rice Naturreis
brown roll Vollkornbrötchen
brown sugar brauner Zucker
brown sauce braune Soße
brussels sprouts Rosenkohl
bubble and squeak zusammengebratene Gemüsereste
buckwheat Buchweizen
buffalo Büffel
buffet Büfett
bulgar wheat, bulgur wheat Bulgur
bun süßes Brötchen, Biskuittörtchen
burbot Aalraupe, Quappe
burdock Klette
Burgundy *[wine]* Burgunder *[wein]*
burn *[verb]* verbrennen
burnet kleiner Wiesenknopf

burnt angebrannt, verbrannt
butcher's shop Metzger
butter Butter
    butterfish Butterfisch
    buttermilk Buttermilch
    butter sauce Buttersoße
    with butter mit Butter
    without butter ohne Butter
cabbage Kohl
cabinet pudding im Wasserbad gebackener Auflauf aus Brot, Butter, Dörrobst und Vanillesoße
Caesar salad Cäsar-Salat: *[mit knoblauch Salatsoße, Croûtons und Parmesankäse]*
café Cafe, Kaffeehaus
caffeine Koffein
    caffeine-free koffeinfrei; entkoffeiniert
cake Kuchen, Torte
    carrot cake Karottenkuchen
    cream cake Sahnetorte, Cremetorte
    fruit cake Früchtekuchen
    sponge cake einfacher Biskuitkuchen
cake shop Konditorei
calamari Tintenfisch
calf Kalb
    calf's brains Kalbsgehirn
    calf's liver Kalbsleber
camomile Kamille
canapés Appetithappen, Canapés
candied kandiert
    candied peel kandierte Fruchtschalen, Zitronat
candle Kerze
candlestick Kerzenhalter, Leuchter
candy *[US]* Bonbon, Süßigkeiten
cane sugar Rohrzucker
canned *[US]* Dosen-, in Dosen
cantaloup *[melon]* Kantalupe, Beutelmelone
capers Kapern
capon Kapaun
capsicum Paprika, spanischer Pfeffer
carafe Karaffe
caramel Karamell
caraway *[seeds]* Kümmel
carbohydrate Kohlenhydrat
carbonara Carbonara
carbonated mit Kohlensäure
cardamom Kardamom
carp Karpfen
carrot Karotte, Möhre
    carrot cake Karottenkuchen
carve tranchieren, aufschneiden, zerteilen
cassata Cassata
cashew nut Cashewnuss
cashier Kassierer, Kassiererin
casserole Kasserolle, Schmortopf
caster sugar Raffinade, Kastorzucker
catfish Katfisch, Seewolf
cauliflower Blumenkohl

English-German

    cauliflower cheese *[überbackener]* Blumenkohl mit Käsesoße
caviar Kaviar
cayenne pepper Cayennepfeffer
celeriac Knollensellerie
celery Stangensellerie, Eppich
cereal *[breakfast]* Cerealien, *[Getreide]* flocken
chair Stuhl
champagne Champagner; Sekt
change *[coins]* Kleingeld
change *[verb]* ändern, wechseln
chantilly Chantilly-Soße
chanterelle Pfifferling
char Saibling
charcoal Holzkohle
    charcoal-grilled über Holzkohle gegrillt
chard Mangold
charlotte Charlotte
    apple charlotte Apfelcharlotte
cheap billig; günstig
check *[US: bill]* Rechnung
cheddar *[cheese]* Chedder-Käse
Cheers! Prost!
cheese Käse
    cheddar *[cheese]* Cheddar
    cheese board Käsebrett; Käseplatte
    cheesecake Käsekuchen
    cream cheese Frischkäse, Rahmkäse
    cheese sandwich Käsebrötchen
    cheese sauce Käsesoße
    cheese soufflé Käsesoufflé, Käseauflauf
    cheese straw Käsestange
chef Koch
cherry Kirsche
    cherry brandy Cherry Brandy, Kirschlikör
    cherry tomato Kirschtomaten
chervil Kerbel
chestnut *[sweet]* Kastanie
    water chestnut Wasserkastanie
chickpea Kichererbse
chicken Hähnchen
    roast chicken im Ofen gebackenes Huhn
    breast of chicken Hühnerbrust
    chicken gumbo Hühnergumbo
    chicken Kiev panierte Hühnerbrust mit Knoblauchfüllung
    chicken liver Hühnerleber
    chicken salad Hühnersalat, Geflügelsalat
    chicken soup Hühnersuppe
chicory Chicorée, Zichorie
children's menu Kindermenü
chilled eisgekühlt
chilli Chili
    chilli con carne Chili con carne
    chilli pepper Chilipfeffer, Peperoni
    chilli powder Chilipulver
    chilli without meat fleischloses Chili
china *[service]* Porzellan
China tea Chinatee
Chinese cabbage Chinakohl

chipped *[glass, plate]* angeschlagen
chips Pommes frites
chips *[US]* *[Kartoffel]* chips
chitterlings Schweinedünndarm, Schweinesaitling
chives Schnittlauch
chocolate Schokolade
   chocolate cake Schokoladenkuchen
   chocolate croissant Schokoladencroissant
   chocolate éclair Éclair, Liebesknochen
   chocolate mousse Schokoladenmousse
   chocolate sauce Schokoladensoße
   chocolate truffle Schokoladentrüffel
   milk chocolate Vollmilchschokolade
   plain chocolate Bitterschokolade
choose (aus)wählen, aussuchen
chop *[cutlet]* Kotelett
chop *[verb]* schneiden
chopped *[into pieces]* (zer)hackt, zerkleinert
chopsticks Essstäbchen
choux pastry Brandteig
chowder sämige Fischsuppe
Christmas cake Weihnachtskuchen
Christmas Day erster Weihnachtsfeiertag
Christmas dinner Weihnachtsessen
Christmas Eve Heiligabend
Christmas log Weihnachtsblock, Julblock
Christmas menu Weihnachtsmenü
Christmas pudding Plumpudding
cider Apfelwein, Cidre
   cider vinegar Apfelessig
cigar Zigarre
cigarettes Zigaretten
cinnamon Zimt, Kaneel
citron Zitronat; Zitrone
citrus Zitrus
clam Venusmuschel, Sandklaffmuschel
   clam chowder sämige Muschelsuppe
claret roter Bordeauxwein
clean sauber
clean up abräumen
clear soup klare Brühe, Kraftbrühe
clementine Klementine
clove (Gewürz)nelke
   clove of garlic Knoblauchzehe
club sandwich Club Sandwich
cobnut Haselnuss
cock-a-leekie *[soup]* Hühnerlauchsuppe
cockles Herzmuscheln
cocktail Cocktail
cocoa Kakao *[pulver]*
   cocoa butter Kakaobutter
   cup of cocoa *[eine]* Tasse Kakao
coconut Kokosnuss
   coconut cream Kokoscreme
   coconut milk Kokosmilch
   desiccated coconut Kokosraspeln
cod Kabeljau, Dorsch

English-German

coffee Kaffee
    cappucino coffee Cappuccino
    coffee parfait Kaffee-Parfait
    coffee pot Kaffeekanne
    coffee spoon Kaffeelöffel
    coffee whitener Kaffeeweißer
    coffee with whipped cream Kaffee mit Sahne
    decaffeinated coffee entkoffeinierter Kaffee
    espresso/expresso coffee Espresso
    filter coffee Filterkaffee
    instant coffee Pulverkaffee
    latte coffee Kaffee mit Milch
cold kalt
    cold cuts kalter Aufschnitt
    cold drink Kaltgetränk
    cold meat kaltes Fleisch; Aufschnitt
    cold water kaltes Wasser
coley *[coalfish]* Seelachs, Köhler
collared beef Rinderroulade
comb honey Wabenhonig
complimentary Gratis-; frei
condensed milk Kondensmilch
condiment Gewürz, Würze
confectioner's cream Puddingmasse
confectionery Süssigkeiten
conger eel Meeraal
consommé *[soup]* Kraftbrühe
    cold consommé gekühlte Kraftbrühe
continental breakfast kontinentales Frühstuck
cook, chef Koch/Köchin
cookies *[US]* Kekse, Plätzchen
coriander Koriander
corkscrew Korkenzieher
corn Korn, Getreide; Mais
    corn bread Maisbrot
    corn oil Meiskeimöl
    corn on the cob Maiskolben
    corn syrup Maissirup
    cornflakes Cornflakes
    cornflour Speisestärke, Stärkemehl
    sweetcorn *[Zucker]* mais
corned beef Corned beef
cornet *[ice cream]* Eistüte
cos lettuce Romagna-Salat, römischer Salat
cottage cheese Hüttenkäse
courgette Zucchini
couscous Kuskus
cover charge Gedeck
crab Krabbe, Krebs
    dressed/prepared crab farcierter Krebs
crackling *[Schweinebraten]* kruste
cranberry Preiselbeere, Moosbeere, Kronsbeere
    cranberry sauce Preiselbeersoße
crawfish Languste
crayfish Flusskrebs
cream Rahm, Sahne
    double cream fettreiche Sahne
    single cream einfache Sahne

sour cream saure Sahne, Sauerrahm
whipped cream Schlagsahne
cream cheese Frischkäse, Rahmkäse
cream cake Sahnetorte, Cremetorte
cream sauce Rahmsoße, Sahnesoße
cream slice Blätterteigschnitte mit Sahnefüllung
cream tea Tee mit Scones, Sahne und Marmelade
cream of -creme
  cream of asparagus soup Spargelcremesuppe
  cream of chicken soup Hühnercremesuppe
  cream of tomato soup Tomatencremesuppe
creamed puriert
  creamed potato *[US]* Kartoffelpüree
  creamed spinach Spinatpüree
creamy sahnig; cremig
crème caramel Caramelcreme, karamelisierter Vanillepudding
crème fraîche Crème fraîche
cress Gartenkresse
crispbread Knäckebrot
crisps *[Kartoffel]* chips
croissant Croissant
croquette potatoes Kroketten
croûtons Croûtons
crumble mit Streuseln bestreutes, überbackenes Obstdessert
crumpet flaches Hefeküchlein zum Toasten
crystallised fruit kandierte Früchte
cucumber (Salat)gurke
  cucumber sandwich Gurkenbrot
cumin *[seed]* Kreuzkümmel
cup Tasse
  cup and saucer (Ober)tasse und Untertasse; Gedeck
  cup of coffee Tasse Kaffee
  cup of tea Tasse Tee
  coffee cup Kaffeetasse
  tea cup Teetasse
curd Quark
cured geräuchert; gepökelt; gesalzen
currants Korinthen
curry Curry
  curry powder Currygewürz
custard Custard, Vanillepudding
  baked custard Caramelcreme, karamelisierter Vanillepudding
custard apple Zimtapfel, Schuppenannone
custard sauce Custard, Vanillesoße
custard tart Puddingtörtchen
cut schneiden
cutlery Besteck
cutlet Schnitzel, Kotelett
cuttlefish gemeiner Tintenfisch
dab Kliesche, Scharbe, Blieschen
dairy products Milchprodukte
damson Damaszenerpflaume
date Dattel
date plum Dattelpflaume
debone filetieren
decaffeinated/decaf entkoffeiniert
deep-fried fritiert
deer/venison Hirsch, Reh *[fleisch]*

English-German

defrost auftauen
delicatessen Delikatessen
delicious köstlich, lecker
demerara sugar brauner Zucker
dessert Dessert, Nachspeise, Nachtisch
    dessert spoon Dessertlöffel
    dessert wine Dessertwein
devilled scharf gewürzt und gebraten
    devilled kidneys pikante Nieren
    devilled sauce pikante Soße
diced in Würfel geschnitten
dill Dill
    dill sauce Dillsoße
dining car Speisewagen
dining room Speisesaal, Esszimmer
dinner Abendessen
    dinner party Essen, Dinner Party
    dinner time Essenszeit
dip *[verb]* (ein)tunken, stippen
dip *[noun]* Dip
dirty *[adj]* schmutzig
dirty *[verb]* beschmutzen, schmutzig machen
discount Nachlass, Rabatt
dish Schüssel; Gericht
    dish of the day Tagesgericht
dogfish Katzenhai, Dornhai, Glatthai
done gar; durch
    under-done nicht durchgebraten; blutig
    well-done durchgebraten
doner kebab Dönerkebap
dory, John Dory Petersfisch, Heringskönig
double *[shot of spirits]* ein Doppelter
double cream fettreiche Sahne
dough Teig
doughnut Berliner
    jam doughnut *[mit Marmelade]* gefüllter Krapfen
Dover sole Seezunge
draught beer Fassbier, Schankbier
dressing Dressing, Salatsoße
dried getrocknet
    sun-dried *[tomatoes]* sonnengetrocknet
drink Getränk
    drink *[verb]* trinken
    drinkable trinkbar
    drinks included Getränke inclusive
drinking water Trinkwasser
dripping Bratenfett
drumstick Geflügelunterschenkel; Keule, Schlegel
dry *[wine]* trocken
Dublin bay prawn Kaisergranat, Tiefseekrebs
duchesse potatoes Duchesse-Kartoffeln
duck *[domestic]* Hausente, Ente
duck *[wild]* Wildente
duck paté Entenleberpastete
duck with orange Orangen-Ente
duckling junge Ente

dumpling Kloß, Knödel
   potato dumpling Kartoffelkloß
eat essen
éclair Eclair, Liebesknochen
eel Aal
egg Ei
   boiled egg gekochtes Ei
   egg and bacon Spiegelei mit Frühstücksspeck
   egg cup Eierbecher
   egg white Eiweiß
   egg yolk Eigelb, Eidotter
   fried egg Spiegelei
   hardboiled egg hartgekochtes Ei
   poached egg pochiertes/verlorenes Ei
   scrambled eggs Rührei
   soft-boiled egg weich *[gekocht]* es Ei
eggplant Aubergine, Eierfrucht
elderberry Holunderbeere
endive Endivie
enough genug
entrée Zwischengericht
escalope scaloppina
   turkey escalope Putenschnitzel
   veal escalope Kalbsschnitzel
espresso Espresso
essence Essenz
ewe's milk Schafmilch
   ewe's milk cheese Schaf(s)käse
excellent ausgezeichnet
expensive teuer
extra-virgin olive oil Olivenöl
faggot Leberfrikadelle
falafel Falafel
farm *[eggs, chickens]* Land-
fast *[not eat]* fasten
fat *[adj]* fett
fat *[noun]* Fett
   fat-free fettfrei
feet, trotters Füße
fennel Fenchel
feta cheese Fetakäse
fig Feige
filbert Haselnuss
fillet Filet
   fillet steak Filetsteak
   fillet of beef Rinderfilet
fillet *[verb]* filetieren
filleted filetiert
filo pastry Filo-Teig
filter coffee Filterkaffee
fine beans Delikatessbohnen
first course Vorspeise
fish Fisch
   fish and chips Backfisch mit Pommes frites
   fish shop Fischgeschäft
   fish stew Fischragout
   fish stock Fischbestand
   fish soup Fischsuppe

fish cake Fischfrikadelle
fishmonger Fischhändler
anchovy Anschovis, Sardelle
angel fish Engelhai, gemeiner Meerengel
bass, sea bass Seebarsch; Flussbarsch
bloater Lachshering, Räucherhering
bream Brachse(n), Brassen
brill Glattbutt
burbot Aalraupe, Quappe
catfish Katfisch, Seewolf
cod Kabeljau, Dorsch
coley Seelachs, Köhler
conger eel Meeraal
crayfish Flusskrebs
cuttlefish gemeiner Tintenfisch
dogfish Katzenhai, Dornhai, Glatthai
dory, John Dory Petersfisch, Heringskönig
Dover sole Seezunge
eel Aal
flounder Flunder
flying fish fliegender Fisch
grey mullet Meeräsche
haddock Schellfisch
hake Seehecht, Hechtdorsch
halibut Heilbutt
herring Hering
kipper Räucherhering, Kipper
lemon sole Limande, Rotzunge
mackerel Makrele
monkfish Seeteufel
pike Hecht
pike-perch Zander
pilchard Pilchard, Sardine
redfish Rotbarsch
red mullet Meerbarbe, Streifenbarbe
rockfish Katfisch, Seewolf
roe Fischlaich, Rogen, Milch
sea bass Meerbarsch, Seebarsch
sea bream Meerbrassen
sea trout Lachsforelle
shark Hai
skate Rochen, Glattrochen
skipjack echter Bonito
smelt Stint
sole Seezunge
sturgeon Stör
swordfish Schwertfisch
tench Schleie
trout Forelle
tunny, tuna Thun, T(h)unfisch
turbot Steinbutt
whitebait *[sprats]* Sprotten, Breitling
whiting Wittling, Merlan
fisherman's pie Fischauflauf
fixed price zu festen Preisen
fixed-price menu Festpreismenü
fizzy sprudelnd, kohlensäurehaltig
flageolet *[beans]* Flageolettbohnen

flakes Flocken
flambé flambiert
flan *[cheese]* Käseboden
flan *[fruit]* Obstboden
flat fish Plattfisch
flavour Geschmack
    flavoured gewürzt
floating island(s) Île(s) flottante(s): *[kalte, dünne Vanillesoße mit löffelgroßen Baiserstücken]*
flounder Flunder
flour Mehl
flying fish fliegender Fisch
fondant Fondant
fondue Fondue
food Essen, Lebensmittel
    food poisoning Lebensmittelvergiftung
fool Süßspeise aus Obstpüree und Sahne
fork Gabel
fowl Geflügel
    boiling fowl Suppenhuhn
frankfurter Frankfurter Würstchen
free *[of charge]* kostenlos, frei, gratis
free-range Freiland-
French beans Gartenbohnen, Buschbohnen, Brechbohnen
French dressing Vinaigrette
French fries Pommes frites
French toast arme Ritter
fresh frisch
freshwater *[fish]* Süßwasser *[fisch]*
fried gebraten
    fried chicken Backhähnchen, Backhuhn, Backhendl
    fried egg Spiegelei
    fried fish gebratener Fisch
    fried food Gebratenes
    mixed fried fish gebratene/fritierte Fischplatte
frisée *[salad]* krause Endivien, Friséesalat
fritter Beignet, Reibekuchen
    apple fritter Apfel-Beignet
frog's legs Froschschenkel
frozen gefroren, tiefgekühlt
fruit Frucht; Obst
    fruit bread/loaf Früchtebrot
    fruit cocktail Fruchtcocktail
    fruit juice Fruchtsaft, Obstsaft
    fruit salad Fruchtsalat, Obstsalat
fry *[in der Pfanne]* braten
fudge weiche Karamelle
full *[restaurant]* voll
full *[after eating]* satt
full-bodied *[wine]* vollmundig, körperreich
full-cream milk Vollmilch
full-fat *[cheese]* vollfett
fungi Pilze, Funghi
galantine Galantine, Sülzplatte
galeeny Perlhuhn
game Wild, Wildbret
    game pie selvaggina in crosta

gammon leicht geräucherter Vorderschinken
garden mint Gartenminze
garden peas Gartenerbsen
garlic Knoblauch
  garlic bread Knoblauchbrot
  garlic mayonnaise Knoblauchmayonnaise
  garlic mushrooms Knoblauchpilze
garlicky Knoblauch-, knoblauchhaltig
garnished garniert
gassy *[water]* mit Kohlensäure
gâteau Kuchen, Torte
gazpacho Gazpacho
gelatine Gelatine
general store Lebensmittelgeschäft
genetically modified *[GM]* genetisch modifiziert
gents' toilets Herrentoiletten
gherkin Essiggurke, Gewürzgurke
giblets Geflügelinnereien, Hals und Innereien
gin Gin, Genever
  gin and tonic Gin Tonic
ginger Ingwer
  ginger beer Ingwerbier, Ingwerlimonade
  gingerbread Ingwerbrot
  ginger cake Ingwerkuchen
glacé cherry Cocktail-Kirsche
glass Glas
  clean glass sauberes Glas
  glass of water Glas Wasser
  wine glass Weinglas
glazed glasiert
gluten-free glutenfrei
gnocchi Gnocchi
goat Ziegenfleisch, Ziege, Geiß
  goat's cheese Ziegenkäse
  goat's milk Ziegenmilch
good gut
goose Gans
  goose liver Gänseleber
gooseberry Stachelbeere
goulash Gulasch
gourmet Gourmet; Feinschmecker
granary loaf Körnerbrot
granita auf Sirup aufgesetztes Sorbet
granulated sugar feinkörniger Zucker, Raffinade
grape(s) Weintraube(n)
grapefruit Grapefruit, Pampelmuse
grapeseed oil Traubenkernöl
grated gerieben, geraspelt
gratuity Gratifikation, Trinkgeld
gravy Soße, Bratensoße
gravy boat Sauciere, Soßenschüssel
grease Fett
Greek yoghurt griechischer Jogurt
green beans grüne Bohnen
green olives grüne Oliven
green peas grüne Erbsen
green pepper grüner Paprika

English-German

green salad grüner Salat
green tea grüner Tee
greengage *[plum]* grüne Reneklode, Reineclaude
greengrocer Gemüsehändler
Greenland halibut schwarzer Heilbutt
greens Grüngemüse
grenadine Grenadine
grey mullet Meeräsche
grill *[verb]* grillen
grill *[noun]* Grill
   mixed grill Grillteller, Grillplatte
grilled gegrillt
grind mahlen; zerkleinern
gristle Knorpel
grits *[US]* Grütze
groats Hafergrütze
grocer's Lebensmittelgeschäft
grocery Gemüseladen
ground gemahlen; zerkleinert
   ground beef Rinderhackfleisch
   ground coffee Kaffee
groundnut oil Erdnussöl
grouper Zackenbarsch
grouse Birkhuhn, Schottisches Moorschneehuhn
guacamole Guacamole
guava Guave, Guajave
gudgeon Gründling
guinea fowl Perlhuhn
gumbo Gumbo
gurnard Knurrhahn
haddock Schellfisch
haggis Haggis: *[im Schafsmagen gekochte, gehackte Schafsinnereien und Haferschrot]*
hake Seehecht, Hechtdorsch
half halb-
   half a litre Halbliter
   half bottle halbe Flasche
   half done halbgekocht
   half-cooked halbgekocht
halibut Heilbutt
ham Schinken
   boiled ham gekochter Schinken
ham sandwich Schinkenbrot
hamburger Hamburger
hangover Kater
hard hart
hard-boiled egg hartgekochtes Ei
hard cheese Hartkäse
hard roe Rogen, Fischlaich
hare Hase
haricot beans weiße Bohnen
hash browns *[US]* Kartoffelpuffer
haunch Keule
hazelnut Haselnuss
health Gesundheit
health shop Gesundheitsladen
healthy gesund

heart Herz
heat up heiß machen, aufwärmen
herbs Kräuter
herbal tea Kräutertee
herring Hering
hickory nut Hickorynuss
highchair Hochstuhl
high-fibre ballaststoffreich
hollandaise sauce holländische Soße
home-made hausgemacht
hominy grits *[US]* Maisgrütze
honey Honig
   comb honey Wabenhonig
honeycomb Honigwabe
honeydew melon Honigmelone
hors d'oeuvre Horsd'oeuvre, Vorspeise
horse mackerel Stöcker
horse meat Pferdefleisch
horseradish Meerrettich, Kren
hot *[not cold; strong]* heiß; scharf
   hot drink heisses Getränk
   hot water heisses Wasser
hot dog Hot dog
hotpot Fleischeintopf mit Kartoffeleinlage
house specialities Hausspezialitäten
hummus Humus
hungry hungrig
ice Eis
   bucket of ice Eiskübel, Eiskühler
ice cream Eiskrem, Speiseeis
   ice-cream cone Eistüte
   ice-cream scoop Eiskugel
ice cube Eiswürfel
ice lolly Eis am Stiel
iceberg lettuce Eisbergsalat
icing Zuckerguss
   icing sugar Puderzucker
ide *[fish]* Aland
ingredients Zutaten
inside innen
instant coffee Pulverkaffee
Irish stew Irish-Stew: *[Eintopfgericht aus Hammelfleisch und Gemüse]*
Irish whiskey irischer Whiskey
jam Marmelade, Konfitüre
Japanese tea japanischer Tee
jellied mit Gelee
jelly *[savoury]* Gelee
jelly *[sweet/pudding]* Götterspeise, Wackelpeter, Wackelpudding
jelly *[US]* Marmelade
jello *[US]* Götterspeise, Wackelpeter, Wackelpudding
Jerusalem artichoke Erdartischocke, Topinambur
John Dory Petersfisch, Heringskönig
jug Kanne, Kännchen, Krug
jugged hare Hasenpfeffer
juice Saft
   juicer Entsafter
julienne Julienne, Suppengemüse

kaki Kaki *[frucht]*
kale Grünkohl, Krauskohl
kebab Kebab
kedgeree Schellfischrisotto mit Currysoße und hartgekochten Eiern
ketchup Ketchup
kettle Wasserkocher, Kessel
key lime pie Limettepastete
kidney Niere
kidney bean rote/weiße Bohne, Kidneybohne
king prawn Riesengarnele, Hummerkrabbe
kipper Räucherhering, Kipper, Bückling
kitchen Küche
kiwi fruit Kiwi
knife Messer
knuckle Hachse, Haxe; Eisbein
kohlrabi Kohlrabi
kosher koscher
kumquat Kumquat
label Etikett
lactose Lactose, Milchzucker
    lactose intolerance Lactoseunverträglichkeit
ladies fingers Okra
ladies' toilets Damentoiletten
ladle Schöpfkelle
lager Lager, helles Bier
    lager shandy Alsterwasser; Radler
lamb Lamm
    lamb chop Lammkotelett
lamb's lettuce Feldsalat
langoustine aragostella
lard *[Schweine]* schmalz
lark Lerche
lasagne Lasagne
latte *[coffee]* Milchkaffee
lavatory Toilette, Waschraum
lavender Lavendel
lean mager
leek Lauch, Porree
leg Keule, Hachse
    leg of lamb Lammkeule
legumes Gemüse
lemon Zitrone
    lemon balm *[Zitronen]* melisse
    lemon grass Zitronengras
    lemon juice Zitronensaft
    lemon sole Limande, Rotzunge
    lemon zest geriebene Zitronenschale
    lemonade *[Zitronen]* limonade
lentil _Linse
lettuce Gartensalat, Kopfsalat
lime Limone, Limette
ling Leng
light-bodied wine leichter Wein
liqueur Likör
liquorice Lakritze; Süßholz
litre Liter
liver Leber

liver sausage Leberwurst
loaf Brot, *[Brot]* laib
   meat loaf Hackbraten
   white loaf Weißbrot
lobster Hummer
   lobster bisque Hummersuppe
local regional; der Region
   local cheese Käse der Region
   local specialities Spezialitäten der Region
loganberry Loganbeere
loin *[of veal, pork]* Lende
long-grained rice Langkornreis
low-fat *[diet]* fettarm
low in fat fettarm
low-salt salzarm
lunch Mittagessen, Lunch
luncheon meat Frühstücksfleisch
lunchtime Mittagessenzeit
lychee Litschi
lythe Pollack
macadamia nuts Macadamia-Nüsse
macaroni Maccaroni
   macaroni cheese Maccaroni-Auflauf
macaroon Makrone
mace Muskatblüte, Mazis
mackerel Makrele
macrobiotic makrobiotisch
Madeira Madeira *[wein]*
   Madeira cake Madeirakuchen
   Madeira sauce Madeirasoße
main course Hauptspeise/ Hauptgang
maize Mais
malt Malz
mandarin Mandarine
mangetout Zuckererbse
mango Mango
mangosteen Mangostane
maple syrup Ahornsirup
maple sugar Ahornzucker
margarine Margarine
marinade Marinade
marinated mariniert
marjoram Majoran
market Markt
marmalade Orangenmarmelade
marrow *[vegetable]* Gemeiner Kürbis
marrow bone Markknochen
   bone marrow Knochenmark
Marsala wine Marsalawein
marshmallow Marshmallow
marzipan Marzipan
mashed zerdrückt, zerstampft
mashed potatoes Kartoffelbrei
matches Streichhölzer, Zündhölzer
matchstick potatoes Streichholzkartoffeln
mature reif; gereift
mayonnaise Majonäse

mead Honigwein, Met
meal Mahlzeit Essen
meat Fleisch
    meat ball Fleischkloß
    meat-free fleischlos
    meat loaf Hackbraten
    meat pie Fleischpastete
medallion Medaillon
medlar Mispel
medium cooked halbgekocht
medium rare *[steak]* halb durchgebraten
medium wine halbtrockener Wein
melon Melone
melted butter zerlassene Butter
menu Speisekarte
    children's menu Kindermenü
meringue Baiser, Meringe
mild mild
milk Milch
    cow's milk Kuhmilch
    ewe's milk Schafmilch
    goat's milk Ziegenmilch
    milk chocolate Vollmilchschokolade
    milkshake Milchmixgetränk, Milchgetränk
    poached in milk in Milch pochiert
    soya milk Sojamilch
    with milk mit Milch
    without milk ohne Milch
minced meat Hackfleisch, Gehackte(s), Faschierte
mincemeat süße Füllung aus Dörrobst, Nüssen und Gewürzen
mince pie mit Mincemeat gefülltes Weihnachtsgebäck
mineral water Mineralwasser
    fizzy mineral water Sprudelwasser
    still mineral water stilles Mineralwasser
minestrone *[soup]* Minestrone
mint Minze
    mint sauce Minzsoße
    mint jelly Minzgelee
    mint tea Minztee
mixed grill Grillteller, Grillplatte
mixed herbs gemischte Kräuter
mixed salad gemischter Salat
mixed vegetables verschiedene Gemüse
mollusc Molluske, Weichtier
monkfish Seeteufel
monosodium glutamate *[MSG]* Mononatriumglutamat
morels Morcheln
moussaka Moussaka
mousse Mousse
muesli Müsli
muffin *[UK]* Mini-Hefepfannkuchen
muffin *[US]* Muffin: Ruhrteigplätzchen *[mit verschiedenen Füllungen]*
mug Becher; Krug
mulberry Maulbeere
mullet Meeräsche; Meerbarbe
mulligatawny *[soup]* Mulligatawnysuppe, Currysuppe
mushroom *[Speise]* pilz, Champignon
    button mushrooms junge Zuchtchampignons

mushy peas Erbsenbrei, Erbspüree
mussel *[Mies]* muschel, Pfahlmuschel
mustard Senf, Mostrich
mutton Hammelfleisch
napkin Serviette
natural Natur-
Neapolitan ice-cream Fürst-Pückler-Eis
neat pur
nectarine Nektarine
nettle Nessel
no smoking Nichtraucher, Rauchen verboten
noisettes mit Speck umwickelte Medaillons
non-alcoholic drink alkoholfreies Getränk
non-smoking area Nichtraucher *[zone]*
noodles Nudeln
   noodle soup Nudelsuppe
nut Nuss
   almond Mandel
   brazil nut Paranuss
   cashew nut Cashewnuss
   chestnut Kastanie
   cobnut Haselnuss
   coconut Kokosnuss
   hazelnut Haselnuss
   peanut Erdnuss
   pecan nut Pekannuss
   sweet chestnut Edelkastanie, Esskastanie, Marone
   walnut Walnuss
nutmeg Muskat *[nuss]*
oatcake Haferkeks
oatmeal Haferschrot, Hafermehl
oats Haferflocken
   porridge/rolled oats *[kernige]* Haferflocken
octopus Tintenfisch, Gemeiner Krake
off *[food, wine]* verdorben, korkig
offal Innereien
oil Öl
okra Okra
olive Olive
   black olives schwarze Oliven
   green olives grüne Oliven
olive oil Olivenöl
omelette Omelett(e), Eierkuchen
onion Zwiebel
   onion soup Zwiebelsuppe
open *[verb]* öffnen
orange Orange, Apfelsine
   orange juice Orangensaft
   orange sauce Orangensoße
oregano Origano
organic biologisch; organisch
ostrich Strauß
outdoors, outside im Freien, draussen
oven *[Back]* ofen
overdone verbraten; verkocht
oxtail Ochsenschwanz
   oxtail soup Ochsenschwanzsuppe

ox tongue Ochsenzunge
oyster Austern
   oyster mushroom Austernpilz
pancake Pfannkuchen
pan-fried in der Pfanne gebraten
papaya Papaya
paprika Paprika
par-boil ankochen
parfait Parfait
Parma ham Parmaschinken
parmesan *[cheese]* Parmesankäse
parsley Petersilie
   curly parsley krause Petersilie
   flat parsley glatte Petersilie
   parsley sauce Petersiliensoße
parsnip Pastinak(e), Petersilienwurzel
partridge Rebhuhn
party Party
pasta Teigwaren, Nudeln
   fresh pasta frischgemachte Nudeln
pastry Gebäck, Pastete
   filo pastry Filo-Teig
   puff pastry Blätterteig
   shortcrust pastry Mürbeteig
pasty *[Teig]* pastete
pâté Pastete
   liver pâté Leberpastete
pawpaw Papaya
pay *[verb]* bezahlen
pea Erbse
   green peas grüne Erbsen
   green pea soup grüne Erbsensuppe
   split peas getrocknete *[halbe]* Erbsen
   pea soup *[with split peas]* gelbe Erbsensuppe
peach Pfirsich
peanut Erdnuss
   peanut butter Erdnussbutter
pear Birne
pearl barley Gerstengraupen, Perlgraupen
pease-pudding Erbspüree
pecan *[nut]* Pekannuss
   pecan pie Pekannusstorte
peel *[verb]* schälen
peel *[noun]* Schale
   grated peel geriebene Schale
peeled geschält
pepper *[spice]* Pfeffer
   black, green, white pepper schwarzer/grüner/ weißer Pfeffer
   ground pepper gemahlener Pfeffer
   whole pepper Pfefferkörner
   pepper mill Pfeffermühle
   pepper pot Pfefferstreuer
   pepper steak Pfeffersteak
pepper *[vegetable]* Paprika
   green pepper grüner Paprika
   red pepper roter Paprika
   stuffed pepper gefüllter Paprika
peppermint Pfefferminze

perch Flussbarsch
perry Birnenmost
persimmon Persimone
pesto Pesto
petits fours Petits Fours
pheasant Fasan
pickled cabbage Sauerkraut
pickled cucumber saure Gurke
pickled herring eingelegter Hering
pickled onion eingelegte Zwiebel
pickles *[Mixed]* Pickles
picnic Picknick
pie *[Teig]* pastete mit Fleisch- oder Obstfüllung
piece Stück
pig Schwein
   suckling pig Spanferkel
pigeon Taube
pig's trotters Schweinsfüße
pike Hecht
pike-perch Zander
pilchard Pilchard, Sardine
pine nuts Pinienkerne
pineapple Ananas
pistachio nut Pistazie
pitcher Krug
pitta bread Pittabrot
pizza Pizza
plaice Scholle, Goldbutt
plain einfach, Nature-î
   plain chocolate Bitterschokolade
plantain Kochbanane, Mehlbanane, Plantain
plat du jour Tagesgericht
plate Teller, Platte
plum Pflaume, Zwetsch(g)e
plum pudding Plumpudding
plum tomato Flaschentomate
poach pochieren
poached pochiert
poached egg pochiertes Ei, verlorenes Ei
polenta Polenta
pollack Pollack
pomegranate Granatapfel
popcorn Popcorn, Puffmais
porcini mushroom Steinpilz
pork Schweinefleisch
   pork chop Schweinekotelett
   pork crackling Schweinebratenkruste
porridge Haferbrei; Porridge
port Portwein
pot roast Schmorbraten
potato Kartoffel
   baked potato *[in der Schale]* gebackene Kartoffel
   fried potoatoes Bratkartoffeln
   mashed potatoes Kartoffelbrei, Kartofelpüree
   new potatoes neue Kartoffeln
   potato chips Pommes *[frites]*
   potato crisps Kartoffelchips

potato dumpling Kartoffelkloß
potato salad Kartoffelsalat
potted shrimp eingekochte Nordseekrabben
poultry Geflügel
pound cake Pfundkuchen
poussin Brathähnchen
prawn Garnele
preserves Eingemachtes
price Preis
  price list Preisliste
prime rib Hochrippe
profiteroles Profiteroles, Windbeutel
protein Eiweiß
prune Dörrpflaume, Backpflaume
pudding *[savoury]* Pudding *[im Wasserbad gegarte Mehlspeise]*
pudding *[sweet]* Pudding, Süßspeise, Nachtisch
pudding rice Milchreis, Rundkornreis
pudding wine Dessertwein
puff pastry Blätterteig
pulses Hülsenfrüchte
pumpkin *[Garten]* kürbis
pure pur
purée Püree
purslane Portulak
puy lentils Linsen du Puy
quail Wachtel
  quail's eggs Wachteleier
quality Qualität
quark Quark
quarter Viertel
quiche Quiche
  quiche Lorraine Quiche Lorraine
quince Quitte
rabbit Kaninchen
rack vorderes Rippenstück
  rack of lamb Lammkammbraten
  rack of ribs Rippenbraten
radicchio Radicchio
radish Radieschen; Rettich
ragout Ragout
rainbow trout Regenbogenforelle
raisin Rosine
ramekin *[small container]* Auflaufförmchen
rancid ranzig
rare *[steak, meat]* blutig, halb roh, leichtgebraten
raspberry Himbeere
ravioli Ravioli
raw roh
receipt Beleg, Eingzahlung, Quittung
recipe Rezept
recommend empfehlen
red cabbage Rotkohl, Rotkabis
red chilli roter Chili
redcurrant rote Johannisbeere, Ribisel
  redcurrant jelly rote Johannisbeergelee
redfish Rotbarsch
red mullet Meerbarbe, Streifenbarbe

English-German

red pepper   roter Paprika
red wine   Rotwein
regional   regional; der Region
reindeer   Rentier
rennet   Renette
reservation   Reservierung
reserve   reserviert
restaurant   Restaurant
rhubarb   Rhabarber
ribs   Rippen
   rack of ribs   Rippenbraten
   ribs of beef   Rinderrippen
   spare ribs   Schweinsrippchen, Spare Ribs
rice   Reis
   rice paper   Reispapier
   rice pudding   Milchreis
   risotto rice   Risottoreis
   wild rice   Wildreis
rind *[on cheese]*   Rinde
ripe   reif
rissole   Rissole, Frikadelle
river   Fluss
roast *[verb]*   braten; rösten
   roast *[noun]*   Braten
   roast beef   Rinderbraten; Roastbeef
   roast chicken   im Ofen gebackenes Huhn
   roast pork   Schweinebraten
roasted   gebraten; geröstet
rock, on the rocks   mit Eis
rock salt   Steinsalz
rocket   Rucola
rockfish   Katfisch, Seewolf
roe   Fischlaich, Rogen, Milch
   hard roe   Rogen
   soft roe   Milch
roll *[bread]*   Brötchen, Semmel
rolled oats   *[kernige]* Haferflocken
rollmop herring   Rollmops
romaine *[lettuce]*   Romagna-Salat, römischer Salat
room temperature   Zimmertemperatur
root   Wurzel
rosé *[wine]*   Rosé *[wein]*
rosehip   Hagebutte
rosemary   Rosmarin
roulade   Roulade
rum   Rum
   rum baba   Rum-Baba
rump steak   Rumpsteak
runner bean   Stangenbohne
rusk   Zwieback
rye   Roggen
   rye bread   Roggenbrot, Pumpernickel
   rye whiskey   Roggenwhiskey, Rye *[whiskey]*
saccharin   Saccharin
saddle   Rücken
safflower   Saflor, Färberdistel
saffron   Safran

sage   Salbei
sago   Sago
saithe   Seelachs, Köhler
salad   Salat
   green salad   grüner Salat
   mixed salad   gemischter Salat
   side salad   Salat *[als Beilage]*
salad bowl   Salatschüssel
salad cream   Salatcreme, Remoulade
salad dressing   Salatsoße, Salat-Dressing
salami   Salami
salmon   Lachs, Salm
   salmon steak   Lachsfilet
salmon trout   Lachsforelle
salsify   Haferwurz
salt   Salz, Kochsalz, Tafelsalz
   low-salt   salzarm
   salt cellar   Salzstreuer
   salt mill   Salzmühle
   sea salt   Meersalz
salted   gesalzen
salty   salzig
sand sole   Sandzunge
sandwich   Sandwich; belegtes Brot
   cheese sandwich   Käsebrötchen
   club sandwich   Club Sandwich
   ham sandwich   Schinkenbrot
sardine   Sardine
sauce   Soße, Tunke, Sauce
   white sauce   weiße Soße, helle Soße, Mehlsoße
saucer   Untertasse
saury   Makrelenhecht
sausage   Wurst, Würstchen
   liver sausage   Leberwurst
   sausage roll   Würstchen im Schlafrock
sauté   kurz anbraten, sautieren
   sautéed   sautiert
   sauté pan   Bratpfanne
saveloy   Zervelatwurst
savoury   pikantes salziges Häppchen
savoy cabbage   Wirsing*[kohl]*
saxifrage   Körnersteinbrech, Wiesensteinbrech
scald   erhitzen, verbrühen
scallion *[US]*   Frühlingszwiebel
scallop   Jakobsmuschel, Kammmuschel, Pilgermuschel
scalloped chicken *[US]*   überbackenes Hähnchen
scalloped potatoes *[US]*   Kartoffelauflauf
scampi   Kaisergranatschwänze, Tiefseekrebsschwänze, Scampi
scone *[UK]*   brötchenartiges Teegebäck
Scotch   Schottisch; Scotch
   Scotch broth   Graupensuppe mit Lamm- oder Rindfleisch und Gemüse
   Scotch egg   paniertes, in Wurstbrät gerolltes Ei
scrambled eggs   Rührei
sea bass   Meerbarsch, Seebarsch
sea bream   Meerbrassen
sea salt   Meersalz
sea view *[table with a sea view]*   ein Tisch mit Meerblick

seafood Meeresfrüchte
sear rasch anbraten
seasonal saisonal, jahreszeitlich
seasoned gewürzt, gelagert, reif
seasoning Gewürz
sea trout Lachsforelle
seat Stuhl, Sitzplatz
seaweed Tang, Alge
second course Hauptspeise, zweiter Gang
selection Auslese, Auswahl
sell-by date Verfallsdatum
semi-dry halbtrocken
semi-hard cheese halbharter Käse
semi-skimmed milk Halbfettmilch
semi-soft cheese halbweicher Käse
semolina Grieß
service Bedienung, Service
   service charge Bedienungskosten
   service discretionary Trinkgeld im Ermessen des Kunden
   service *[not]* **included** Bedienung *[nicht]* inbegriffen
serviette Serviette
sesame seeds Sesam
set menu festgelegtes Menü
shad Alse, Maifisch
shallot Schalotte
shandy Alsterwasser, Radler
   half of shandy ein halbes Radler
shank Schenkel
shark Hai
sharp scharf
shell Schale
shellfish Meeresfrüchte
shepherd's pie mit Kartoffelbrei überbackenes Hackfleisch
sherbet Sorbet
sherry Sherry, Jerez *[wein]*
shiitake mushrooms Shiitakepilze
shish kebab Schaschlik
shop Geschäft, Laden
shortbread Shortbread, Butterkeks
shortcrust *[pastry]* Mürbeteig
shoulder Bug, Schulter
shrimp Shrimp, Granat, Nordseekrabbe, kleine Garnele
   shrimp cocktail *[Nordsee]* krabbencocktail
shut zu, geschlossen
side dish(es) Beilage
sift *[durch]* sieben
silverside Schwanzstück, Unterschale
simmer köcheln
single cream *[einfache]* Sahne
sippets Croûtons
sirloin Lendenfilet
skate Rochen, Glattrochen
skewer Spieß
skimmed milk Magermilch
skin Haut; Schale
skipjack echter Bonito
slice Scheibe

slice of bread Scheibe Brot
slice of ham Scheibe Schinken
slice of pie Stück Pastete
sliced aufgeschnitten, kleingeschnitten, *[in Scheiben]* geschnitten
sloe Schlehe
sloe gin Schlehenlikör
smell Geruch
smelt Stint
smoke *[a cigarette]* rauchen
smoke *[food]* räuchern
smoke *[noun]* Qualm, Rauch
smoked geräuchert
smoked bacon angeräucherter Bacon Frühstücksspeck, Räucherspeck
smoked cheese Räucherkäse
smoked eel Räucheraal
smoked fish Räucherfisch
smoked haddock geräucherter Schellfisch
smoked kipper Räucherhering
smoked meat Rauchfleisch
smoked salmon Räucherlachs
smoker Raucher
snack *[between meals]* Zwischenmahlzeit
snack *[light meal]* Snack
snail Weinbergschnecke
snipe Schnepfe
soda bread mit Backpulver gebackenes Brot
soda water Sodawasser, Selterswasser
soft weich
soft-boiled egg weichgekocht Ei
soft cheese Weichkäse
soft drink alkoholfreies Getränk, Soft Drink
soft roe Milch
sole Seezunge
sorbet Sorbet
sorghum Sorghum
sorrel Sauerampfer
soufflé Soufflé, Auflauf
cheese soufflé Käsesoufflé, Käseauflauf
soup Suppe
soup spoon Suppenlöffel
beef tea Rindfleischbrühe
broth Fleischbrühe, Kraftbrühe, Bouillon
chowder sämige Fischsuppe
fish broth Fischsud
fish soup Fischsuppe
mulligatawny Mulligatawnysuppe, Currysuppe
onion soup Zwiebelsuppe
soup of the day Tagessuppe
vegetable soup Gemüsesuppe
vichyssoise kalte Lauchkartoffelsuppe
sour sauer
sour cream saure Sahne, Sauerrahm
sourdough Sauerteig
sweet and sour süßsauer
soy bean, soya bean Sojabohne
soy sauce, soya sauce Sojasoße
soya milk Sojamilch
spaghetti Spaghetti

spaghetti bolognese Spaghetti Bolognese
spare ribs Schweinsrippchen, Spare Ribs
sparkling perlend, moussierend
   sparkling water Sprudelwasser
   sparkling wine Schaumwein, Perlwein
speciality Spezialität
spice Gewürz
spicy würzig, pikant
spinach Spinat
spiny lobster Languste
spirits Spirituosen
sponge biscuits Löffelbiskuits, Biskotten
sponge cake Biskuitkuchen, Sandtorte
spoon Löffel
   spoonful Löffel *[voll]*
sprat Sprotte
spring greens Frühkohl
spring onion Frühlingszwiebel
spring roll Frühlingsrolle
spring water Quellwasser
sprouts *[Brussels]* Rosenkohl
squab Jungtaube
squash Kürbisgewächs
squid Kalmar, *[zehnarmiger]* Tintenfisch
stale alt, altbacken
starch Speisestärke
starter course Vorspeise
steak *[beef]* Steak
   steak and kidney pie Rindfleisch-Nieren-Pastete
   steak and kidney pudding Rindfleisch-Nieren-Pudding
steam *[verb]* dünsten
steamed gedämpft, gedünstet
   steamed vegetables gedünstetes Gemüse
stew *[verb]* *[meat]* schmoren; *[fruit]* dünsten
stew *[noun]* Eintopf
   lamb stew Lammeintopf
stewed geschmort; gedünstet
   stewed fruit Obstkompott
   stewed steak geschmorter Rindfleisch
Stilton Stilton *[käse]*
stir-fry *[unter Rühren]* kurz anbraten
stock Brühe
stout Stout
stove Herd, Ofen
strawberry Erdbeere
   strawberry jam Erdbeermarmelade
   strawberry shortcake Erdbeerkuchen aus Mürbeteig
streaky bacon durchwachsener Speck
strip steak Beefsteak
strong kräftig
stuffed gefüllt
   stuffed olives gefüllte Oliven
stuffing Füllung; Farce, Füllsel
sturgeon Stör
suckling pig Spanferkel
suet Nierentalg, Nierenfett, Rindertalg
sugar Zucker

    caster sugar Raffinade, Kastorzucker
    granulated sugar feinkörniger Zucker, Raffinade
    icing sugar Puderzucker
    sugar-coated almonds mit Zucker überzogene Mandeln
sugar snap peas Zuckererbsen
sultana Sultanine
sundae Eisbecher
sun-dried an der Sonne getrocknet
sunflower Sonnenblume
    sunflower oil Sonnenblumenöl
    sunflower seeds Sonnenblumenkerne
supermarket Supermarkt
supper Abendessen, Abendbrot
supplement Zusatz
swede Kohlrübe, Steckrübe
sweet süß
    sweet *[wine]* süßer Wein, Dessertwein
sweet chestnut Edelkastanie, Esskastanie, Marone
sweet potato Süßkartoffel, Batate
sweet trolley Dessertwagen
sweets *[candy]* Süßigkeiten
sweet and sour süßsauer
sweetbreads Bries, Bröschen
sweetcorn Zuckermais, Süßmais
sweetener Süßstoff
Swiss roll Biskuitrolle
swordfish Schwertfisch
syllabub Obstspeise mit Sahne
syrup Sirup
table Tisch; Tafel
    table by the window Tisch am Fenster
    table wine Tafelwein
    tablecloth Tischdecke, Tischtuch
    tablespoon Servierlöffel
tagliatelle Tagliatelle
tangerine Tangerine, Mandarine
take home mit nach Hause nehmen
tap water Leitungswasser
tapioca Tapioka
taragon, tarragon Estragon
tart Törtchen
tartar sauce Tatarensoße
tartare Tartar
taste Geschmack
tasty lecker
tea Tee
    afternoon tea *[Nachmittags]* tee, Teestunde
    beef tea Rindfleischbrühe
    cup of tea Tasse Tee
    green tea grüner Tee
    herbal tea Kräutertee
    high-tea *[frühes]* Abendbrot
    iced tea eisgekühlter Tee
    lemon tea Zitronentee
    teacake Rosinenbrötchen
    teapot Teekanne
    tea spoon Teelöffel
    tea-time Teestunde

English-German

    tea with milk Tee mit Milch
tench Schleie
tender zart
tenderloin Lendenstück
terrine Terrine
thick dick
thirsty durstig
thrush Drossel
thyme Thymian
tin Dose, Büchse
tinned Dosen-, Büchsen-
tip Trinkgeld
toad in the hole Würstchen im Pfannkuchenteig
toast *[tribute]* Trinkspruch
toast Toast
    French toast arme Ritter
toasted getoastet
toffee *[Sahne]* karamel
tofu Tofu
toilet(s) Toiletten
toilet paper Toilettenpapier
tomato Tomate
    cherry tomato Kirschtomaten
    tomato juice Tomatensaft
    tomato ketchup Tomatenketchup
    tomato purée Tomatenpüree
    tomato salad Tomatensalat
    tomato sauce Tomatensoße
tongue Zunge
tonic water Tonikwasser
toothpick Zahnstocher
tope Hundshai
tough *[meat]* zäh
treacle *[Zuckerablauf]* sirup; Melasse
    treacle tart Sirup-Torte
trifle Trifle
trimmings Beilagen
trolley Wagen
trout Forelle
truffle Trüffel
    chocolate truffle Schokoladentrüffel
    truffle butter Trüffelbutter
tuna, tunny Thun, T(h)unfisch
turbot Steinbutt
turkey Truthahn, Pute(r)
    roast turkey im Ofen gebackener Truthahn; Putenbraten
turmeric Kurkuma, Gelbwurzel
turnip Rübe
turnip tops Rübenblätter
turnover Tasche
uncooked ungekocht, roh
underdone nicht durchgebraten, blutig
unsalted butter ungesalzene Butter
upside-down cake Sturzkuchen
use by haltbar bis
vanilla Vanille
    vanilla essence Vanille-Essenz

    vanilla ice cream Vanilleeis
    vanilla pod/bean Vanilleschote
    vanilla sugar Vanillezucker
veal Kalbfleisch
    veal escalope Kalbsschnitzel
vegan Veganer
vegetable Gemüse
    vegetable chilli vegetarisches Chili
    vegetable oil Pflanzenöl
    vegetable soup Gemüsesuppe
    vegetable stock Gemüsebrühe
vegetarian vegetarisch
    vegetarian bolognaise vegetarische Spaghetti Bolognese
    vegetarian burger vegetarischer Hamburger
    vegetarian cooking vegetarische Küche
    vegetarian gravy vegetarische Brühe
    vegetarian lasagne vegetarische Lasagne
    vegetarian sausage Sojasoße
venison Reh *[fleisch]*, Hirsch *[fleisch]*
    venison cutlets Rehkotelett
vermicelli Fadennudeln
very dry *[wine]* sehr trocken
very rare *[of meat]* knapp
very sweet sehr süß
victoria sponge *[cake]* englische Biskuit-Sandtorte
vinaigrette Vinaigrette
vine Rebe, Rebstock
vine leaves Weinblätter
vinegar Essig
vintage Jahrgang, Weinlese
virgin olive oil kaltgepresstes Olivenöl
vol-au-vent Vol-au-vent, Blätterteigpastete
    chicken vol-au-vent Königinpastetchen
wafer Waffel, Eiswaffel
waffles Waffeln
waiter Kellner, Ober
waitress Kellnerin, Fräulein
Waldorf salad Waldorfsalat
walnut Walnuss
warm *[salad etc.]* warm
water Wasser
    bottled water Flaschenwasser
    glass of water Glas Wasser
    iced water eisgekühltes Wasser
    jug of water Krug Wasser
    sparkling/fizzy water Sprudelwasser
    spring/mineral water Quellwasser; Mineralwasser
    still water stilles *[Mineral]* wasser
watercress Wasserkresse
water chestnut Wasserkastanie
water melon Wassermelone
wedding cake Hochzeitstorte
well-done durchgebraten
Welsh rarebit/ rabbit überbackener Käsetoast
whale Walfisch
wheat Weizen
    wheat flour Weizenmehl
    wheatgerm Weizenkeim

whelk Wellhornschnecke
whipped cream Schlagsahne
whisky *[Schottischer]* Whisky
whitebait *[sprats]* Sprotten, Breitling
white *[wine, meat]* weiß
white bread Weißbrot
white truffle Weißer Trüffel
white wine Weißwein
whiting Wittling, Merlan
whole ganz, voll
whole-grain mustard grobkörniger Senf
wholemeal bread Vollkornbrot
wholewheat Vollkorn
  wholewheat flour Vollkornmehl
whortleberry Heidelbeere, Blaubeere
wild wild
  wild boar Wildschwein
  wild rice Wildreis
  wild strawberry Walderdbeere
  wild mushrooms Waldpilze
window table Tisch am Fenster
wine Wein
  bottle of wine Flasche Wein
  glass of wine Glas Wein
  house wine Hauswein
  local wine lokaler Wein, hiesiger Wein
  red wine Rotwein
  sparkling wine Schaumwein
  sweet/pudding wine süßer Wein, Dessertwein
  white wine Weißwein
  wine cooler Weinkühler, Sektkühler
  wine list Weinkarte
  wine vinegar Weinessig
  wine waiter Weinkellner, Sommelier
winkle Strandschnecke
with ice cream mit *[Speise-]* Eis
woodcock Waldschnepfe
Worcestershire sauce Worcestershire Soße
yam Yamswurzel; Batate, Süßkartoffel
yeast Hefe
yoghurt Jogurt
  plain yoghurt Naturjogurt
Yorkshire pudding Yorkshire-Pudding
zabaglione Zabaglione, Weinschaumdessert
zest geriebene Zitrusschale
zucchini *[US]* Zucchini

English-German

Useful Italian Expressions

Types of restaurant

Bar	*serves coffee, pastries, alcohol, wine, snacks*
Caffè	*serves coffee, pastries, sandwiches, snacks*
Hotel	*hotel [often with restaurant]*
Locanda	*typical local restaurant [usually serving local dishes]*
Motel stradale	*highway or motorway motel, often with a restaurant*
Osteria	*local bar serving wine and sometimes food*
Paninoteca	*sandwich bar*
Pizzeria	*pizzeria*
Ristorante	*restaurant*
Snack-bar	*snack bar [serving light snacks and sandwiches, sometimes full meals during lunch time]*
Trattoria	*restaurant [originally very local and cheap, now often fashionable and sometimes expensive]*

Tipping

Restaurants in Italy normally add a service charge of about 10-15% to the bill and, while not expected, leaving an additional 5%-10% tip or small change for good service is well-regarded in most restaurants.

Meals and eating times

07:00 - 10:00	colazione *breakfast*
12:30 - 14:30	pranzo *lunch*
20:00 - 22:00	cena *dinner*

Restaurant rating scheme

Italy: Fork scheme (five forks = de luxe, one fork = fourth-class)

Menu

Menus are normally split into six sections:
Gruppo I: Antipasti, Insalate e Zuppe   *starters, salads and soups*
Gruppo II: Primi Piatti, Pasta, Riso   *first dishes, pasta, Rice*

Gruppo III: Secondi piatti a base di carne	*meat main courses*
Gruppo IV: Secondi piatti a base di pesce	*fish main courses*
Gruppo V: Contorni, Verdure	*side orders as garnish, vegetables*
Gruppo VI: Dolci, Gelati, Frutta, Formaggi	*desserts, ice-cream, fruits and cheeses*

Getting to a restaurant

Can you recommend a good restaurant?	*Potrebbe consigliarmi un buon ristorante?*
I would like to reserve a table for this evening	*Vorrei riservare un tavolo per questa sera*
Do you have a table for three/four people	*Avreste un tavolo per tre/quattro persone?*
We would like the table for 8 o'clock	*Vorremmo il tavolo per le otto*
Could we have a table....?	*È possibile avere un tavolo...?*
by the window	*vicino alla finestra*
outside	*fuori [all'esterno]*
on the terrace	*sulla terrazza*
in the non-smoking area	*nell'area non-fumatori*
What time do you open?	*A che ora aprite?*
Could you order a taxi for me?	*Potreste chiamarmi un taxi?*

Ordering

Waiter/waitress !	*Cameriere/Cameriera !*
What do you recommend?	*Cosa ci consiglia?*
What are the specials of the day?	*Quali sono i piatti del giorno?*
Is this the fixed-price menu?	*Questo è il menu a prezzo fisso?*
Can we see the a-la-carte menu?	*Possiamo vedere il menu alla carta?*
Is this fresh?	*Questo è fresco?*
Is this local?	*Questo è locale?*
I would like a/an …	*Vorrei un...*
Could we have ... please?	*Per favore, potremmo avere ... ?*
an ashtray	*un portacenere*
the bill	*il conto*
our coats	*i nostri soprabiti*
a cup	*una tazza*
a fork	*una forchetta*
a glass	*un bicchiere*
a knife	*un coltello*
the menu	*il menu*
a napkin	*un tovagliolo*
a plate	*un piatto*
a spoon	*un cucchiaio*
a toothpick	*uno stuzzicadenti*
the wine menu	*la lista dei vini*

May I have some ...?	*Potrei avere un pò di ...?*
bread	*pane*
butter	*burro*
ice	*ghiaccio*
lemon	*limone*
milk	*latte*
pepper	*pepe*
salt	*sale*
sugar	*zucchero*
water	*acqua*
I would like it ...	*Lo vorrei ...*
baked	*al forno*
fried	*fritto*
grilled	*alla griglia*
poached	*affogato (for eggs), bollito*
smoked	*affumicato*
steamed	*cotto a vapore*
boiled	*bollito*
fried	*fritto*
roast	*arrosto*
very rare	*molto al sangue*
rare	*al sangue*
medium	*a punto*
well-done	*ben cotto*

Useful phrases for vegetarians

I am ...	*Sono ...*
vegetarian	*vegetariano*
lacto-ovo-vegetarian	*lacto-ovo-vegetariano*
lacto-vegetarian	*lacto-vegetariano*
vegan	*vegetaliano*
I don't eat ...	*Non mangio...*
I don't eat meat/pork/chicken	*Non mangio carne/carne di maiale/pollo*
I don't eat fish	*Non mangio pesce*
I eat eggs/milk/cheese	*Mangio uova/latte/formaggio*
I don't eat eggs/milk/cheese	*Non mangio uova/latte/formaggio*
I don't eat suet/lard/dripping	*Non mangio grasso di rognone/strutto/grasso d'arrosto*
Do you have anything without meat?	*Avete qualcosa senza carne?*
Do you have any vegetarian dishes?	*Avete dei piatti vegetariani?*
Is there a vegetarian restaurant near here?	*C'è un ristorante vegetariano qui vicino?*
Is this cheese made with rennet?	*È un formaggio fatto col caglio?*
Do you have a rennet-free cheese?	*Avete un formaggio fatto senza caglio?*
Do you serve this dish without meat/eggs/cheese?	*Preparate questo piatto anche senza carne/uova/formaggio?*
Does this sauce/soup contain beef/chicken/fish/meat stock?	*In questa salsa/minestra c'è del brodo di manzo/pollo/pesce/carne?*

Does this dish contain gelatine/aspic?	*In questo piatto c'è gelatina animale?*
Does this contain organic ingredients?	*È fatto con ingredienti biologici?*
Do you use GM foods/MSG?	*Usate alimenti geneticamente modificati/glutammato di sodio?*

Useful phrases for people on special diets etc.

I am diabetic	*Sono diabetico*
Does this dish contain nuts?	*Questo piatto contiene frutta a guscio?*
I am allergic to …	*Sono allergico a...*
I have a peanut/seafood/wheat allergy	*Sono allergico alle arachidi/ai frutti di mare/al grano*
I don't eat wheat/gluten	*Non mangio alimenti con grano/glutine*

Drinks

Can I see the wine menu, please?	*Potrei vedere la lista dei vini, per favore?*
I would like a/an	*Vorrei un ...*
aperitif	*aperitivo*
another	*qualcosa d'altro*
I would like a glass of …	*Vorrei un bicchiere di ...*
red wine	*vino rosso*
white wine	*vino bianco*
rose wine	*vino rosato*
sparkling wine	*vino spumante*
still water	*acqua minerale naturale*
sparkling water	*acqua minerale gassata*
tap water	*acqua del rubinetto*
With lemon	*con limone*
With ice	*con ghiaccio*
With water	*con acqua*
Neat	*puro*
I would like a bottle of....	*Vorrei una bottiglia di ...*
this wine	*questo vino*
house red	*vino rosso della casa*
house white	*vino bianco della casa*
Is this wine ...?	*Questo vino è ... ?*
very dry	*molto secco*
dry	*secco*
sweet	*dolce*
local	*locale*
This wine is	*Questo vino è ...*
not very good	*non molto buono*
not very cold	*non abbastanza fresco*
corked (wine)	*sa di tappo*
I would like a …	*Vorrei un/una...*
fruit juice	*succo di frutta*
lemonade	*gazzosa*
non-alcoholic beer	*birra analcolica*

non-alcoholic wine	*vino analcolico*
low-alcohol beer	*birra a bassa gradazione alcolica*
low-alcohol wine	*vino a bassa gradazione alcolica*
non-alcoholic beverage	*bevanda analcolica*
decaffeinated	*decaffeinato*
soft drink	*bibita*

Complaints

This is not what I ordered	*Questo non è quello che avevo ordinato*
I asked for …	*Io avevo ordinato …*
Could I change this?	*Potrei cambiare questo?*
The meat is …	*La carne è …*
overdone	*troppo cotta*
underdone	*non abbastanza cotta*
tough	*dura*
I don't like this	*Questo non mi piace*
The food is cold	*Il mangiare è freddo*
This is not fresh	*Questo non è fresco*
What is taking so long?	*Come mai ci vuole così tanto tempo?*
This is not clean	*Questo non è pulito*

Paying

Could I have the bill?	*Potrei avere il conto?*
I would like to pay	*Vorrei pagare*
Can I charge it to my room?	*È possibile metterlo sul conto della mia camera?*
We would like to pay separately	*Vorremmo pagare separatamente*
There's a mistake in the bill	*C'è un errore nel conto*
What's this amount for?	*Cos'è questo importo?*
Is service included?	*Il servizio è compreso?*
Do you accept traveller's cheques?	*Accettate travellers cheques?*
Can I pay by credit card?	*Posso pagare con carta di credito?*

Numbers

0	*zero*	15	*quindici*
1	*uno*	16	*sedici*
2	*due*	17	*diciasette*
3	*tre*	18	*diciotto*
4	*quattro*	19	*diciannove*
5	*cinque*	20	*venti*
6	*sei*	30	*trenta*
7	*sette*	40	*quaranta*
8	*otto*	50	*cinquanta*
9	*nove*	60	*sessanta*
10	*dieci*	70	*settanta*
11	*undici*	80	*ottanta*
12	*dodici*	90	*novanta*
13	*tredici*	100	*cento*
14	*quattordici*	200 etc.	*duecento ecc.*

Italian-English

abbastanza   enough
abbrustolito   toasted
abramide   bream
accartocciato   twisted, wrapped
acciuga   anchovy
acciughe, burro di   anchovy butter
acciughe, pasta di   anchovy paste
acetini   pickles
aceto   vinegar
   aceto balsamico   balsamic vinegar
   aceto di sidro   cider vinegar
   aceto di vino   wine vinegar
   aceto-dolce   sweetened vinegar
acetosa   sorrel
acido   sour
acini   tiny pasta shapes similar to rice, used in soups
acqua   water
   acqua, bicchiere di   glass of water
   acqua bollente   boiling water
   acqua calda   hot water
   acqua, caraffa dl   jug of water
   acqua cotta   mushroom soup
   acqua del rubinetto   tap water
   acqua di sorgente   spring water
   acqua di sorgente, minerale   spring/mineral water
   acqua fredda   cold water
   acqua dolce, di   freshwater *[fish]*
   acqua ghiacciata   iced water
   acqua in bottiglia   bottled water
   acqua minerale gassata   fizzy mineral water, sparkling water
   acqua minerale naturale, non gassata   still mineral water
   acqua minerale   mineral water
   acqua non gassata   still water
   acqua potabile   drinking water
   acqua tonica   tonic water
acquavite di prugnole   sloe gin
affamato   hungry
affettato   sliced
affogare   poach
affogato   poached
   affogato nel latte   poached in milk
affumicato   smoked
aglio   garlic
   aglio, all'   garlicky
   aglio e olio   garlic and oil sauce or dressing
   aioli   garlic mayonnaise
agnello   lamb
   agnellino   spring lamb
   agnolotti   meat dumplings

agro   sour, tart
agrodolce   sweet and sour
agrume   citrus
alalonga, tonno alalonga   albacore *[tuna]*
albicocca   apricot
albume   egg white
alcol   alcohol
alfredo, all'   tossed in cream and butter
alga   seaweed
alice   fresh anchovy
alimentari   grocery
alimenti   food
   alimenti per l'infanzia   baby food
all'aperto   outside
allergia   allergy
   allergico *[a]*   allergic *[to]*
allevamento a terra, di   free-range
allodola   lark
alloro   bay leaf
alosa   shad
amarena   morello cherry
amaretto   macaroon
amaro   bitter
amatriciana, all'   sauce with tomatoes, onion and salt pork or bacon
amido   starch
analcolico   non-alcoholic drink
ananas   pineapple
anatra *[domestica]*   duck *[domestic]*
anatra *[di Barberia]*   barbary duck
anatra *[selvatica]*   duck *[wild]*
anatra all'arancia   duck with oranges
anatra caramellata   duck coated in caramel
anatroccolo   duckling
andato a male   off *[food, wine]*
anellini   tiny pasta rings used for soup
aneto   dill
angel cake *[torta dolce senza tuorli]*   angel food cake
angelica *[erba curativa]*   angelica
anguilla   eel
   anguilla affumicata   smoked eel
   anguilla al pomodoro   eel in tomato sauce
anguria   water melon
anice   aniseed
animelle   sweetbreads
antipasti   hors d'oeuvre
   antipasti al carrello   hors d'oeuvre trolley
   antipasti assortiti   mixed antipasti of ham, salami, anchovies, olives, fruit, etc.
antipasto   starter, entree
aperitivo   aperitif
apribottiglie   bottle opener
aprire   open *[verb]*
arachide   peanut
aragosta   crawfish, spiny lobster
aragostella   langoustine
arancia   orange
   arancia, succo di   orange juice

arancini di riso al ragù di carne   rice croquettes *[with meat sauce]*
aringa   herring
   aringa affumicata   bloater, *[smoked]* kipper
   aringa sottaceto   pickled herring
arista   loin of pork
aroma   aroma
arrostire   roast *[verb]*
arrosto   roasted
   arrosto di maiale   roast pork
   arrosto di manzo, roastbeef   roast beef
   arrosto in cocotte   pot roast
arsella   clam
Asiago   Asiago *[cow's cheese from Veneto]*
asparago   asparagus
   asparagi, punte di   asparagus tips
aspic   aspic
assenzio   absinthe
assetato   thirsty
assortito   assorted
astice   lobster
avella   hazelnut
avena   oats
   avena, fiocchi di   rolled oats
avocado   avocado
   avocado ai gamberetti   avocado with shrimps
baba al rum   rum baba
baccalà   cod *[salted and dried in the open air]*
   baccalà al forno   oven baked cod
bacchette cinesi   chopsticks
baci di dama   lady's kisses *[almond pastries]*
bacon   bacon
   bacon affumicato   smoked bacon, streaky bacon
   bacon con uova al tegamino   bacon and eggs
bagni   toilet
   bagno degli uomini   gents' toilets
   bagno delle donne   ladies' toilets
balena   whale
banana   banana
   banana flambé   banana flambé
   banana, frittella di   banana fritter
   banana split   banana split
banana verde *[da cuocere]*   plantain
bagna cauda   olive oil dip with chopped anchovies, garlic, butter and seasoning
bar   bar *[pub]*
barattolo, scatola   tin
barbabietola   beetroot
barbecue   barbecue
   barbecue, cotto al   barbecued
barbo   barbel
barchette alla frutta   oval tartlets with fruit
bardana   burdock
basilico   basil
bastoncini al formaggio   cheese straw
bastoncini al cioccolato   chocolate fingers
bavaglino   bib *[child's]*
bavette   thin tagliatelle

bavosa butterfish
beccaccia woodcock
beccaccino snipe
ben cotta well done *[steak]*
bere drink *[verb]*
bergamotto bergamot
berlingozzo cream cake
besciamella béchamel sauce
bevanda drink
   bevanda calda hot drink
   bevande incluse drinks included
bianchetti whitebait *[sprats]*
bianco *[vino, carne]* white *[wine, meat]*
biancomangiare *[budino di latte di mandorle]* blancmange
biberon baby's bottle
bibita a base di vino wine cooler
bibita analcolica soft drink
bibita fresca cold drink
bicchiere glass
   bicchiere da vino wine glass
   bicchiere d'acqua glass of water
   bicchiere di vino glass of wine
   bicchiere pulito clean glass
bietola chard
bigné allungato éclair
biologico organic
birra beer
   birra alla spina draught beer
   birra allo zenzero ginger beer
   birra chiara lager
   birra con gazzosa shandy
   birra rossa real ale
   birra scura bitter *[beer]*
biscotti biscuit
   biscotti alla cannella cinnamon biscuits
   biscotti alle mandorle almond biscuits
   biscotti integrali wholemeal biscuits
   biscotti per neonato rusks
   biscotti savoiardi lady's fingers
   biscotti secchi biscuit, *[US]* cookies
bistecca steak
   bistecca al pepe pepper steak
   bistecca alla tartara steak tartare
   bistecca di manzo rump steak, steak, beefsteak *[US]*
blinis blinis
boga bogue *[fish]*
bollire boil
bollito boiled
bollitore elettrico kettle
Bologna sausage ground spiced pork sausage cooked in wine or tomato sauce
bomba gelato bombe
bombolone alla crema doughnut with custard filling
borragine borage
bottatrice burbot
bottiglia bottle
   bottiglia di vino bottle of wine
bouquet garni *[erbe aromatiche legate a mazzetti]* bouquet garni

brace, carbone di legna charcoal
    brace, alla charcoal grilled
braciola chop *[cutlet]*
    braciola di maiale pork chop
brandy brandy
branzino bass, sea bass
    branzino al cartoccio sea bass oven baked in foil
    branzino alle erbe sea bass with herbs
brasare braise *[verb]*
brasato braised
bresaola dry-salted beef
brindisi toast *[tribute]*
brioche brioche
    brioche alla crema cream-filled brioche
brocca pitcher
broccoli broccoli
brodo broth, stock
    brodo di legumi castor broth
    brodo di manzo beef tea
    brodo di pesce fish broth
    brodo di pollo chicken soup
    brodo di verdure vegetable broth
    brodo scozzese *[zuppa con montone, legumi e orzo]* scotch broth
    brodo vegetale vegetable stock
bruciare burn *[verb]*
    bruciato burnt
bruschetta toasted bread with garlic, tomatoes and olive oil
bucatini all'amatriciana hollow spaghetti amatriciana style *[bacon, onion, tomato sauce]*
buccia peel *[noun]*
buccina whelk
budduzze Sicilian meat balls in tomato sauce
budino *[dolce]* pudding *[sweet]*
    budino *[salato]* pudding *[savoury]*
    budino di Natale *[Inglese]* Christmas pudding
    budino di prugne plum pudding
    budino di pesche peach pudding
    budino di riso, riso e latte rice pudding
    budino diplomatico *[con crema inglese, frutta candita e savoiardi]* cabinet pudding
bufala buffalo
buffet buffet
bulgur bulgar wheat, bulgur wheat
buongustaio gourmet
buono good
burro butter
    burro chiarificato clarified butter
    burro, con with butter
    burro di arachidi peanut butter
    burro di cacao cocoa butter
    burro di tartufi truffle butter
    burro fuso melted butter
    burro nero black butter
    burro nocciola brown butter
    burro non salato unsalted butter
    burro, senza without butter
cacao cocoa
caco kaki, persimmon, date plum

caffè coffee
    caffè all'americana filter coffee
    caffè con panna coffee with whipped cream
    caffè decaffeinato decaffeinated coffee
    caffè filtro filter coffee
    caffè istantaneo, solubile instant coffee
    caffellatte latte *[coffee]*
    caffè macinato ground coffee
    caffè nero black coffee
    caffellatte latte coffee
caffè café
caffeina caffeine
    caffeina, senza caffeine-free
    decaffeinato decaffeinated
caffettiera coffee pot
caglio rennet
calamaro squid
    calamari ripieni stuffed calamari, squid
caldo hot *[not cold]*
calzone pizza folded over and baked or fried
cambiare to change
cameriera waitress
cameriere waiter
camicia *[uova]*, in poached *[eggs]*
camomilla camomile
candela candle
candelabro candlestick
candito candied
canederli in brodo large bread dumplings in stock
canesca tope
cannellini white beans
cannella cinnamon
cannelloni al forno oven-baked cannelloni pasta *[with meat filling]*
    cannelloni ricotta e spinaci oven-baked cannelloni pasta *[with ricotta cheese and spinach filling]*
cannoli pastry cornet filled with cream, custard or chocolate
cannoli siciliani sicilian cornets *[with ricotta cheese and candied fruits]*
cantucci small almond biscuits traditionally eaten dunked in wine
capasanta scallop
capelli d'angelo angel hair pasta
capellini in brodo noodle soup
capone, gallinella gurnard
cappelletti in brodo little tortellini in stock
capperi capers
cappone capon
    cappone farcito con le noci capon stuffed with walnuts
cappuccino cappuccino coffee
capra goat
capriolo venison
caprino fresh goat's cheese *[soft]*
caraffa carafe, pitcher, jug
    caraffa d'acqua jug of water
caramelle sweets, candy
caramella candy *[US]*
caramella mou toffee
caramello caramel
carboidrato carbohydrate

carbonara   sauce with bacon, eggs, cream and Parmesan cheese, served with fresh spaghetti
carciofo   artichoke
   carciofini sottaceto   artichoke hearts in vinegar
   carciofini sottolio   artichoke hearts in olive oil
cardamomo   cardamom
carne   meat
   agnolotti   meat dumplings
   carne affumicata   smoked meat
   carne di cavallo   horse meat
   carne di maiale   pork
   carne fredda   cold meat
   carne e verdure in umido coperte da fette di patate   hotpot
   carne in scatola pressata   luncheon meat
   carne in scatola   corned beef
   carne magra   lean meat
   carne trita, macinata   minced meat
   fondo di cottura di arrosto   gravy
caro   expensive
carota   carrot
carpa   carp
carpaccio di manzo   thin slices of raw beef fillet, marinated
carrè   rack
   carrè *[d'agnello o di maiale]*   rack of ribs
   carrè d'agnello   rack of lamb
carrello   dessert trolley
carta igienica   toilet paper
cartamo   safflower
cartilagine   gristle
cartoccio, al   baked in foil
cassata   cassata
   cassata siciliana   Sicilian cassata *[sponge cake filled with ricotta cheese, chocolate and candied fruit]*
casseruola   casserole
cassiere/cassiera   cashier
castagna   chestnut
   castagna d'acqua   water chestnut
   marrone   sweet chesnut
cattivo *[sapore]*   bad
cavatappi   corkscrew
caviale   caviar
cavolfiore   cauliflower
   cavolfiore gratinato al formaggio   cauliflower cheese
cavolini di Bruxelles   brussels sprouts
cavolo   cabbage
   cavolo cinese   Chinese cabbage
   cavolo rapa   kohlrabi
   cavolo verza, cavolo di Milano   savoy cabbage
cece   chickpea
cedrone   grouse
cefalo   grey mullet, mullet
cena   dinner, supper; dinner party
   cena leggera *[Scozia e nord dell'Inghilterra]*   high-tea
centrifuga   juicer
cereali   cereal *[breakfast]*
cerfoglio   chervil
cernia   grouper

cervella brains
    cervella alla milanese brains Milanese style *[breaded]*
    cervella di vitello calf's brains
cervo, capriolo deer, venison
cetriolo cucumber
cetriolini sottaceto gherkins
champagne champagne
charlotte *[bavarese ricoperta con savoiardi]* charlotte
    charlotte alle mele apple charlotte
cheddar *[tipo di formaggio]* cheddar *[cheese]*
chef, cuoco chef, cook
chiacchiere carnival knots *[sweet]*
chilli con carne chilli con carne
chiodo di garofano clove
chiuso shut/closed
ciabatta bread made with olive oil
cialde waffles
ciambella doughnut
ciambellone ring cake
cibo food
cieche baby eels
ciliegia cherry
    ciliegia nera black cherry
    ciliegia candita glacé cherry
cinghiale boar
cioccolato chocolate
    cioccolato al latte milk chocolate
    cioccolato fondente plain chocolate
    cioccolato, mousse al chocolate mousse
ciotola bowl
cipolla onion
    cipollina spring onion
    cipollina sottaceto pickled onion
    cipollotto scallion *[US]*
civet di lepre jugged hare
clementina clementine
climatizzato air-conditioned
club-sandwich club sandwich
coca coke
cocotte ramekin *[food]*
cocktail cocktail
cocktail di gamberetti, gamberetti in salsa rosa shrimp cocktail
coda alla vaccinara oxtail soup
coda di bue oxtail
coda di rospo monkfish
cognac cognac
colazione breakfast
    colazione continentale continental breakfast
colomba pasquale Easter dove *[leavened cake]*
colombaccio wood pigeon
colostro beestings
coltello knife
    coltello da pane bread knife
commensale/commensali dining companion/s
completo, al full *[restaurant]*
composta di frutta stewed fruit
    composta di mele apple puree

con gelato with ice cream
concentrato di pomodoro tomato purée
conchiglia shell
condimento *[per insalata]* salad dressing
    condimento seasoning, condiment
    condimento tipo maionese per l'insalata salad cream
condito seasoned
confetteria confectionery
confetti sugar-coated almonds
congelato frozen
coniglio rabbit
cono *[di gelato]* cone *[ice cream]*
conserve preserves
consigliare recommend
consommé clear soup, consommè
    consommé di astice lobster bisque
    consommé freddo cold consommé
consumare entro, da use by
conto *[al ristorante]* bill, *[US]* check
conto account
contorno/contorni side dish/es
coperto service charge, cover charge
coppa coppa *[cold cured meat]*
coppa gelata mixed ice cream
coque, alla soft boiled *[egg]*
coriandolo coriander
cornetto croissant
cosce di rana frog's legs
coscia leg, haunch
cosciotto d'agnello leg of lamb
costata o lombata di manzo sirloin
costata strip steak
costata di manzo sirloin steak
costine ribs
    costine di maiale spare ribs
    costole di manzo ribs of beef
costoletta d'agnello lamb chop
cotoletta di cervo venison cutlets
costoletta di maiale pork chop
cotechino cotechino *[boiled salami]*
    cotechino con lenticchie e purè di patate cotechino with lentils and mashed potatoes
cotenna di maiale arrosto pork crackling
cotoletta cutlet
    cotoletta di vitello alla milanese breaded cutlet of veal
cotto done
    cotto a puntino medium cooked
    cotto, molto *[ben cotto]* well-done
    cotto, non abbastanza underdone
    cotto, non uncooked
    cotto, troppo overdone
cotto al forno baked
couscous couscous
cozza mussel
    cozze alla marinara mussels with onion, garlic and white wine
    cozze alla napoletana mussels in tomato sauce
crauti pickled cabbage

crema   cream
   crema, alla   creamed
crema bavarese   bavarian cream
crema di   cream of
crema di asparagi   cream of asparagus soup
crema di cioccolato e pere   cream of chocolate and pear
crema di cocco   coconut cream
crema di gamberi   cream of prawn soup
crema di patate con tartufo   potato cream with truffle
crema di pollo   cream of chicken soup
crema di pomodoro   cream of tomato soup
crema inglese   custard, custard sauce
crema pasticciera   confectioner's cream
crème caramel   crème caramel *[baked custard]*
crème fraîche   crème fraîche
cremoso   creamy
cren, barbaforte, rafano   horseradish
crêpe   pancake
crescione d'acqua   watercress
crescione   cress
   crescione, risotto al   risotto with cress
crespella   pancake
crespella *[spessa e salata]*   crumpet
crespelle al salmone   crepes filled with salmon
croccante   praline
crocchette di patate   croquette potatoes
croissant   croissant
   croissant al cioccolato   chocolate croissant
crosta   rind *[cheese]*
crostata, crostatina   pie, tart
crostata di mele   apple tart
crostata di selvaggina   game pie
crostini   croutons; toasted bread with a savoury topping
crostino di formaggio fuso   Welsh rarebit/rabbit
crudo   raw
crusca   bran
cucchiaiata   spoonful
cucchiaio   spoon
   cucchiaino da caffè   coffee spoon
   cucchiaino da tè   tea spoon
   cucchiaio da dessert   dessert spoon
   cucchiaio da minestra   soup spoon
   cucchiaio da tavola   tablespoon
cucina   kitchen
   cucina economica   stove
   cucina vegetariana   vegetarian cooking
cucurbita   marrow *[vegetable]*, squash
cumino   cumin *[seed]*
cuocere a fuoco lento   simmer
cuocere a vapore   steam *[verb]*
cuoco, chef   cook, chef
cuore   heart
cuori di mare   cockles
curcuma   turmeric
curry *[miscela di spezie]*   curry
   curry in polvere   curry powder
cuscinetti   toasted or fried cheese sandwich

custard apple   custard apple
dattero   date
decaffeinato   decaffeinated
delicato   mild
delizioso   delicious
demi-sec   semi-dry
dente, al   pasta or vegetables cooked firm to the bite
dentro   inside
diavola, alla   spicy dish, devilled
diplomatico   rum and coffee flavoured chocolate cake
disossare   debone
disossato   boned
   disossato, non   on the bone *[meat]*
dolce   sweet
dolce al cioccolato   fudge cake
dolce al Madera   madeira cake
dolce arrotolato   Swiss roll
dolce con gelato e meringa al forno   baked Alaska
dolce da tè *[grigliato, tagliato, imburrato, da servire con il tè]*   teacake
dolce di Natale *[inglese]*   Christmas cake
dolce tipo pandispagna   Victoria sponge *[cake]*
dolce, torta   cake, gateau
dolce quattro quarti   pound cake
dolcetto all'uva passa *[tostato e imburrato, da servire con il tè]*   teacake
dolcetto ripieno di frutta secca e noci   mince pie
dolci   desserts
dolci, carrello dei   sweet trolley
dolcelatte   mild, soft blue cheese
dolci   *see dolce*
dolcificante   sweetener
dolcissimo   very sweet
dorare, far   sear
dragoncello   tarragon
drogheria   general store, grocer's
duro   tough *[meat]*
eccellente   excellent
economico   cheap
eglefino   haddock
eglefino affumicato   smoked haddock
erbe, spezie   herbs
   erbe aromatiche   mixed herbs
   erba cipollina   chives
espresso, caffè espresso   espresso, expresso coffee
essenza   essence
   essenza di vaniglia   vanilla essence
essiccato   sun-dried
etichetta   label
fagiano   pheasant
fagiolo   bean, haricot bean
   fagioli borlotti   borlotti beans
   fagioli con salsina di pomodoro   baked beans
   fagioli larghi   runner beans
   fagioli neri   black beans
   fagioli rossi   kidney beans, red beans
   fagiolini   French beans, green beans, string beans, fine beans
   fagiolini molto fini   fine beans
   fagiolo nano   flageolet *[beans]*

fagiolo pinto   pinto bean
fagottino alle mele   apple turnover
falafel   falafel
faraona   guinea fowl
farcito   stuffed
farina   flour
   farina d'avena   oatmeal
   farina di mais   cornflour
   farina integrale   wholewheat flour
fatto in casa   home-made
fattoria, [uova, polli] di   farm [eggs, chickens]
fava   broad bean
favo   honeycomb
fegato   liver
   fegatini di pollo   chicken liver
   fegato alla veneziana   liver Venetian style [with onions]
   fegato di vitello   calf's liver
   fegato, patè di   liver pâté
felino   salami
ferri, ai   grilled on an open fire
festa   party
fetta   slice
   fetta biscottata   crispbread, French toast
   fette, a   sliced
fettina alla pizzaiola   steak pizzaiola style
fettuccine   flat, ribbon pasta
fiammiferi   matches
fico   fig
filetto [di carne, pesce]   fillet
   filetto [di manzo]   fillet steak
   filetto alla Wellington   beef Wellington
   filetto stroganoff   beef stroganoff
finocchio   fennel
fiocchi d'avena   rolled oats
fiocco   flakes
fiume   river
flambè   flambé
flan, budino   baked custard, flan
focaccia   flat herb bread often stuffed with cheese, vegetables or meat
foglie di vite   vine leaves
foglie tenere di cavolo, broccolo, ecc.   spring greens
fondente   fondant
fonduta   fondue
forchetta   fork
formaggio   cheese
   formaggi, assortimento di   cheese board
   formaggio a pasta dura   hard cheese
   formaggio affumicato   smoked cheese
   formaggio Asiago   cow's cheese from Veneto
   formaggio bianco [magro]   quark
   formaggio caprino   goat's cheese
   formaggio cremoso   cream cheese
   formaggio di latte di capra   ewe's milk cheese
   formaggio duro   hard cheese
   formaggio erborinato   blue cheese
   formaggio feta   feta cheese
   formaggio, fiocchi di   cottage cheese
   formaggio a pasta morbida   soft cheese

174

formaggio pecorino   ewe's cheese *[hard]*
formaggio Stilton   stilton
formaggio, soufflè al   cheese soufflé
gorgonzola   gorgonzola cheese *[blue]*
mascarpone   creamy and mild cheese
ricotta   ricotta cheese
forno   oven
   cotto al forno   baked
   forno *[con la buccia]***, patata al**   baked potato
   forno, cuocere al   bake
   forno, mela al   baked apple
forte   strong
fragola   strawberry
   fragola di bosco   wild strawberry
   marmellata di fragole   strawberry jam
frascati   white wine
frattaglie   offal
   frattaglie di maiale   chitterling *[US]*
freddo   cold
fresco   fresh
friggere   fry
frittata   omelette
   frittata con prosciutto e formaggio   omelette with ham and cheese
   frittata con spinaci   omelette with spinach
frittella   fritter
   frittella di banana   banana fritter
   frittella di mele   apple fritter
   frittella salata   fritter, pancake
fritto   fried, fried food
   fritto *[in padella]*   pan-fried
   fritto *[nella friggitrice, in molto olio]*   deep-fried
   fritto misto *[di pesce]*   mixed fried fish
   fritto, uovo   fried egg
frizzante   sparkling, fizzy
frollino   shortbread
frullato   milkshake
frumento   wheat
frutta   fruit
   frutta a guscio   nuts
   frutta candita   crystallised fruit
   frutta, succo di   fruit juice
frutta *[budino]***, gelatina di**   jelly *[sweet/pudding]*
frutti di bosco   berries
frutti di mare   seafood, shellfish
fruttivendolo/a   greengrocer
fumare   smoke *[food]*
fumare *[una sigaretta]*   smoke *[a cigarette]*
   fumatore   smoker
   fumare, vietato   no smoking
   fumatori, zona non   non-smoking area
fumo   smoke *[noun]*
funghi   mushrooms
   funghi cantarelli   chanterelle
   funghi champignons   button mushroom
   funghi porcini   porcini mushroom
   funghi selvatici   wild mushrooms
fuori   outdoors
fusi   drumsticks

fusi di pollo   chicken drumsticks
fusilli   pasta shaped like a corkscrew
fuso, sciolto   smelt
galantina   galantine
gallette di farina d'avena   oatcake
galletto   poussin, young rooster, cockerel
gallina faraona   guinea fowl
gallina   chicken, hen
gamberetti   shrimps
gamberi   prawns
   gamberi di fiume   crayfish
   gamberoni   king prawns
garretto   shank
gassato   carbonated, gassy
gattuccio   dog fish
gazpacho   gazpacho
gelatina   gelatine
   gelatina di frutta *[budino]*   jelly *[sweet/pudding]*
   gelatina di ribes rossi   redcurrant jelly
   gelatina di menta   mint jelly
   gelatina tipo marmellata   jello *[US]*
gelato   ice cream
   gelato alla vaniglia   vanilla ice cream
   gelato, com   with ice cream
   gelato, cono   ice cream cone
   gelato con praline e sciroppo   sundae
   gelata, coppa   mixed ice cream
gelone *[fungo]*   oyster mushroom
geneticamente modificato   genetically modified *[GM]*
germe di grano   wheatgerm
germogli di Alfalfa   alfalfa sprouts
germogli di bambù   bamboo shoots
germogli di soia   bean sprouts
ghiaccio, con   with ice
   con ghiaccio *[on the rocks]*   on the rocks *[with ice]*
   ghiaccio, cubetto di   ice cube
   ghiacciolo   ice lolly
gin   gin
   gin tonic   gin and tonic
girasole   sunflower
girello di manzo   silverside
glassato   glazed
glassatura   icing
glutammato di sodio   monosodium glutamate *[MSG]*
gnocchi   dumpling
   gnocchi al gorgonzola   potato dumplings with gorgonzola sauce
   gnocchi alla romana   Roman dumplings *[baked semolina dumplings]*
   gnocchi di patate   potato dumpling
gobione   gudgeon
gombo, ibisco   okra
gorgonzola   creamy, blue veined cheese
goulash   goulash
granaglia   groats
granatina   grenadine
granchio   crab
   granchio farcito   dressed crab
   granchio preparato, pulito   prepared crab
grande   big

granita   granita, water-ice
   granita alla siciliana   Sicilian water-ice
grano   wheat
   grano saraceno   buckwheat
granturco   corn, maize
   granturco, pannocchietta di   baby corn *[cob]*
grasso *[aggettivo]*   fat *[adj]*
   grasso *[formaggio]*   full-fat *[cheese]*
   grasso *[nome]*   fat *[noun]*
   grasso d'arrosto   dripping
   grasso di rognone   suet
   grassi, senza   fat-free
gratinato   au gratin *[US]*
gratis   free *[of charge]*
   omaggio   complimentary
grattugiato   grated
griglia   grill *[noun]*
griglia, cucinare alla   grill *[verb]*
grigliata mista   mixed grill
grigliato   grilled
   grigliato alla brace   charcoal-grilled
grissino   breadstick
grongo   conger eel
guacamole   guacamole
guaiava   guava
guarnito   garnished
guarnizioni   trimmings
gumbo   gumbo
guscio   shell
gusto, al   flavoured
   gustoso   tasty
halibut   halibut
   halibut della Groenlandia   black halibut, Greenland halibut
hamburger   hamburger
   hamburger vegetariano   vegetarian burger
hot dog   hot dog
hummus   hummus
ide   ide *[fish]*
idromele   mead
igname   yam
impanato   breaded
impastellato   in batter
impasto   dough
incluso   included
   incluso, non   not included
indivia   endive
   indivia belga   chicory
infuso, tisana   herbal tea
ingredienti   ingredients
insalata   salad
   insalata Caesar   Caesar salad
   insalata caprese   mozzarella, tomato and basil salad
   insalata di contorno   side salad
   insalata di patate   potato salad
   insalata di pollo   chicken salad
   insalata di polpo   octopus salad
   insalata di pomodoro   tomato salad
   insalata mista   mixed salad

insalata riccia   frisée *[salad]*
insalata russa   Russian salad
insalata verde   green salad
insalata Waldorf *[mele, sedano, noci, maionese]*   Waldorf salad
insalatiera   salad bowl
integrale   wholewheat
integratore   supplement
intero   whole
intolleranza al lattosio   lactose intolerance
intossicazione alimentare   food poisoning
involtini di pesce   fish rolls
involtini di vitello   veal rolls
involtini di melanzana   aubergine roll
involtino primavera   spring roll
inzuppare   dip *[verb]*
iposodico   low-salt
Irish whisky   Irish whiskey
irrorare col fondo di cottura   baste
julienne, *[verdure]* **alla**   julienne
kasher   kosher
ketchup   ketchup, tomato ketchup
kiwi   kiwi fruit
krapfen   doughnut
krapfen alla marmellata   jam doughnut
kumquat, mandarino cinese   kumquat
lacerto   mackerel
lampone   raspberry
lamponi con panna   raspberries with cream
lasagne   lasagne *[flat, wide sheets of pasta]*
lasagne al forno   lasagne
lasagne alla bolognese   pasta sheets layered with meat sauce, bechamel sauce and cheese
lasagne vegetariane   vegetarian lasagne
lasagne verdi   green lasagne
latte   milk
latte, affogato nel   poached in milk
latte, con   with milk
latte condensato   condensed milk
latte di capra   goat's milk
latte di cocco   coconut milk
latte di mucca   cow's milk
latte di pecora   ewe's milk
latte di soia   soya milk
latte in polvere *[per il caffè]*   coffee whitener
latte intero   full-cream milk
latte parzialmente scremato   semi-skimmed milk
latte scremato   skimmed milk
latte, senza   without milk
latticello *[siero di latte acido]*   buttermilk
latticini   dairy products
lattosio   lactose
lattuga   lettuce
lattuga iceberg   iceberg lettuce
lattuga romana   cos lettuce
lattuga romana   romain *[lettuce]*
lattughella, dolcetta   lamb's lettuce
lavanda   lavender
lavarelli al vino bianco   white fish in butter, wine and parsley sauce

legumi pulses
lemon grass lemon grass
lenticchia lentil
  lenticchie di Puy puy lentils
lepre hare
lepudrida rich stew with meat and vegetables
lesso boiled
lievito yeast
limanda dab
lime, limetta lime
limonata lemonade
limone citron, lemon
  limone, succo di lemon juice
lingua tongue
  lingua di bue ox tongue
  lingua di manzo salmistrata cured beef tongue
linguine flat spaghetti
  linguine al pesto flat spaghetti with pesto sauce
liquirizia liquorice
liquore liqueur
lische bones *[of fish]*
lista dei vini wine list
listino prezzi price list
litchi, lici, ciliegia cinese lychee
litro litre
locale local
loganberry loganberry
lombata loin, tenderloin
  lombata carrè *[di vitello, maiale, capriolo]* loin *[of veal, pork, venison]*
luccio pike
lucioperca pike-perch
lumaca, lumache snail(s)
lumachina di mare winkle
maccheroni macaroni
macedonia di frutta fruit salad
macelleria butcher's shop
macinare grind
macinasale salt mill
macinato, tritato ground
macinino per il pepe pepper mill
macis mace
macrobiotico macrobiotic
maggiorana marjoram
magro, dietetico low-fat *[diet]*
maiale pig
  maiale, piedini di pig's trotters
  maialino da latte suckling pig
maionese mayonnaise
mais sweetcorn
malto malt
mancia gratuity, tip
mandarino mandarin, tangerine
mandorla almond
  mandorle, alle with almonds
mandorle, pasta di almond paste
mango mango
mangosta mangosteen

mangiare eat
manzo beef
    manzo, arrosto di roast beef
    manzo, bistecca di beefsteak
    manzo, brodo di beef tea
    manzo alla Wellington, filetto di beef Wellington
maranta, fecola arrowroot
maraschino cherry brandy
margarina margarine
marinara, alla tomato sauce with garlic, herbs and olive oil
marinato marinated
    marinata marinade
marmellata jam, jelly
    marmellata di arance marmalade
    marmellata salata jelly *[savoury]*
marrone sweet chesnut
marsala fortified wine
mascarpone soft, sweet creamy cheese, used often in desserts
marzapane marzipan
mattonella di gelato Neapolitan ice-cream
maturo ripe
medaglione medallion
mela apple
    mela, succo di apple juice
    mele, composta di apple puree
    mele, crostata di apple tart
    mele, fagottino alle apple turnover
    mele, frittella alle apple fritter
    mele, salsa di apple sauce
    mele, strudel di apple strudel
    mele, torta di apple pie
    mela al forno baked apple
mela cotogna quince
melagrana pomegranate
melanzana aubergine, eggplant
    melanzane alla parmigiana aubergine bake
    melanzane, involtino di aubergine roll
melassa treacle
melissa lemon balm
melone melon
    melone Cantaloupe cantaloup *[melon]*
    melone Cavaillon honeydew melon
    melone, prosciutto e cured ham and melon
melù blue whiting
menta mint
    menta, gelatina di mint jelly
    menta piperita peppermint
    menta verde garden mint
menu menu
    menu a prezzo fisso fixed price menu, set menu
    menu di Natale Christmas menu
mercato market
meringa meringue
merlano whiting
merluzzo cod
merluzzo giallo pollack, lythe
merluzzo nero coley *[coalfish]*, saithe
mestolo ladle

mezza bottiglia   half bottle
mezzo   half
   mezzo crudo   half done, half cooked
   mezzo litro   half a litre
midollo   bone marrow
miele   honey
millefoglie   cream slice
mincemeat *[preparato zuccherato a base di frutta e noccioline secche]*
   mincemeat
minestra del giorno   soup of the day
minestrone   minestrone *[soup]*
mirtillo   bilberry, blueberry, whortleberry
mirtillo rosso   cranberry
mischiare, incorporare   blend
mollusco   mollusc
molva   ling
montone   mutton
morbido   soft
more di gelso   mulberry
more di rovo   blackberry
mortadella   bologna *[sausage]*
moussaka   moussaka
mousse   mousse
mousse di frutta, crema e panna montata   fool
mozzarella   mozzarella cheese
   mozzarella di bufala   buffalo mozzarella
muesli   muesli
muffin *[piccolo dolce con uvette]*   muffin *[US]*
muggine   mullet
napoletana, alla   style of cooking, using tomatoes and garlic
naturale   natural
navone   swede
negozio   shop
nocciola   hazelnut, cobnut
nocciola di Dalmazia   filbert
nocciole   noisettes
noce   nut
   noce   walnut
   noce d'America   hickory nut
   noce del Brasile   brazil nut
   noce di acagiù   cashew nut
   noce di cocco   coconut
   noce di cocco essiccata   desiccated coconut
   noce macadamia   macadamia nut
   noce moscata   nutmeg
   noce pecan   pecan nut
non troppo cotta   medium rare *[steak]*
oca   goose
odore   smell
olio   oil
   olio d'oliva   olive oil
   olio di mais   corn oil
   olio di semi   vegetable oil
   olio di semi d'arachide   groundnut oil
   olio di semi di girasole   sunflower oil
   olio di semi di vinaccioli   grapeseed oil
   olio extra vergine di olive   extra virgin olive oil

oliva olive
    olive farcite stuffed olives
    olive nere black olives
    olive verdi green olives
omaggio complimentary
omelette omelette
on the rocks on the rocks
ora di pranzo lunchtime
ora di pranzo/cena dinner time
orecchia marina, abalone abalone
origano oregano
ortica nettle
orzata barley water
orzo barley
    orzo mondato pearl barley
    orzo, sciroppo di barley water
    orzo, zucchero di barley sugar
osso bone
    carne con l'osso on the bone *[meat]*
    osso con midollo marrow bone
ossobuco knuckle
ossobuco di vitello veal ossobuco *[braised veal shank slice]*
ostie di riso rice paper
ostrica oyster
paesana, alla country style cooking
pagare pay *[verb]*
paglia e fieno yellow and green tagliatelle *[fresh egg pasta]*
pagnotta loaf
    pagnotta bianca white loaf
palamita bonito
pallina di gelato ice cream scoop
palombo alla todina roasted pigeon
pancetta salt-cured bacon
pandispagna sponge cake
    pandispagna, fette di sponge biscuits
pan di spezie gingerbread
pancetta bacon
    pancetta affumicata smoked bacon
pandoro Christmas yeast cake
pane bread
    pane al bicarbonato di soda soda bread
    pane all'uva fruit bread/loaf
    pane bianco white bread
    pane, coltello per il bread knife
    pane di mais corn bread
    pane di segale rye bread
    pane dolce sweet bread
    pane, fetta di slice of bread
    pane grattugiato breadcrumbs
    pane integrale wholemeal bread, brown bread
    pane pitta pitta bread
    pane speziato gingerbread
panetteria bakery
panettone Christmas yeast cake with raisin and candied fruit
panforte hard cake with dried and candied fruit
panino bun, roll *[bread]*
    panino integrale brown roll
panna cream

panna acida   sour cream
panna cotta   cooked cream *[cream pudding]*
panna da cucina   single cream
panna montata   chantilly, whipped cream
panna per dolci   double cream
pannocchia di mais   corn on the cob
papaia   papaya, pawpaw
papalina   sprat
pappardelle   wide flat pasta
parfait   parfait
parfait al caffè   coffee parfait
parmigiana, alla   served with cheese sauce
parmigiano   parmesan cheese
passato di verdura   vegetable soup
passera, pianuzza   flounder
pasta   pasta
pasta al gratin   macaroni cheese
pasta choux   choux pastry
pasta all'uovo   egg pasta
pasta *[dolce]*   pastry
pasta e fagioli   pasta & bean soup
pasta fermentata   sour dough
pasta fillo   filo pastry
pasta fresca   fresh pasta
pasta frolla   shortcrust *[pastry]*
pasta sfoglia   puff pastry
pasta di altea   marshmallow
pastella per frittura   batter
pasticceria   cake shop
pasticcini, biscottini   petits fours, pastries
pasticcio di manzo e rognone in crosta   steak and kidney pie
pasticcio di pesce   fisherman's pie
pastinaca   parsnip
patata   potato
patata al forno con la buccia   baked potato
patata americana   sweet potato
patate al rosmarino   sauteed potatoes with rosemary
patate alla duchessa   duchesse potatoes
patate bollite   boiled potatoes
patate, crocchette di   croquette potatoes
patate, gnocchi di   potato dumpling
patate, insalata di   potato salad
patate fritte   chips
patate gratinate con panna   scalloped potatoes *[US]*
patate lesse   boiled potatoes
patate novelle   new potatoes
patatine fritte   crisps, potato crisps
patatine fritte *[tagliate a bastoncino]*   matchstick potatoes, French fries *[US]*
paté   paté
paté d'anatra   duck paté
paté di fegato d'oca   goose liver pâté
paté di fegato   liver pâté
paté di fegato al tartufo   liver pâté with truffle
pelare, sbucciare   peel *[verb]*
pelle   skin
penne   penne *[pasta tubes]*
penne al gorgonzola   penne pasta with gorgonzola sauce
penne all'arrabbiata   penne with a spicy tomato sauce

pepe [spezia] pepper [spice]
    macinino per il pepe pepper mill
    pepe di Caienna cayenne pepper
    pepe in grani whole pepper
    pepe macinato ground pepper
    pepe nero black pepper
    pepe bianco white pepper
    pepe verde green pepper
    peperonata pepper stew
    peperoncino chilli pepper
    peperoncino in polvere chilli powder
    peperoncino rosso red chilli
    peperone pepper [vegetable], capsicum
    peperone ripieno stuffed pepper
    peperone rosso red pepper
    peperone verde green pepper
    pepiera pepper pot
pera pear
perlano smelt
pernice partridge
pesca peach
    pesca noce nectarine
pescatora, alla with seafood sauce
pesce fish
    acciuga anchovy
    anguilla eel
    aringa herring
    aringa affumicata kipper
    bianchetti whitebait
    branzino bass, sea bass
    bonita skipjack
    bottatrice burbot
    cefalo grey mullet
    coda di rospo monkfish
    dentice bream, sea bream
    dorata dory, John Dory
    eglefino haddock
    frittella di pesce fish cake
    gamberi di fiume crayfish
    gattuccio dog fish
    grongo conger eel
    halibut halibut
    luccio pike
    lucioperca pike-perch
    merlano whiting
    merluzzo cod
    merluzzo nero coley [coalfish]
    nasello hake
    passera, pianuzza flounder
    perlano smelt
    pesce affumicato smoked fish
    pesce angelo angel fish
    pesce fritto e patatine fish and chips
    pesce fritto fried fish
    pesce gatto catfish
    pesce in umido fish stew
    pesce persico perch
    pesce piatto flat fish

pesce, pasticcio di fisherman's pie
pesce, polpetta di fish cake
pesce spada swordfish
pesce, uova di roe
pesce volante flying fish
pesce, zuppa di fish soup
pescheria fishmonger
razza skate
rombo chiodato turbot
rombo liscio brill
San Pietro dory, John Dory
sarago white bream
sardina, sardella sardine, pilchard
scorfano rockfish
scorfano del nord redfish
seppia cuttlefish
sgombro mackerel
sogliola Dover sole, sole
sogliola limanda lemon sole
squalo, pescecane shark
storione sturgeon
tinca tench
tonno tunny, tuna
triglia red mullet
trota trout
trota di mare sea trout
pesto basil pesto, pesto
pesto, linguine al flat spaghetti with pesto sauce
petto breast
petto *[di manzo]* brisket *[of beef]*
petto di agnello, di vitello breast of lamb, veal
petto di pollo breast of chicken, chicken breast
petto di tacchino turkey breast
petto di vitello arrotolato rolled veal breast
pezzo piece
piattino saucer
piatto dish, plate
piatto del giorno dish of the day
piatto di carni fredde, affettati cold cuts *[US]*
piccante hot *[strong]*
piccata al limone veal escalopes with lemon sauce
piccioncino squab
piccione pigeon
picnic picnic
piedini di maiale feet, trotters
pieno full *[stomach]*
pimento della Giamaica *[detto anche "4 spezie"]* allspice
pinoli pine nuts
piselli garden peas, green peas, peas
piselli secchi split peas
pistacchio pistachio nut
pitta flatbread
pizza pizza
pizza ai frutti di mare with seafood
pizza alla siciliana with tomato sauce, mozzarella, olives, capers, anchovies
pizza capricciosa with tomato sauce, mozzarella, artichokes, olives, anchovies

pizza Margherita   with tomato sauce and mozzarella
pizza prosciutto e funghi   with tomato sauce, mozzarella, ham, mushrooms
platessa, passera di mare   plaice
poco cotta   rare *[steak]*
polenta   thick cornmeal porridge, usually served cooled, sliced and grilled or
   with sauce
pollame   poultry, fowl
pollo   chicken
   pollo alla diavola   chicken devilled style
   pollo alla Kiev   chicken kiev
   pollo arrosto   roast chicken
   pollo, fegatini di   chicken liver
   pollo fritto   fried chicken
   pollo, insalata di   chicken salad
polpetta di pesce   fish cake
polpette di patate rifritte   hash browns *[US]*
polpette fritte di cavolo e patate   bubble and squeak
polpettina di carne   faggot, meat ball
   polpettine al sugo   meat balls in tomato sauce
   polpettine di pollo   meat balls *[chicken]*
polpettone di carne   meat loaf
polpo   octopus
   polpo, insalata di   octopus salad
pomodoro   tomato
   pomodori secchi   sun-dried *[tomatoes]*
   pomodorini ciliegia   cherry tomato
   pomodoro di San Marzano   plum tomato
   pomodoro, insalata di   tomato salad
   pomodoro, salsa di   tomato sauce
   pomodoro, succo di   tomato juice
pompelmo   grapefruit
popcorn   popcorn
porchetta   porchetta *[roast whole pig]*
porridge   porridge
porro   leek
   porri piccoli   baby leeks
portacenere   ashtray
portare a casa   take home
portauovo   egg cup
porto *[vino]*   port
portulaca   purslane
posate   cutlery
posto *[a sedere]*   seat
postumi della sbornia   hangover
potabile   drinkable
pranzo   lunch, meal
   pranzo di Natale, il   Christmas dinner
precotto   par-boiled
prenotare   reserve
   prenotazione   reservation
prezzemolo   parsley
   prezzemolo piatto   flat parsley
   prezzemolo riccio   curly parsley
prezzo   price
   prezzo fisso, a   fixed price
primo piatto   first course, entree *[US]*
profiteroles   profiteroles
prosciutto   ham

prosciutto bollito boiled ham
prosciutto cotto boiled ham
prosciutto cotto affumicato gammon
prosciutto di Parma Parma ham
prosciutto San Daniele San Daniele ham
prosciutto e melone cured ham and melon
prosciutto, fetta di slice of ham
prugna plum
prugna claudia greengage *[plum]*
prugna di Damasco damson
prugna secca prune
prugnola sloe
pulito clean
purè purée
purè, ridotto a mashed
purè di piselli secchi pease-pudding
purè di piselli mushy peas
purè di patate mashed potatoes, creamed potatoes *[US]*
puro pure
puttanesca, alla sauce with tomatoes, black olives and chilli
quaglia quail
qualità quality
quarto quarter
quattro formaggi four cheese sauce
quiche, torta salata quiche
quiche lorraine quiche lorraine
rabarbaro rhubarb
radicchio radicchio
rafano tedesco horseradish
ragù ragout, *[a meat or vegetable sauce]*
ragù alla bolognese bolognaise sauce
rana pescatrice angler
rancido rancid
rapa turnip
rapa, punte di turnip tops
rapa svedese swede
ravanello radish/radishes
ravioli ravioli
ravioli di ricotta e spinaci ravioli with ricotta cheese and spinach
ravioli di zucca pumpkin ravioli
razza skate
refrigerato chilled
renna reindeer
ribes nero blackcurrant
ribes rosso redcurrant
ricetta recipe
ricciarelli almond biscuits
ricco di fibre high-fibre
ricevuta receipt
ricotta soft cheese
rigaglie giblets
ripieno stuffing
riscaldare heat up
riservare *[un tavolo]* to book *[a table]*
riso rice
ostie di riso rice paper
riso a chicchi lunghi long-grained rice
riso al latte fatto al forno, budino di riso baked rice, rice pudding

riso basmati   basmati rice
riso bollito   boiled rice
riso, budino di   rice pudding
riso integrale   brown rice
riso per budino   pudding rice
riso selvaggio   wild rice
risotto   risotto rice
risotto ai funghi porcini   risotto with porcini mushrooms
risotto al crescione   risotto with cress
risotto alla milanese   Milanese risotto *[with saffron]*
rissole *[polpettina di carne speziata]*   rissole
ristorante   restaurant
rognone   kidney
rognone, grasso di   suet
rognoni alla diavola   devilled kidneys
rollata   roulade
rombo chiodato   turbot
rombo liscio   brill
rosa canina   rosehip
rosbif   roast beef
rosolare, far   sear
rosmarino   rosemary
rostbeef arrotolato   collared beef
rotolini di aringa *[marinata]*   rollmop herring
rotolino di salsiccia in crosta *[stuzzichino salato]*   sausage roll
rucola   rocket
rum   rum
rye, whisky di segale   rye whisky
saccarina   saccharin
sagù   sago
saira *[del Pacifico]*   saury
sala da pranzo   dining room
salame   salami
salame Milano   salami Milano style
salame tipo cervellata   saveloy
salamino cacciatore   small salami
salame di cioccolato   chocolate log
salamoia   brine
salato   salted, salty
salato; marinato; affumicato   cured
sale   salt
sale grosso   rock salt
sale marino   sea salt
saliera   salt cellar
salmerino   char
salmone   salmon
salmone affumicato   smoked salmon
salmone, medaglione di   salmon steak
salmone, trancio di   salmon steak
salsa   sauce
salsa aïoli   garlic mayonnaise
salsa al cioccolato   chocolate sauce
salsa al formaggio   cheese sauce
salsa al Madera   madeira sauce
salsa al prezzemolo   parsley sauce
salsa all'aneto   dill sauce
salsa all'arancia   orange sauce
salsa alla crema, salsa alla panna   cream sauce

salsa alla diavola devilled sauce
salsa alla menta mint sauce
salsa alla panna cream sauce
salsa bernese béarnaise sauce
salsa besciamella béchamel sauce, white sauce
salsa bordolese bordelaise sauce
salsa bruna o demi-glace brown sauce
salsa di burro butter sauce
salsa di mele apple sauce
salsa di mirtillo rosso cranberry sauce
salsa di pomodoro tomato sauce
salsa di soia soy sauce, soya sauce
salsa olandese hollandaise sauce
salsa tartara tartar sauce
salsa verde Italian green sauce *[olive oil, garlic, parsley, anchovies, capers, gherkins]*
salsa vinaigrette vinaigrette
salsa Worcestershire Worcestershire sauce
salsefrica, barba di becco salsify
salsiccia sausage
salsiccia di fegato liver sausage
salsiccia di soia vegetarian sausage
salsiccia in pastella cotta al forno toad in the hole
salsiera gravy boat
salsina dip *[noun]*
saltare in padella *[alla cinese]* stir-fry
saltato *[in padella]* sautéed
saltimbocca alla romana escalopes with ham and sage
salutare healthy
salute health
Salute! Cheers!
salvastrella burnet
salvia sage
sambuco, bacca di sambuco elderberry
San Pietro dory, John Dory
sangue blood
sangue, al rare *[steak, meat]*
sangue, quasi al medium-rare
sanguinaccio black pudding
sapore di flavoured
sarago white bream
sarde a scapece deep-fried sardines
sardella pilchard
sardina sardine
sassifraga saxifrage
sbollentato blanched
sbriciolare crumble
sbucciare, pelare peel *[verb]*
sbucciato peeled
scadenza sell-by date
scalogno shallot
scaloppina escalope
scaloppine al marsala escalope with Marsala wine
scaloppine di pollo scalloped chicken *[US]*
scaloppine di tacchino turkey escalope
scaloppine di vitello veal escalope
scampi Dublin bay prawn, langoustine
scampo langoustine

scatola, in *[conserva]*   tinned, canned *[US]*
scegliere   to choose
scelta   selection
scheggiato *[bicchiere, piatto]*   chipped *[glass, plate]*
sciroppo   syrup
   sciroppo d'orzo   barley water
   sciroppo di acero   maple syrup
scone *[dolcetto che si mangia con marmellata e panna]*   scone *[UK]*
scongelare   defrost
sconto   discount
scorfano   rockfish
scorfano del nord   redfish
scorza   zest
   scorza candita   candied peel
   scorza di limone   lemon zest
   scorza grattugiata   grated peel
scottare   blanch, scald
Scozzese, alla   Scotch
secchiello per il ghiaccio   ice bucket
secco *[vino]*   dry *[wine]*
secco, molto *[vino]*   very dry *[wine]*
secco   dried
secondo *[piatto]*   main course, second course
sedano   celery
sedano rapa   celeriac
sedia   chair
segale   rye
seggiolone   highchair
sella   saddle
selvaggina   game
   selvaggina in crosta   game pie
selvatico   wild
seme di carvi   caraway *[seeds]*
semi di faggio, faggiole   beech nuts
semi di girasole   sunflower seeds
semi di sesamo   sesame seeds
semifreddo alla ricotta   ricotta cheese parfait
semolino   semolina, grits *[US]*, hominy grits *[US]*
semplice   plain
senape   mustard
   senape in grani   whole grain mustard
senza glutine   gluten-free
seppia   cuttlefish
servizio   service
servizio di porcellana   china *[service]*
setacciare   sift
sfilettato   filleted
   sfilettato   off the bone *[fish]*
   sfilettato, non   on the bone *[fish]*
sgombro   mackerel
sherry   sherry
shiitake *[funghi cinesi]*   shiitake mushrooms
sidro   cider
   sidro, aceto di   cider vinegar
   sidro di pere   perry
sigarette   cigarettes
sigaro   cigar

snack snack (between meals)
soda, seltz soda water
soffriggere shallow-fry
sogliola Dover sole, sole
   sogliola *[piccola]* sand sole
   sogliola limanda lemon sole
soia soy
   soia, germogli di bean sprouts
   soia, seme di soy bean, soya bean
sommelier wine waiter
sorbetto sherbet, sorbet
   sorbetto allo yogurt yoghurt sorbet
sorgo sorghum
sottaceti pickles
soufflé soufflé
   soufflé al formaggio cheese soufflé
spaghetti spaghetti
   spaghetti al ragù spaghetti bolognese
   spaghetti alla carbonara spaghetti carbonara *[bacon, egg, cream and parmesan]*
spalla shoulder
sparecchiare clear up
specialità speciality
   specialità della casa house specialities
   specialità locali local specialities
specialità alimentari delicatessen
speck smoked, aged ham
speziato spicy
spezie spices
spezzatino, carne in umido casserole
spezzatino di agnello lamb stew
spezzatino di manzo stewed steak
spiedino kebab
spiedino *[di legno, di metallo]* skewer
spinaci spinach
   spinaci al burro spinach with butter
   spinaci alla panna creamed spinach
spine, lische bones *[of fish]*
sporcare dirty *[verb]*
sporco dirty *[adj]*
spremiagrumi juicer
spesso thick
spicchio d'aglio clove of garlic
spiccioli change *[coins]*
spugnola *[fungo]* morels
spuntino snack *[light meal]*
squalo, pescecane shark
stagionato aged, mature
stagione, di seasonal
stantio stale
storione sturgeon
stout *[birra scura]* stout
stufato stew
strudel di mele apple strudel
strutto lard
struzzo ostrich
stufato di montone all'Irlandese Irish stew

stuzzicadenti toothpick
stuzzichini per aperitivo appetizer
   stuzzichino salato savoury
succo juice
   succo d'arancia orange juice
   succo di frutta fruit juice
   succo di limone lemon juice
   succo di mela apple juice
   succo di pomdoro tomato juice
supermercato supermarket
surgelato frozen
suro, sugarello horse mackerel
swiss roll *[dolce di pandispagna farcito e arrotolato]* Swiss roll
tacchino turkey
   tacchino, scaloppine di turkey escalope
tacchino arrosto roast turkey
taccole mangetout, sugar snap peas
tagliare cut
   tagliare a pezzi to chop *[meat]*
tagliare la carne carve
tagliatelle noodles, tagliatelle
   tagliatelle al salmone tagliatelle with salmon
tagliato a dadi diced *[cubed]*
tagliato a pezzi chopped *[into pieces]*
tagliente, affilato sharp
tagliolini al nero di seppia thin tagliatelle with cuttlefish ink
tapioca tapioca
tartara tartare
tartelletta alla crema maids of honour
tartine canapés
tartufo truffle
   tartufo al cioccolato chocolate truffle *[sweet]*
   tartufo bianco white truffle
   tartufo nero black truffle
tavolo table
   tavolo con vista window table, table by the window
tazza cup, mug
   tazza da caffè coffee cup
   tazza da tè tea cup
   tazza di caffè cup of coffee
   tazza di cioccolata cup of cocoa
   tazza di tè cup of tea
   tazza e sottotazza *[o piattino]* cup and saucer
tè tea
   tè accompagnato da scones con marmellata e crème fraîche cream tea
   tè al limone lemon tea
   tè alla menta mint tea
   tè delle 5 afternoon tea
   tè cinese china tea
   tè con latte tea with milk
   tè freddo iced tea
   tè Giapponese Japanese tea
   tè, ora del tea-time
   tè verde green tea
teiera teapot
temperatura ambiente room temperature
tenero tender

terrina terrine
   terrina di gamberetti potted shrimp
timballo di carne meat pie
timo thyme
tinca tench
tiramisù tiramisù *[pudding with sponge biscuits, coffee, amaretto liquor, mascarpone]*
tisana herbal tea
toast toasted sandwich
tofu tofu
toilettes lavatory
tonno tunny, tuna
topinambur, patata del Canada, tartufo di canna Jerusalem artichoke
tordo thrush
torrone nougat
torta, dolce gateau, cake
   torta *[anche salata]* pie, tart
   torta, fetta di *[anche salata]* slice of pie
   torta al cioccolato chocolate cake
   torta al formaggio *[dolce]* cheesecake
   torta alla crema cream cake
   torta alla frutta candita fruit cake
   torta alla melassa treacle tart
   torta alla noci pecan pecan pie
   torta alle mandorle almond tart
   torta allo zenzero ginger cake
   torta di carote carrot cake
   torta di compleanno birthday cake
   torta di fragole con panna montata strawberry shortcake
   torta di lime key lime pie
   torta di mele apple pie
   torta nuziale wedding cake
   torta foresta nera Black Forest cake/gateau
   torta rovesciata upside-down cake
   tortina alla crema custard tart
tortellini pasta stuffed with meat or cheese
   tortellini alla panna tortellini with cream
   tortellini in brodo tortellini in stock
tovaglia tablecloth
tovagliolo napkin, serviette
tramezzino sandwich
   tramezzino al cetriolo cucumber sandwich
   tramezzino al formaggio cheese sandwich
   tramezzino al prosciutto ham sandwich
trenette allo scoglio flat spaghetti with seafood sauce
triglia red mullet
trippa tripe
   trippa pressata in gelatina brawn
tritato *[di manzo]*, **macinato** ground beef
tronchetto di Natale Christmas log
trota trout
   trota arcobaleno, iridea rainbow trout
   trota di mare sea trout
   trota salmonata salmon trout
tuorlo *[d'uovo]* egg yolk
umido, in stewed
uovo egg
   uova al tegamino fried egg

uova alla coque *[bollite 3-4 minuti]* soft-boiled eggs
uova Benedict eggs Benedict
uova di pesce hard roe
uova di pesce *[morbide, tenere]* soft roe
uova di quaglia quail's eggs
uova e asparagi eggs and asparagus
uova marce bad eggs
uova strapazzate scrambled eggs
uovo, albume di egg white
uovo al tegamino con bacon egg and bacon
uovo al tegamino fried egg
uovo alla scozzese *[sodo, ricoperto di salsiccia, impanato e fritto]* scotch egg
uovo bollito boiled egg
uovo fritto fried egg
uovo in camicia poached egg
uovo sodo boiled egg, hard boiled egg
uovo, tuorlo di egg yolk
uva grape(s)
uva passa di Corinto, ribes currants
uva spina gooseberry
uva sultanina sultanas
uvetta, uva passa raisin
vagone ristorante dining car
vaniglia vanilla
vaniglia, gelato alla vanilla ice cream
vaniglia, stecca di vanilla pod/bean
vapore, al steamed
vassoio cheese board
vegetaliano vegan
vegetariano vegetarian
veloce fast *[not eat]*
verdura vegetables
verdure a bastoncino batons *[vegetables]*
verdure cotte al vapore steamed vegetables
verdure lesse boiled vegetables
verdura mista assorted vegetables, mixed vegetables
vermicelli vermicelli
verza cabbage
verza rossa red cabbage
Vin Santo sweet dessert wine
vinaigrette French dressing
vino wine
vino bianco white wine
vino corposo full-bodied wine
vino da dolce, vino da dessert dessert wine, pudding wine
vino da tavola table wine
vino della casa house wine
vino Bordeaux Burgundy *[wine]*
vino dolce sweet *[wine]*
vino leggero light-bodied wine
vino locale, regionale local wine
vino Madera Madeira
vino Marsala Marsala wine
vino non troppo corposo medium wine
vino rosato rosé *[wine]*
vino rosso red wine, claret
vino spumante sparkling wine

vista sul mare *[tavolo con]*   sea view *[i.e. table with]*
vite   vine
vitello   calf, veal
   vitello, fegato di   calf's liver
   vitello, involtini di   veal rolls
   vitello, scaloppine di   veal escalope
   vitello tonnato   cold veal slices with a tuna sauce
vol au vent   vol au vent
   vol au vent di pollo   chicken vol au vent
vongola   clam
wafer   wafer
whisky   whisky
wurstel   frankfurter
   wurstel e crauti   frankfurter with sauerkraut
yogurt   yoghurt
   yogurt alla Greca   Greek yoghurt
   yogurt naturale   plain yoghurt
Yorkshire pudding   Yorkshire pudding
zabaglione   zabaglione
zafferano   saffron
zampe   feet, trotters
zampetto   pig's leg
zenzero   ginger
   zenzero, birra allo   ginger beer
   zenzero, torta allo   ginger cake
ziti   thick macaroni
zucca   pumpkin
zucchero   sugar
   zucchero a velo   icing sugar
   zucchero cristallizzato   granulated sugar
   zucchero d'orzo   barley sugar
   zucchero di acero   maple sugar
   zucchero di canna   cane sugar, demerara sugar, brown sugar
   zucchero per glassa   icing sugar
   zucchero semolato   caster sugar
   zucchero vanigliato   vanilla sugar
zucchina   courgette
zucchine ripiene   stuffed courgettes
zuppa   soup
   zuppa aromatizzata al curry   mulligatawny *[soup]*
   zuppa con pollo e porri   cock-a-leekie *[soup]*
   zuppa di cipolla   onion soup
   zuppa di pesce   fish soup
   zuppa di pesce e legumi a base di latte   chowder
   zuppa di piselli   green pea soup
   zuppa di piselli secchi   pea soup *[with split peas]*
   zuppa di pollo e gombo   chicken gumbo
   zuppa di verdura, passato di verdura   vegetable soup
   zuppa di vongole   clam chowder
   zuppa vichyssoise   vichyssoise
   zuppetta di mare   chowder *[US]*
zuppa inglese   trifle

Italian-English

English-Italian

abalone   orecchia marina, abalone
absinthe   assenzio
account   conto
aged   stagionato
aïloli sauce   salsa aïoli
air-conditioned   climatizzato
albacore *[tuna]*   alalonga, tonno Alalonga
alcohol   alcol
ale   birra rossa real
alfalfa sprouts   germogli di Alfalfa
allergic *[to]*   allergico *[a]*
allergy   allergia
allspice   pimento della Giamaica *[detto anche "4 spezie"]*
almond   mandorla
   almond biscuits   biscotti alle mandorle
   almond paste   pasta di mandorle
   almond tart   torta alle mandorle
   with almonds   alle mandorle
anchovy   acciuga
   anchovy butter   burro di acciughe
   anchovy paste   pasta di acciughe
angel food cake   angel cake *[torta dolce senza tuorli]*
angel fish   pesce angelo
angel hair pasta   capelli d'angelo
angels on horseback   angels on horseback *[ostriche con bacon, fatte alla griglia, e poi su toast]*
angelica   angelica *[erba curativa]*
angler   rana pescatrice
anise   anice
aniseed   anice
aperitif   aperitivo
appetizer   stuzzichini per aperitivo
apple   mela
   apple fritter   frittella di mele
   apple juice   succo di mele
   apple pie   torta di mele
   apple puree   composta di mele
   apple sauce   salsa di mele
   apple strudel   strudel di mele
   apple turnover   fagottino alle mele
   apple tart   crostata di mele
   baked apple   mela al forno
apricot   albicocca
aroma   aroma
arrowroot   fecola di maranta
artichoke   carciofo
   artichoke hearts in olive oil   carciofini sottolio
   artichoke hearts in vinegar   carciofini sottaceto
ashtray   portacenere

asparagus asparago
   asparagus tips asparagi, punte di
aspic aspic
assorted vegetables verdura mista
aubergine melanzana
au gratin [US] gratinato
avocado avocado
baby corn [cob] granturco, pannocchietta di
baby eels cieche
baby food alimenti per l'infanzia
baby leeks porri piccoli
baby's bottle biberon
bacon pancetta
   bacon and eggs pancetta con uova al tegamino
   streaky bacon bacon affumicato
bad cattivo [sapore]
   bad egg uova marcia
bake forno, cuocere al
baked cotto al forno
   baked Alaska dolce con gelato e meringa al forno
   baked apple mela al forno
   baked custard flan, budino
   baked potato patata al forno
   baked rice, rice pudding riso al latte fatto al forno, budino di riso
baked beans fagioli con salsina di pomodoro
bakery panetteria
balsamic vinegar aceto balsamico
bamboo shoots germogli di bambù
banana banana
   banana fritter banana, frittella di
   banana split banana split
   banana flambé banana flambé
bar [pub] bar
barbary duck anatra di Barberia
barbecue barbecue
barbecued cotto al barbecue
barbel barbo
barley orzo
   barley sugar zucchero di orzo
   barley water sciroppo di orzo
basil basilico
   basil pesto pesto
basmati rice riso basmati
bass, sea bass branzino
baste irrorare col fondo di cottura
bathroom bagno, toilette
batter pastella per frittura
bavarian cream crema bavarese
bay leaf alloro
bean fagiolo
   bean sprouts germogli di soia
   broad bean fava
   French bean, green bean, string bean fagiolino
   kidney bean, red bean fagioli rossi
   runner beans fagiolini
   soya bean [fava] di soia
béarnaise [sauce] salsa bernese
béchamel [sauce] salsa besciamella

English-Italian

beech nuts   semi di faggio, faggiole
beef   manzo
   beef stroganoff   filetto stroganoff
   beef tea   brodo di manzo
   beef Wellington   filetto alla Wellington
   beefsteak *[US]*   bistecca dimanzo
   roast beef   arrosto dimanzo
beer   birra
   draught beer   birra alla spina
beestings   colostro
beetroot   barbabietola
bergamot   bergamotto
berries   frutti di bosco
bib *[child's]*   bavaglino
big   grande
bilberry   mirtillo
bill   conto *[all'uscita del ristorante]*
birthday cake   torta di compleanno
biscuits   biscotti
bitter   amaro
bitter *[beer]*   birra scura, birra rossa
black beans   fagioli neri
black butter   burro nero
blackberry   more, more di rovo
black cherry   ciliege nere
black coffee   caffè nero
blackcurrant   ribes nero
Black Forest cake/gateau   torta foresta nera
black halibut   halibut della Groenlandia
black pepper   pepe nero
black pudding   sanguinaccio
black truffle   tartufo nero
blaeberry   mirtillo
blanch   scottare *[immergere in acqua bollente per pochissimi minuti]*
   blanched   sbollentato
blancmange   biancomangiare *[budino di latte di mandorle]*
blend   mischiare, incorporare
blinis   blinis
bloater   aringa affumicata
blood   sangue
blue cheese   formaggio erborinato
blue whiting   melù
boar   cinghiale
bogue *[fish]*   boga
boil   bollire
boiled   bollito
   boiled egg   uovo sodo
   boiled ham   prosciutto bollito
   boiled potatoes   patate lesse
   boiled rice   riso bollito
   boiled vegetables   verdure lesse
   hard boiled egg   uovo sodo
boiling water   acqua bollente
bombe   bomba gelato
bone   osso
   boned   disossato
   bone marrow   midollo

on the bone *[meat]* con l'osso; *[fish]* senza aver tolto le spine, lische
bones *[of fish]* spine, lische
bonito tonnetto
book *[a table]* riservare *[un tavolo]*
borage borragine
bordelaise sauce salsa bordolese *[salsa di carne con midollo di manzo]*
borlotti beans fagioli borlotti
bouquet garni bouquet garni *[erbe aromatiche legate a mazzetti]*
bottle bottiglia
   bottle opener apribottiglie
bowl ciotola
brains cervella
braise *[verb]* brasare
braised brasato
bran crusca
   bran flakes fiocchi di avena integrali
brandy brandy
   cherry brandy cherry brandy, liquore di ciliegie
brawn trippa pressata in gelatina
brazil nut noce del Brasile
bread pane
   bread knife coltello per il pane
   bread roll panino
   breadcrumbs pane grattugiato
   breadstick grissino
breaded impanato
breakfast colazione
   breakfast cereal cereali
bream, sea bream dentice
breast petto
   breast of lamb, veal petto di agnello, di vitello
   chicken breast petto di pollo
brill rombo liscio
brioche brioche
brisket *[of beef]* petto *[di manzo]*
brittle croccante, croccantino
broad bean fava
broccoli broccoli
broth brodo
brown *[verb]* rosolare
brown butter burro nocciola
brown rice riso completo, integrale
brown roll panino integrale
brown sugar zucchero di canna
brown sauce salsa bruna o demi-glace
brussels sprouts cavolini di Bruxelles
bubble and squeak polpette fritte di cavolo e patate
buckwheat grano saraceno
buffalo bufala
buffet buffet
bulgar wheat, bulgur wheat bulgur
bun panino
burbot bottatrice
burdock bardana
burgundy *[wine]* vino di Borgogna
burn *[verb]* bruciare
burnet salvastrella

burnt bruciato
butchers shop macelleria
butter burro
    butterfish bavosa
    buttermilk latticello *[siero di latte acido]*
    butter sauce salsa di burro
    with butter con burro
    without butter burro, senza
cabbage verza
cabinet pudding budino diplomatico *[con crema inglese, frutta candita e
    savoiardi]*
Caesar salad insalata Caesar
café caffè/bar
caffeine caffeina
    caffeine-free caffeina, senza
    decaffeinated decaffeinato
cake torta, dolce
    cake shop pasticceria
    carrot cake torta di carote
    cream cake torta alla crema
    fruit cake torta alla frutta candita
    sponge cake pandispagna
calamari calamari fritti
calf vitello
    calf's brains cervella di vitello
    calf's liver fegato di vitello
camomile camomilla
canapés tartine
candied candito
    candied peel scorza candita
candle candela
candlestick candelabro
candy *[US]* caramella
cane sugar zucchero di canna
canned *[US]* in scatola *[conserva]*
cantaloup *[melon]* melone cantaloupe
capers capperi
capon cappone
cappuccino coffee cappuccino
carafe caraffa
caramel caramello
caraway *[seeds]* seme di carvi
carbohydrate carboidrato
carbonara alla carbonara
carbonated gassato
cardamom cardamomo
carp carpa
carrot carota
    carrot cake torta di carota
carve tagliare
cashier cassiere/cassiera
cassata cassata
cashew nut noce di acagiù
casserole spezzatino, carne in umido
caster sugar zucchero semolato
castor broth brodo di legumi
catfish pesce gatto

cauliflower cavolfiore
   cauliflower cheese cavolfiore gratinato al formaggio
caviar caviale
cayenne pepper pepe di Caienna
celeriac sedano rapa
celery sedano
cereal *[breakfast]* cereali
chair sedia
champagne champagne
change *[coins]* spiccioli, monete
change *[verb]* cambiare
chantilly panna montata
chanterelle funghi cantarelli
char salmerino
charcoal brace, carbone di legna
   charcoal-grilled alla brace
chard bietola
charlotte charlotte *[bavarese ricoperta con savoiardi]*
   apple charlotte charlotte alle mele
cheap economico
check *[US]* conto
cheddar *[cheese]* cheddar *[tipo di formaggio]*
Cheers! Salute!
cheese formaggio
   cheddar *[cheese]* cheddar
   cheese board assortimento di formaggi
   cheese sandwich tramezzino al formaggio
   cheese sauce salsa al formaggio
   cheese soufflé soufflé al formaggio
   cheese straw bastoncini al formaggio
   cheesecake torta al formaggio *[dolce]*
   cream cheese formaggio cremoso
chef chef, cuoco
cherry ciliegia
   cherry brandy maraschino
   cherry tomato pomodorini ciliegia
chervil cerfoglio
chestnut *[sweet]* castagna
   sweet chestnut marrone
   water chestnut castagna d'acqua
chickpea cece
chicken pollo
   roast chicken pollo arrosto
   breast of chicken petto di pollo
   chicken drumsticks fusi di pollo
   chicken gumbo zuppa di pollo e gombo *[ibiscus]*
   chicken kiev pollo alla Kiev
   chicken liver fegatini di pollo
   chicken salad insalata di pollo
   chicken soup brodo di pollo *[zuppa di pollo]*
chicory indivia belga
chilled refrigerato
chilli peperoncino
   chilli-con-carne chilli con carne
   chilli pepper peperoncino
   chilli powder peperoncino in polvere
china *[service]* servizio di porcellana
China tea tè cinese

English-Italian

Chinese cabbage   cavolo cinese
chipped [glass, plate]   scheggiato
chitterling [US]   frittura di trippe
chives   erba cipollina
chocolate   cioccolato
   chocolate cake   torta al cioccolato
   chocolate croissant   croissant al cioccolato
   chocolate eclair   bignè al cioccolato
   chocolate mousse   mousse al cioccolato
   chocolate sauce   salsa al cioccolato
   chocolate truffle   tartufo al cioccolato
   milk chocolate   cioccolato al latte
   plain chocolate   cioccolato fondente
choose   scegliere
chop [cutlet]   braciola
chop [verb]   tagliare a pezzi
chopped [into pieces]   tritato, tagliato a pezzi
chopsticks   bacchette cinesi
choux pastry   pasta choux
Christmas cake   dolce di Natale [inglese]
Christmas Day   il giorno di Natale
Christmas dinner   il pranzo di Natale
Christmas Eve   la vigilia di Natale
Christmas log   tronchetto di Natale [inglese]
Christmas menu   menu di Natale
Christmas pudding   budino di Natale [inglese]
cider   sidro
   cider vinegar   aceto di sidro
cigar   sigaro
cigarettes   sigarette
cinnamon   cannella
citron   limone
citrus   agrume
clam   vongola
   clam chowder   zuppa di vongola
clean   pulito
clear up   pulire [riordinare la tavola]
clear soup   consommè, minestra chiara
clementine   clementina
clove   chiodo di garofano
   clove of garlic   spicchio d'aglio
club sandwich   club-sandwich
cock-a-leekie [soup]   zuppa con pollo e porri
cockles   cuori di mare
cocktail   cocktail
cocoa   cacao
   cocoa butter   burro di cacao
   cup of cocoa   tazza di cioccolata
coconut   noce di cocco
   coconut cream   crema di cocco
   coconut milk   latte di cocco
   desiccated coconut   noce di cocco seccata
cod   merluzzo
coffee   caffè
   cappuccino coffee   cappuccino
   coffee cup   tazza da caffè
   coffee parfait   parfait, semifreddo al caffè
   coffee pot   caffettiera

coffee spoon   cucchiaino da caffè
coffee whitener   latte in polvere *[per il caffè]*
coffee with whipped cream   caffè con panna
decaffeinated coffee   caffè decaffeinato
espresso / expresso coffee   espresso / caffè espresso
filter coffee   caffè all'americana
instant coffee   caffè istantaneo, solubile
latte coffee   caffellatte
cognac   cognac
coke   coca
cold   freddo
cold cuts *[US]*   piatto di carni fredde, affettati
cold drink   bibita fresca
cold meat   carne fredda
cold water   acqua fredda
coley *[coalfish]*   merluzzo nero
collared beef   rostbeef arrotolato
complimentary   gratis, omaggio
condensed milk   latte condensato
cone *[ice cream]*   cono *[di gelato]*
confectionery   confetteria
confectioner's cream   crema pasticciera
conger eel   grongo
consommé *[soup]*   consommè
continental breakfast   colazione continentale
cook, chef   cuoco, chef
coriander   coriandolo
corkscrew   cavatappi
corn   granturco
corn bread   pane di mais
corn oil   olio di mais
corn on the cob   pannocchia di mais
cornflakes   fiocchi di mais
cornflour   farina di mais
sweetcorn   mais
corned beef   carne in scatola
cornet *[ice cream]*   cono *[di gelato]*
cos lettuce   lattuga romana
cottage cheese   formaggio, fiocchi di
courgette   zucchina
couscous   couscous
cover charge   coperto
crab   granchio
dressed crab   granchio farcito
prepared crab   granchio preparato, pulito
crackling *[pork]*   cotenna di maiale arrosto
cranberry   mirtillo rosso
cranberry sauce   salsa di mirtillo rosso
crawfish   aragosta
crayfish   gamberi di fiume
cream   panna
double cream   panna per dolci
single cream   panna da cucina
sour cream   panna acida
whipped cream   panna montata
cream cheese   formaggio cremoso, alla crema
cream cake   torta alla crema
cream sauce   salsa alla panna

English-Italian

cream slice   millefoglie
cream tea   te accompagnato da scones con marmellata e crème fraîche
cream of   crema di
   cream of asparagus soup   crema di asparagi
   cream of chicken soup   crema di pollo
   cream of tomato soup   crema di pomodoro
creamed   alla crema
   creamed spinach   spinaci alla panna
creamy   cremoso
crème caramel   crème caramel
crème fraîche   crème fraîche
cress   crescione
crispbread   fetta biscottata
crisps   patatine
croissant   croissant, cornetto
croquette potatoes   crocchette di patate
croutons   crostini
crumble   sbriciolare
crumpet   crespella *[spessa e salata]*
crystallised fruit   frutta candita
cucumber   cetriolo
   cucumber sandwich   tramezzino al cetriolo
cumin *[seed]*   cumino
cup   tazza
   cup and saucer   tazza e sottotazza *[o piattino]*
   cup of coffee   tazza di caffè
   cup of tea   tazza di tè
   coffee cup   tazza da caffè
   tea cup   tazza da tè
curd   caglio
cured   salato; marinato; affumicato
currants   uva passa di Corinto, ribes
curry   curry *[miscela di spezie]*
   curry powder   curry in polvere
custard   crema inglese
   baked custard   flan, budino
custard apple   custard apple
custard sauce   crema inglese
custard tart   tortina alla crema
cut   tagliare
cutlery   posate
cutlet   cotoletta
cuttlefish   seppia
dab   limanda
dairy products   latticini
damson   prugna di Damasco
date   dattero
date plum   caco
debone   disossare
decaffeinated/decaf   decaiffenato
deep-fried   fritto *[nella friggitrice, in molto olio]*
deer/venison   cervo, capriolo
defrost   scongelare
delicatessen   specialità alimentari
delicious   delizioso
demerara sugar   zucchero di canna
desiccated coconut   noce di cocco essiccata

dessert dolci
   dessert spoon cucchiaio da dessert
   dessert wine vino da dolce, vino da dessert
devilled alla diavola
   devilled kidneys rognoni alla diavola
   devilled sauce salsa alla diavola
diced [cubed] tagliato a dadi
dill aneto
   dill sauce salsa all'aneto
dining car vagone ristorante
dining companion(s) commensale/commensali
dining room sala da pranzo
dinner cena
   dinner party cena
   dinner time ora di pranzo/cena
dip [noun] salsina
dip [verb] inzuppare
dirty [adj] sporco
dirty [verb] sporcare
discount sconto
dish piatto
   dish of the day piatto del giorno
dog fish gattuccio
done cotto
   under-done non cotto abbastanza
   well-done molto cotto
double [shot of spirits] doppio
double cream panna per dolci
dough impasto
doughnut ciambella
   jam doughnut krapfen alla marmellata
dover sole sogliola
draught beer birra alla spina
dressing condimento [per insalata]
dried secco
   sun-dried [tomatoes] pomodori essiccati al sole
drink bevanda
   drink [verb] bere
   drinkable potabile, bevibile
   drinking water acqua potabile
   drinks included bevande incluse
dripping grasso d'arrosto
drumsticks fusi
dry [wine] secco [vino]
Dublin bay prawn scampi
duchesse potatoes patate alla Duchessa
duck [domestic] anatra [domestica]
duck [wild] anatra [selvatica]
   duck paté patè d'anatra
   duck with oranges anatra all'arancia
   duckling anatroccolo
dumpling gnocco
   meat dumpling agnolotti
   potato dumpling gnocchi di patate
eat mangiare
éclair bigné allungato
eel anguilla
egg uovo

boiled egg   uovo bollito
egg and bacon   uova al tegamino con bacon
egg cup   portauovo
egg white   albume
egg yolk   tuorlo d'uovo
eggs Benedict   uova Benedict
eggs florentine   uova affogate alla fiorentina
fried egg   uovo al tegamino
hard boiled egg   uovo sodo
omelette   frittata, omelette
poached egg   uovo affogato
scrambled eggs   uova strapazzate
soft boiled egg   uovo alla coque *[3-4 minuti]*
eggplant *[US]*   melanzana
elderberry   sambuco, bacca di sambuco
endive   indivia
enough   abbastanza
entree   antipasto
entree *[US]*   primo *[come piatto principale]*
escalope   scaloppine
   turkey escalope   tacchino, scaloppine di
   veal escalope   scaloppine di vitello
espresso   espresso
essence   essenza
ewe's milk   latte di capra
ewe's milk cheese   formaggio di latte di capra
excellent   eccellente
expensive   caro
extra virgin olive oil   olio extra vergine di oliva
faggot   polpettina di carne
falafel   falafel
farm *[eggs, chickens]*   di fattoria
fast *[not eat]*   veloce
fat *[adj]*   grasso *[aggettivo]*
fat *[noun]*   grasso *[nome]*
   fat-free   senza grassi
feet, trotters   piedini di maiale
fennel   finocchio
feta cheese   formaggio feta
fig   fico
filbert   nocciola di Dalmazia
fillet   filetto
   fillet steak   filetto *[di manzo]*
filleted   sfilettato
filo pastry   pasta fillo
filter coffee   caffè filtro
first course   primo *[piatto]*
fish   pesce
   fish and chips   pesce fritto e patatine
   fish cake   polpetta di pesce
   fishmonger   pescheria
   fish soup   zuppa di pesce
   fish stew   pesce in umido
   fish stock   brodo di pesce
   anchovy   acciuga
   angel fish   pesce angelo
   bass, sea bass   branzino
   bloater   aringa affumicata

bream abramide
brill rombo liscio
burbot bottatrice
catfish pesce gatto
cod merluzzo
coley merluzzo nero
conger eel grongo
crayfish gamberetti di fiume
cuttlefish seppie
dog fish gattuccio
dover sole sogliola
eel anguilla
flounder passera, pianuzza
grey mullet cefalo
haddock eglefino
halibut halibut
herring aringa
kipper *[smoked]* aringa affumicata
lemon sole sogliola limanda
mackerel sgombro
monkfish coda di rospo
pike luccio
pike-perch lucioperca
pilchard sardina, sardella
redfish scorfano del nord
red mullet triglia
rockfish scorfano
sea bass branzino
sea bream dentice
sea trout trota di mare
shark squalo, pescecane
skate razza
smelt perlano
sole sogliola
sturgeon storione
swordfish pesce spada
tench tinca
trout trota
tunny, tuna tonno
turbot rombo chiodato
whitebait *[sprats]* bianchetti
whiting merlano
fisherman's pie torta di pesce in crosta
fixed price a prezzo fisso
  fixed price menu menu a prezzo fisso
fizzy frizzante
flageolet *[beans]* fagiolo nano
flakes fiocco
flambé flambè
flan flan, budino
flat fish pesce piatto
flavour gusto, sapore
  flavoured al gusto/sapore di
floating island(s) uova montate a neve
flounder passera, pianuzza
flour farina
fondant fondente
fondue fonduta

food cibo, alimenti
   food poisoning intossicazione alimentare
fool mousse di frutta, crema e panna montata
fork forchetta
   boiling fowl gallina
frankfurter wurstel
free [of charge] gratis
free-range di allevamento a terra
French beans fagiolini
French dressing vinaigrette
French fries [US] patatine fritte [tagliate a bastoncino]
French toast fetta biscottata
fresh fresco
freshwater [fish] di acqua dolce
fried fritto
   fried chicken pollo fritto
   fried egg uova al tegamino
   fried fish pesce fritto
   fried food fritto [frittura]
   mixed fried fish fritto misto [di pesce]
frisée [salad] insalata riccia
fritter frittella
   apple fritter frittella di mele
   banana fritter frittella di banana
frog's legs cosce di rana
frozen surgelato
fruit frutta
   fruit bread/loaf pane all'uva
   fruit juice frutta, succo di
   fruit salad macedonia di frutta
fry friggere
fudge dolce al cioccolato
fudge cake dolce al cioccolato
full [restaurant] al completo
full [after eating] pieno
full-bodied wine vino corposo
full-cream milk latte intero
full-fat [cheese] grasso [formaggio]
fungi funghi
galantine galantina
galeeny gallina faraona
game selvaggina
   game pie crostata di selvaggina
gammon pancetta affumicata
garden mint menta verde
garden peas piselli
garlic aglio
   garlic mayonnaise aioli
garlicky all'aglio
garnished guarnito
gassy [water] gassato
gateau dolce, torta
gazpacho gazpacho
gelatine gelatina
genetically modified [GM] geneticamente modificato
gents' toilets bagno degli uomini
ghee burro fuso [di latte di bufala]

English-Italian

gherkins   cetriolini sottaceto
giblets   rigaglie
gin   gin
   gin and tonic   gin tonic
ginger   zenzero
   ginger beer   birra allo zenzero
   gingerbread   pane speziato
   ginger cake   torta allo zenzero
glacé cherry   ciliegia candita
glass   bicchiere
   clean glass   bicchiere pulito
   glass of water   bicchiere d'acqua
   wine glass   bicchiere per vino
glazed   glassato
gluten-free   senza glutine
gnocchi   gnocchi
goat   capra
   goat's cheese   formaggio caprino
   goat's milk   latte di capra
good   buono
goose   oca
   goose liver pâté   paté di fegato d'oca
gooseberry   uva spina
goulash   goulash
gourmet   buongustaio
granary loaf   pane integrale
granita   granita
granulated sugar   zucchero cristallizzato o cristallino
grape(s)   uva
grapefruit   pompelmo
grapeseed oil   olio di semi di vinaccioli
grated   grattugiato
gratuity   mancia
gravy   fondo di cottura di arrosto
   gravy boat   salsiera
grease   grasso
Greek yoghurt   yoghurt alla Greca
green beans   fagiolino
green olives   olive verdi
green peas   pisello
green pepper   pepe verde
green salad   insalata verde
green tea   tè verde
greengage *[plum]*   prugna claudia
greengrocer   fruttivendolo/a
greenland halibut   ippoglosso nero, halibut di Groenlandia
grenadine   granatina
grey mullet   cefalo
grill *[verb]*   cucinare alla griglia
grill *[noun]*   griglia
   mixed grill   grigliata mista
grilled   grigliato
grind   macinare
gristle   cartilagine
grits *[US]*   semolina
groats   granaglia
grocery   alimentari

ground macinato, tritato
    ground beef tritato di manzo, macinato
    ground coffee caffè macinato
groundnut oil olio di semi d'arachide
grouper cernia
grouse cedrone
guacamole guacamole
guava guaiava
gudgeon gobione
guinea fowl faraona
gumbo gumbo
gurnard capone, gallinella
haddock eglefino
half mezzo
    half a litre mezzo litro
    half bottle mezza bottiglia
    half done mezzo crudo
    half-cooked mezzo crudo
halibut halibut
ham prosciutto
    boiled ham prosciutto cotto
    ham sandwich tramezzino al prosciutto
hamburger hamburger
hangover postumi della sbornia
hard duro
hard boiled egg uovo sodo
hard cheese formaggio a pasta dura
hard roe uova di pesce
hare lepre
haricot beans fagiolo
hash browns *[US]* polpette di patate rifritte
haunch coscia
hazelnut nocciola
health salute
    health shop negozio di macrobiotica
    healthy salutare
heart cuore
heat up riscaldare
herbs erbe, spezie
herbal tea tisana
herring aringa
hickory nut noce d'America
highchair seggiolone
high-fibre ricco di fibre
high tea cena leggera *[Scozia e nord dell'Inghilterra]*
hollandaise sauce salsa olandese
home-made fatto in casa
hominy grits *[US]* semolina
honey miele
honeycomb favo
honeydew melon melone Cavaillon
hors d'oeuvre antipasti
horse mackerel suro, sugarello
horse meat carne di cavallo
horseradish cren, barbaforte, rafano
hot *[not cold; strong]* caldo
hot dog hot dog

hot drink   bevanda calda
hotpot   carne e verdure in umido coperte da fette di patate
hot water   acqua calda
house specialities   specialità della casa
hummus   hummus
hungry   affamato
ice   ghiaccio
   bucket of ice   secchio per il ghiaccio *[per tenere il vino in fresco]*
   with ice   con ghiaccio
ice cream   gelato
   ice cream cone   cono di gelato
   ice cream scoop   pallina di gelato
   ice cream sundae   gelato con praline e sciroppo
ice cube   ghiaccio, cubetto di
ice lolly   ghiacciolo
iceberg lettuce   lattuga iceberg
icing   glassatura
   icing sugar   zucchero per glassatura
ide *[fish]*   ido
in batter   impastellato
ingredients   ingredienti
inside   dentro
instant coffee   caffè istantaneo
Irish stew   stufato di montone all'Irlandese
Irish whiskey   irish whisky
jam   marmellata
Japanese tea   te giapponese
jellied   in gelatina
jelly *[savoury]*   marmellata salata
jelly *[sweet/pudding]*   gelatina di frutta
jello *[US]*   gelatina tipo marmellata
Jerusalem artichoke   topinambur, patata del Canada, tartufo di canna
jug   piccola caraffa
jugged hare   civet di lepre
juice   succo
   juicer   centrifuga, spremiagrumi
julienne   julienne, *[verdure]* alla
kaki   caco
kale   cavolo
kebab   spiedino
kedgeree   kedgeree *[riso al pesce affumicato, con uova sode, aromatizzato al curry]*
ketchup   ketchup
kettle   bollitore elettrico
key lime pie   torta alla crema di limone verde o limetta
kidney   rognoni
kidney beans   fagioli rossi
king prawn   gamberoni
kipper *[smoked]*   aringa affumicata
kitchen   cucina
kiwi fruit   kiwi
knife   coltello
knuckle   ossobuco
kohlrabi   cavolo rapa
kosher   kasher
kumquat   kumquat, mandarino cinese
label   etichetta

lactose lattosio
    lactose intolerance intolleranza al lattosio
ladies fingers biscotti savoiardi
ladies' toilets bagno delle donne
ladle mestolo
lager birra chiara
    lager shandy birra con gazzosa
lamb agnello
    lamb chop costoletta d'agnello
lamb's lettuce lattughella, dolcetta
langoustine scampo
lard strutto
lark allodola
lasagne *[flat sheets of pasta]* lasagne
lasagne lasagne al forno
latte *[coffee]* caffellatte
lavatory toilettes, lavabo, locale per lavarsi le mani
lavender lavanda
lean *[meat]* carne magra
leek porro
leg coscia
    leg of lamb cosciotto d'agnello
legumes legumi, verdure
lemon limone
    lemon balm melissa
    lemon grass lemon grass
    lemon juice succo di limone
    lemon sole sogliola limanda
    lemon zest scorza di limone
    lemonade limonata
lentil lenticchia
lettuce lattuga
lime lime, limetta
ling molva
light-bodied wine vino leggero
liqueur liquore
liquorice liquirizia
litre litro
liver fegato
    liver pâté patè di fegato
    liver sausage salsiccia di fegato
loaf pagnotta
    meat loaf polpettone di carne
    white loaf pagnotta bianca
lobster astice
    lobster bisque consommé di astice
local locale
    local cheese formaggio locale
    local specialities specialità locali
loganberry loganberry
loin *[of veal, pork, venison]* lombata carrè
long-grained rice riso a chicchi lunghi
low-fat *[diet]* magro, dietetico
low in fat contenente poco grasso, magro
low-salt iposodico
lunch pranzo
luncheon meat carne in scatola pressata

lunchtime   ora di pranzo
lychee   litchi, lici, ciliegia cinese
lythe   merluzzo giallo
macadamia nut   noce macadamia
macaroni   maccheroni
   macaroni cheese   pasta al gratin
macaroon   amaretto
mace   macis
mackerel   sgombro
macrobiotic   macrobiotico
madeira   vino Madera
   madeira cake   dolce al Madera
   madeira sauce   salsa al Madera
maids of honour   tartelletta alla crema
main course   secondo *[piatto]*
maize   granturco
mallard   germano reale
malt   malto
mandarin   mandarino
mangetout   taccole
mango   mango
mangosteen   mangosta
maple syrup   sciroppo di acero
maple sugar   zucchero di acero
margarine   margarina
marinade   marinata
   marinated   marinato
marjoram   maggiorana
market   mercato
marmalade   marmellata di arance
marrow *[vegetable]*   cucurbita
marrow bone   osso con midollo
   bone marrow   midollo
marsala wine   vino di Marsala, vino Marsala
marshmallow   altea, pasta di altea
marzipan   marzapane
mashed   purè, ridotto a
mashed potatoes   puree di patate
matches   fiammiferi
matchstick potatoes   patatine fritte *[tagliate a bastoncino]*
mature   stagionato
mayonnaise   maionese
mead   idromele
meal   pranzo
meat   carne
meat ball   polpettine di carne
meat dumplings   agnolotti
meat loaf   polpettone
meat pie   torta di carne *[salata]*
medallion   medaglione
medium cooked   cotto a puntino
medium-rare   non troppo cotta
medium wine   vino non troppo corposo
medlar   nespola
melon   melone
   cantaloup melon   melone cantaloupe
   honeydew melon   melone Cavaillon

melted butter   burro fuso
menu   menu
meringue   meringa
mild   delicato
milk   latte
    cow's milk   latte di mucca
    ewe's milk   latte di capretto
    goat's milk   latte di capra
    milk chocolate   cioccolato al latte
    milkshake   frullato
    poached in milk   affogato nel latte
    semi-skimmed milk   latte parzialmente scremato
    soya milk   latte di soia
    with milk   con latte
    without milk   senza latte
minced meat   carne trita, macinata
mincemeat   *[preparato zuccherato a base di frutta e noccioline secche]*
mince pie   tortina a base di mincemeat
mineral water   acqua minerale
    fizzy mineral water   acqua minerale gassata
    still mineral water   acqua minerale naturale, non gassata
minestrone *[soup]*   minestrone
mint   menta
    mint sauce   salsa alla menta
    mint jelly   menta, gelatina di
    mint tea   te alla menta
mixed grill   grigliata msta
mixed herbs   erbe aromatiche
mixed salad   insalata mista
mixed vegetables   verdure miste
mollusc   mollusco
monkfish   coda di rospo
monosodium glutamate *[MSG]*   glutammato di sodio
morels   spugnola *[fungo]*
moussaka   moussaka
mousse   mousse
muesli   muesli
muffin   muffin *[piccolo dolce con uvette]*
mug   tazza
mulberry   more di gelso
mullet   cefalo
mulligatawny *[soup]*   zuppa aromatizzata al curry
mushroom   funghi
    button mushrooms   funghi champignons
    porcini mushrooms   funghi porcini
mushy peas   purè di piselli
mussel   cozza
mustard   senape
mutton   montone
napkin   tovagliolo
natural   naturale
Neapolitan ice-cream   trancio di gelato Napoletano
nectarine   pesca noce
nettle   ortica
no smoking   fumare, vietato
noisettes   nocciole
non-alcoholic drink   analcolico

non-smoking area   fumatori, zona non
noodles   tagliatelle
   noodle soup   capellini in brodo
nut   frutta a guscio
   almond   mandorla
   brazil nut   noce del Brasile
   cashew nut   noce di acagiù
   chestnut   castagna
   cobnut   nocciola
   coconut   noce di cocco
   hazelnut   nocciola
   peanut   arachide
   pecan nut   noce pecan
   sweet chestnut   castagna
   walnut   noce
nutmeg   noce moscata
oatcake   gallette di farina d'avena
oatmeal   farina d'avena
oats   avena
   porridge/rolled oats   fiocchi di avena
octopus   polipo, polpo
off *[food, wine]*   andato a male
off the bone *[fish]*   sfilettato
offal   frattaglie
oil   olio
okra   gombo, ibisco
olive   oliva
   black olives   olive nere
   green olives   olive verdi
olive oil   olio d'oliva
omelette   omelette
on the rocks *[with ice]*   con ghiaccio, on the rocks
on the bone *[meat]*   non disossato
onion   cipolla
   onion soup   zuppa di cipolle
open *[verb]*   aprire
orange   arancia
   orange juice   succo di arancia
   orange sauce   salsa all'arancia
oregano   origano
organic   biologico
ostrich   struzzo
outdoors/outside   fuori, all'aperto
oven   forno
overdone   troppo cotto
oxtail   coda di bue
   oxtail soup   coda alla vaccinara
ox tongue   lingua di bue
oyster   ostrica
oyster mushroom   gelone *[fungo]*
pancake   crepe
pan-fried   fritto *[in padella]*
papaya   papaia
paprika   paprika *[spezia di origine ungherese, meno piccante del peperoncino]*
par-boil   precotto
parfait   parfait
parma ham   prosciutto di Parma

parmesan *[cheese]* parmigiano *[formaggio]*
parsley prezzemolo
   curly parsley prezzemolo riccio
   flat parsley prezzemolo piatto
   parsley sauce salsa al prezzemolo
parsnip pastinaca
partridge pernice
party festa
pasta pasta
   fresh pasta pasta fresca
pastry pasta *[dolce, sfoglia, frolla]*
   choux pastry pasta choux
   filo pastry pasta fillo
   puff pastry pasta sfoglia
pâté paté
   liver pâté paté di fegato
pawpaw papaia
pay *[verb]* pagare
pea pisello
   green peas pisello
   green pea soup zuppa di piselli
   split peas piselli secchi tagliati a metà
   pea soup *[with split peas]* zuppa di piselli secchi tagliati a metà
peach pesca
peanut arachide
   peanut butter burro di arachidi
pear pera
pearl barley orzo mondato
pease-pudding purè di piselli secchi
pecan nut noce pecan
   pecan pie torta alla noce di pecan
peel *[verb]* pelare, sbucciare
peel *[noun]* buccia
   grated peel scorza grattuggiata
peeled sbucciata
pepper *[spice]* pepe *[spezia]*
   black, green, white pepper pepe nero, verde, bianco
   ground pepper pepe macinato
   whole pepper pepe in grani
   pepper mill macinino per il pepe
   pepper pot pepiera
   pepper steak bistecca al pepe
pepper *[vegetable]* peperone
   green pepper peperone verde
   red pepper peperone rosso
   stuffed pepper peperoni ripieno
peppermint menta piperita
perch pesce persico
perry sidro di pere
persimmon caco
pesto pesto
petits fours pasticcini, biscottini
pheasant fagiano
pickled cabbage crauti
pickled cucumber cetriolini sottoaceto
pickled herring aringa sottaceto
pickled onion cipollina sottaceto
pickles sottaceti

picnic picnic
pie torta *[anche salata]*
piece pezzo
pig maiale
   suckling pig maialino da latte
pigeon piccione
pig's trotters piedini di maiale
pike luccio
pike-perch lucioperca
pilchard sardina, sardella
pine nuts pinoli
pineapple ananas
pinto bean fagiolo pinto
pistachio *[nut]* pistacchio
pitcher caraffa, brocca
pitta bread pane pitta
pizza pizza
plaice platessa, passera di mare
plain semplice
plain chocolate cioccolato fondente
plantain banana verde *[da cuocere]*
plat du jour piatto del giorno
plate piatto
plum prugna
plum pudding budino di prugne
plum tomato pomodoro di San Marzano
poach affogare
poached *[egg]* in camicia
polenta polenta
pollack merluzzo giallo
pomegranate melagrana
popcorn popcorn
porcini mushroom funghi porcini
pork carne di maiale
   pork chop braciola di maiale
   pork crackling cotenna di maiale arrosto
porridge porridge
port porto *[vino]*
pot roast arrosto in cocotte
potato patata
   baked potato patata al forno
   fried potoatoes patate fritte
   mashed potatoes pureè di patate
   new potatoes patate novelle
   potato chips patatine fritte
   potato crisps patatine
   potato dumpling gnocchi di patate
   potato salad insalata di patate
potted shrimp terrina di gamberetti
poultry pollame
poussin galletto
praline croccante
prawns gamberi
preserves conserve
price prezzo
   price list listino prezzi
prime rib costoletta

profiteroles profiteroles
protein proteina
prune prugna secca
pudding *[savoury]* budino *[salato]*
pudding *[sweet]* budino *[dolce]*
pudding rice budino di riso
pudding wine vino da dessert
puff pastry pasta sfoglia
pulses legumi
pumpkin zucca
pure puro
purée purè
purslane portulaca
puy lentils lenticchie di Puy
quail quaglia
   quail's eggs uova di quaglia
quality qualità
quark formaggio bianco *[magro]*
quarter quarto
quiche quiche, torta salata
   quiche lorraine quiche lorraine
quince mela cotogna
rabbit coniglio
rack carrè
   rack of lamb carrè d'agnello
   rack of ribs carrè *[d'agnello o di maiale]*
radicchio radicchio
radish/radishes ravanello
ragout ragù
rainbow trout trota arcobaleno, iridea
raisin uvetta, uva passa
ramekin *[food]* ramequin, tartelletta
ramekin *[small container]* piccola forma *[da usare anche nel forno, di solito in porcellana]*
rancid rancido
rare *[steak, meat]* al sangue *[bistecca, carne]*
raspberry lampone
ravioli ravioli
raw crudo
receipt ricevuta, scontrino
recipe ricetta
recommend consigliare
red cabbage verza rossa
red chilli peperoncino rosso
redcurrant ribes rossi
   redcurrant jelly gelatina di ribes rossi
redfish scorfani del nord
red mullet triglie
red pepper peperone rosso
red wine vino rosso
reindeer renna
rennet caglio
reservation prenotazione
   reserve prenotare
restaurant ristorante
rhubarb rabarbaro
ribs costine

rack of ribs carrè *[d'agnello, di maiale]*
rib of beef costole di manzo
spare ribs costine di maiale
rice riso
    rice paper ostie di riso
    rice pudding budino di riso
    risotto rice risotto
    wild rice riso selvatico
rind *[cheese]* crosta
ripe maturo
rissole rissole *[sfogliatina ripiena]*
river fiume
roast *[verb]* arrostire
    roast *[noun]* arrosto
    roast beef arrosto di manzo
    roast chicken pollo arrosto
    roast meats arrosti
    roast pork arrosto di maiale
roasted arrosto
rock salt sale grosso
rocket rucola
rockfish scorfano
roe *[hard]* uova di pesce
    soft roe uova di pesce *[morbide, tenere]*
roll *[bread]* panino
rolled oats fiocchi d'avena
rollmop herring rotolini di aringa *[marinata]*
romain *[lettuce]* lattuga romana
room temperature temperatura ambiente
root radice
rosé *[wine]* vino rosato
rosehip rosa canina
rosemary rosmarino
roulade rollata
rum rum
    rum baba baba al rum
rump steak bistecca di manzo
runner beans fagioli larghi
rusk biscotti per neonato
rye segala
rye bread pane di segale
rye whisky rye, whisky di segala
saccharin saccarina
saddle sella
safflower cartamo
saffron zafferano
sage salvia
sago sago, sagù
salad insalata
    green salad insalata verde
    mixed salad insalata mista
    side salad insalata di contorno
salad bowl insalatiera
salad cream condimento tipo maionese per l'insalata
salad dressing condimento per insalata
salami salame
salmon salmone

English-Italian

salmon steak salmone, trancio di
salmon trout trota salmonata
salsify salsefrica, barba di becco
salt sale
    low-salt che contiene poco sale
    salt cellar saliera
    salt mill macinasale
    salted salato
    salty **salato**
    sea salt sale marino
sand sole sogliola *[piccola]*
sandwich tramezzino
    cheese sandwich tramezzino al formaggio
    club sandwich club-sandwich
    ham sandwich tramezzino al prosciutto
sardine sardina, sardella
sauce salsa
    white sauce salsa bianca, salsa besciamella
saucer piattino
saury saira *[del Pacifico]*
sausage salsiccia
    liver sausage salsiccia di fegato
    sausage roll rotolino di salsiccia in crosta *[stuzzichino salato]*
sauté in padella
    sauté pan padella
    sautéed saltato *[in padella]*, sauté
saveloy salame tipo cervellata
savoury stuzzichino salato
savoy cabbage cavolo verza, cavolo di Milano
saxifrage sassifraga
scald scottare
scallion *[US]* cipollotto
scallop capasanta
scalloped chicken *[US]* scaloppine di pollo
scalloped potatoes *[US]* patate gratinate con panna
scampi scampi
scone scone *[piccolo panino che si mangia con marmellata e crema]*
Scotch alla Scozzese
    Scotch broth brodo scozzese *[zuppa con cappone,legumi e orzo]*
    Scotch egg uovo alla scozzese *[uovo sodo con carne di salsiccia, impanato e fritto]*
scrambled eggs uova strapazzate
sea bass, bass branzino
sea bream dentice
sea salt sale marino
sea view *[i.e. table with]* vista sul mare *[tavolo con]*
seafood frutti di mare
seafood sauce, with alla pescatora
sear rosolare, far
seasonal di stagione
seasoning condimento
    seasoned condito
seat posto *[a sedere]*
sea trout trota di mare
seaweed alga
second course secondo *[piatto]*
selection scelta

sell-by date   scadenza
semi-dry   demi-sec
semi-hard cheese   formaggio a pasta semi-dura
semi-skimmed milk   latte parzialmente scremato
semi-soft cheese   formaggio a pasta semi-molle
service   servizio
   service charge   coperto
   service discretionary   a discrezione
   service included   incluso
   service not included   non incluso
serviette   tovagliolo
sesame seeds   semi di Sesamo
set menu   menu a prezzo fisso
shad   alosa
shallot   scalogno
shallow-fry   soffriggere
shandy   birra con gazzosa
shank   garretto
shark   squalo, pescecane
sharp   tagliente, affilato
shell   guscio, conchiglia
shellfish   frutti di mare
shepherd's pie   pasticcio di carne di agnello macinata *[in umido, ricoperto di purè e gratinato]*
sherbet   sorbetto
sherry   sherry
shiitake mushrooms   shiitake *[funghi cinesi]*
shop   negozio
shortbread   frollino
shortcrust *[pastry]*   pasta frolla
shoulder   spalla
shrimp   gamberetti
   shrimp cocktail   cocktail di gamberetti, gamberetti in salsa rosa
shut/closed   chiuso
side dish(es)   contorno/contorni
sift   passare al setaccio, setacciare
silverside   girello di manzo
simmer   cuocere a fuoco lento
single cream   panna da cucina
sippets   crostini
sirloin steak   costata di manzo
skate   razza
skewer   spiedino
skimmed milk   latte scremato
skin   pelle
slice   fetta
   slice of bread   fetta di pane
   slice of pie   fetta di torta *[anche salata]*
   slice of ham   fetta di prosciutto
sliced   a fette
sloe   prugnola
   sloe gin   acquavite di prugnole
smell   odore
smelt   fuso, sciolto
smoke *[a cigarette]*   fumare *[una sigaretta]*
   smoker   fumatore
smoke *[food]*   fumare

smoke *[noun]* fumo
smoked affumicato
   smoked bacon bacon affumicato
   smoked cheese formaggio affumicato
   smoked eel anguilla affumicata
   smoked fish pesce affumicato
   smoked haddock eglefino affumicato
   smoked kipper aringa affumicata
   smoked meat carne affumicata
   smoked salmon salmone affumicato
snack *[between meals]* snack
snack *[light meal]* spuntino
snail lumaca
snipe beccaccino
soda bread pane al bicarbonato di soda
soda water soda, seltz
soft morbido
soft-boiled egg uova alla coque *[bollite 3-4 minuti]*
soft cheese formaggio a pasta morbida
soft drink bibita analcolica
soft roe uova di pesce *[morbide, tenere]*
sole sogliola
sorbet sorbetto
sorghum sorgo
sorrel acetosa
soufflé soufflé
   cheese soufflé soufflé al formaggio
soup zuppa
   beef tea brodo di manzo
   broth brodo
   chowder zuppa di pesce e legumi a base di latte
   fish broth brodo di pesce
   fish soup zuppa di pesce
   mulligatawny zuppa aromatizzata al curry
   onion soup zuppa di cipolla
   soup of the day minestra del giorno
   soup spoon cucchiaio da minestra
   vegetable soup zuppa di verdura, passato di verdura
   vichyssoise zuppa vichyssoise
sour acido
   sour cream panna acida
   sour dough pasta fermentata
   sweet and sour agrodolce
soy bean, soya bean seme di soia
soy sauce, soya sauce salsa di soia
soya milk latte di soia
spaghetti spaghetti
   spaghetti bolognese spaghetti al ragù
spare ribs costine di maiale
sparkling frizzante
   water acqua
   wine vino
speciality specialità
spice spezie
spicy speziato
spinach spinaci
spiny lobster aragosta
spirits alcolici

sponge biscuits   fetti di pandispagna
sponge cake   pandispagna
spoon   cucchiaio
   spoonful   cucchiaiata
sprat   papalina
spring greens   foglie tenere di cavolo, broccolo, ecc.
spring onion   cipollina
spring lamb   agnellino
spring roll   involtino primavera
spring water   acqua di sorgente
sprouts *[Brussels]*   cavolini di Bruxelles
squab   piccioncino
squash   cucurbita, zucca, zucchina
squid   calamaro
starch   amido
stale   stantio
starter   antipasto
steak   bistecca di manzo
   steak and kidney pie   torta di manzo e rognone in crosta
   steak and kidney pudding   torta di manzo e rognone in crosta
steam *[verb]*   cuocere a vapore
   steamed   a vapore
   steamed vegetables   verdure cotte al vapore
stew *[meat]*   stufato
   lamb stew   spezzatino o intingolo di agnello
stewed   in umido, intingolo
   stewed fruit   composta di frutta
   stewed steak   spezzatino di manzo
still water   acqua non gassata
Stilton   formaggio Stilton
stir-fry   saltare in padella *[alla cinese]*
stock   brodo
stout   stout *[birra scura]*
stove   cucina economica
strawberry   fragola
   strawberry jam   marmellata di fragole
   strawberry shortcake   torta di fragole, con panna montata
streaky bacon   bacon affumicato
strip steak   costata
strong   forte
stuffed   ripieno, farcito
   stuffed olives   olive farcite
stuffing   ripieno
sturgeon   storione
suckling pig   maialino di latte
suet   grasso di rognone
sugar   zucchero
   caster sugar   zucchero semolato
   granulated sugar   zucchero cristallizzato, cristallino
   icing sugar   zucchero a velo
   sugar-coated almonds   confetti
sultanas   uva sultanina
sundae *[ice cream]*   gelato con praline e sciroppo
sun-dried   essiccato
sunflower   girasole
   sunflower oil   olio di semi di girasole
   sunflower seeds   semi di girasole

supermarket supermercato
supplement integratore
supper cena
swede rapa svedese
sweet dolce
  sweet *[wine]* vino dolce
  sweet chesnut castagna, marrone
  sweet potato patata americana
  sweet trolley carrello dei dolci
  sweets *[candy]* caramelle
sweet and sour agrodolce
sweetbreads animelle
sweetcorn mais
sweetener dolcificante
Swiss roll swiss roll *[dolce di pandispagna farcito e arrotolato]*
swordfish pesce spada
syllabub zabaglione
syrup sciroppo
table tavolo
  table by the window tavolo con vista
  tablecloth tovaglia
  tablespoon cucchiaio da tavola
  table wine vino da tavola
tagliatelle tagliatelle
  thin tagliatelle bavette
take home portare a casa
tangerine mandarino
tap water acqua del rubinetto
tapioca tapioca
taragon, tarragon dragoncello
tartar sauce salsa tartara
tartare tartara
taste gusto, sapore
tasty gustoso, saporito
tea tè
  afternoon tea il te delle 5
  beef tea manzo, brodo di
  cup of tea tazza di tè
  green tea tè verde
  herbal tea tisana
  high-tea cena leggera *[Scozia e nord dell'Inghilterra]*
  iced tea tè freddo
  lemon tea tè al limone
  teacake dolce da tè *[grigliato, tagliato, imburrato, da servire con il tè]*
  tea cup tazza da tè
  tea spoon cucchiaino da tè
  tea with milk tè con latte
  teapot teiera
tea time tè, ora del
tench tinca
tender tenero
tenderloin lombata
terrine terrina
thick spesso, denso
thirsty assetato
thrush tordo
thyme timo
tin barattolo, scatola

tinned in scatola
tip mancia
toad in the hole salsiccia in pastella cotta al forno
toast *[tribute]* brindisi
toast toast
   French toast pane dorato
toasted abbrustolito
toffee caramella mou
tofu tofu, patè di soia
toilet(s) bagni
toilet paper carta igienica
tomato pomodoro
   cherry tomato pomodorini ciliegia
   tomato juice succo di pomdoro
   tomato ketchup ketchup
   tomato purée concentrato di pomodoro
   tomato salad insalata di pomodoro
   tomato sauce salsa di pomodoro
tongue lingua
tonic water acqua tonica
toothpick stuzzicadenti
tope canesca
treacle melassa
treacle tart torta allo sciroppo di mais
trifle trifle*[biscotti inzuppati, frutta e panna montata]*
trimmings guarnizioni
tripe trippa
tough *[meat]* duro
trolley carrello
trout trota
truffle tartufo
   chocolate truffle *[sweet]* tartufo al cioccolato
truffle butter burro di tartufi
tuna, tunny tonno
turbot rombo chiodato
turkey tacchino
   roast turkey tacchino arrosto
turmeric curcuma
turnip rapa
turnip tops punte di rapa
uncooked non cotto
underdone non abbastanza cotto
unsalted butter burro non salato
upside-down cake torta rovesciata *[sottosopra]*
use by da consumare entro
vanilla vaniglia
   vanilla essence essenza di vaniglia
   vanilla ice cream gelato alla vaniglia
   vanilla pod/bean stecca di vaniglia
   vanilla sugar zucchero vanigliato
veal vitello
   veal escalope scaloppine di vitello
vegan vegetaliano
vegetable verdura
   vegetable oil olio di semi
   vegetable soup zuppa di verdure
   vegetable stock brodo vegetale

vegetable broth   brodo di verdure
vegetarian   vegetariano
  vegetarian burger   hamburger vegetariano
  vegetarian cooking   cucina vegetariana
  vegetarian lasagne   lasagne vegetariane
  vegetarian sausage   salsiccia di soia
venison   capriolo
  venison cutlets   cotoletta di cervo
vermicelli   vermicelli
very dry *[wine]*   molto secco *[vino]*
very rare *[of meat]*   al sangue
very sweet   dolcissimo
victoria sponge *[cake]*   dolce tipo Pan di Spagna
vinaigrette   salsa vinaigrette
vine   vite
  vine leaves   foglie di vite
vinegar   aceto
vintage   annata
virgin olive oil   olio extra vergine di oliva
vol au vent   vol au vent, cestini di pasta sfoglia salati
  chicken vol au vent   vol au vent al pollo
wafer   wafer
waffles   cialde
waiter   cameriere
waitress   cameriera
Waldorf salad   insalata Waldorf *[mele, sedano, noci, maionese]*
walnut   noce
warm *[salad etc.]*   caldo
water   acqua
  bottled water   acqua in bottiglia
  glass of water   bicchiere di acqua
  iced water   acqua ghiacciata
  jug of water   caraffa di acqua
  sparkling water/fizzy water   acqua minerale gassata
  spring/mineral water   acqua di sorgente, minerale
  still water   acqua non gassata
watercress   crescione d'acqua
water melon   anguria
wedding cake   torta nuziale
well done   molto cotto, ben cotto
Welsh rarebit, rabbit   crostino di formaggio fuso
whale   balena
wheat   grano
  wheat flour   farina di grano
  wheatgerm   germe di grano
whelk   buccina
whipped cream   panna montata
whisky   whisky
whitebait *[sprats]*   bianchetti
white *[wine, meat]*   bianco
white bread   pane bianco
white truffle   tartufo bianco
white wine   vino bianco
whiting   merlano
whole   intero
wholewheat   integrale
  wholewheat flour   farina integrale

whole grain mustard   senape in grani
wholemeal bread   pane completo, integrale
wild   selvatico
   wild boar   cinghiale
   wild rice   riso selvatico
   wild mushrooms   funghi selvatici
window table   tavolo con vista
wine   vino
   bottle of wine   bottiglia di vino
   wine cooler   bibita a base di vino
   glass of wine   bicchiere di vino
   house wine   vino della casa
   local wine   vino locale, regionale
   red wine   vino rosso
   sparkling wine   vino spumante
   wine glass   bicchiere da vino
   wine list   lista dei vini
   wine vinegar   aceto di vino
   wine waiter   sommelier
   white wine   vino bianco
winkle   lumachina di mare
with ice cream   con gelato
woodcock   beccaccia
Worcestershire sauce   salsa Worcestershire
yam   igname
yeast   lievito
yoghurt   yoghurt
   plain yoghurt   yoghurt naturale
Yorkshire pudding   Yorkshire pudding *[frittella salata]*
zabaglione   zabaglione
zest   scorza

English-Italian

Useful Spanish Expressions

Types of restaurant

Autoservicio	*self-service restaurant*
Bar	*bar (snack-bar, light meals, tapas)*
Bodega	*bar (in Spain, it is mainly used for a wine shop/off-licence or a wine cellar but in some Latin American countries can also mean a grocery)*
Brasería	*charcoal-grill restaurant (popular in Latin America)*
Café	*coffee shop (also bar; cafetería)*
Cafetería	*café (= snack bar; restaurant)*
Cantina	*snack-bar (cheap restaurant, usually with fixed-price menu)*
Cervecería	*bar (with emphasis on beer, light meals, some offer special lunch menu)*
Crepería	*pancakes (often with bar service)*
Frankfurt	*mainly hot-dogs and toasted sandwiches and bar service*
Granja	*teashop, coffee house (popular for breakfast and tea-time snacks [also means farm])*
Heladería	*ice-cream parlour*
Mesón	*inn, pub (also light meals and tapas)*
Parador/Paradores de Turismo	*state-run high-quality tourist hotels normally sited in places of historical interest in beauty spots. They offer good quality at reasonable prices. Often specialising in local cuisine.*
Pensión	*guest house (bed & breakfast); in some Latin American countries can also mean bar*
Pizzería	*pizzeria*
Posada	*inn, restaurant*
Quesería	*cheese shop, dairy produce*
Restaurante	*restaurant*
Snack-bar	*snack bar (tapas, light meals)*
Taberna	*bar, pub (light meals, tapas)*

Tipping

Restaurants in Spain are required by law to include their service charges in the menu price, however up to a 5% tip is still recommended where the quality of service has been high. It is customary to leave small change in bars and cafes and don't forget to account for the obligatory 7% IVA (pronounced ee-vah) sales tax added to your bill.

Menu

Menus are normally split into five sections:
Grupo I: Entremeses, Ensaladas y Sopas
starters, salads and soups
Grupo II: Verduras, Huevos, Pastas y Arroces
vegetables, egg dishes, pasta and rice dishes
Grupo III: Pescados y Mariscos *fish and seafood*
Grupo IV: Carnes *meat and main dishes*
Grupo V: Postres, Pasteleria, Helados, Frutas y Quesos
desserts, pastries, ice-creams, fruits and cheeses

Meals and eating times

07:00 - 10:00	*el desayuno*
	breakfast
13:00 - 15:30	*la comida o el almuerzo*
	lunch
21:00 - 00:00	*la cena*
	dinner

There is also la merienda *(early evening tea or mid-afternoon snack), which is very popular with children*

Restaurant rating scheme

Spain: Fork scheme (five forks = deluxe, one fork = fourth-class)

Getting to a restaurant

Can you recommend a good restaurant?	*¿me podría recomendar un buen restaurante?*
I would like to reserve a table for this evening	*desearía reservar una mesa para esta noche*
Do you have a table for three/four people	*¿tienen una mesa para tres/ cuatro personas?*
We would like the table for 9 o'clock	*queremos la mesa para las 9*
Could we have a table...?	*¿tienen una mesa ... ?*
by the window	*cerca de la ventana*
outside	*fuera*
on the terrace	*en la terraza*
in the non-smoking area	*en la zona de no fumadores*
What time do you open?	*¿a qué hora abren?*
Could you order a taxi for me?	*¿me podría llamar un taxi?*

Ordering

| Waiter/waitress ! | *¡camarero/camarera!* |
| What do you recommend? | *¿Qué me/nos recomienda?* |

What are the specials of the day?	*¿Cuál es la especialidad del día?*
Is this the fixed-price menu?	*¿Es este el menú del día?*
Can we see the a-la-carte menu?	*¿Puede traer la carta?*
Is this fresh?	*¿Es del día?*
Is this local?	*¿Es de la región?*
I would like a/an …	*¿Me podría traer un/una ...?*
Could we have ... please?	*¿Nos puede traer ..., por favor?*
an ashtray	*un cenicero*
the bill	*la cuenta*
our coats	*los abrigos*
a cup	*una taza*
a fork	*un tenedor*
a glass	*un vaso / una copa*
a knife	*un cuchillo*
the menu	*el menú / la carta*
a napkin	*una servilleta*
a plate	*un plato*
a spoon	*una cuchara*
a toothpick	*un palillo*
the wine menu	*la carta de los vinos*
May I have some ...?	*¿Me puede traer ...?*
bread	*pan*
butter	*mantequilla*
ice	*hielo*
lemon	*limón*
milk	*leche*
pepper	*pimienta*
salt	*sal*
sugar	*azúcar*
water	*agua*
I would like it …	*Lo quiero ....*
baked	*al horno*
fried	*frito*
grilled	*a la parrilla*
poached	*hervido / escalfado*
smoked	*ahumado*
steamed	*al vapor*
boiled	*hervido*
roast	*asado*
very rare	*muy crudo*
rare	*poco hecho*
medium	*no muy hecho*
well-done	*muy hecho*

Useful phrases for vegetarians

I am …	*soy ...*
vegetarian	*vegetariano, -a*
lacto-ovo-vegetarian	*ovo-lacto vegetariano, lacto-ovo vegetariano*

lacto-vegetarian	*lacto vegetariano*
vegan	*vegano*
I don't eat …	*no como …*
I don't eat meat, pork or chicken	*no como carne, cerdo o pollo*
I don't eat fish	*no como pescado*
I eat eggs/milk/cheese	*como huevos/leche/queso*
I don't eat eggs/milk/cheese	*no como huevos/leche/queso*
I don't eat suet/lard/dripping	*no como grasas o mantecas*
Do you have anything without meat?	*¿tienen algo (de comer) sin carne?*
Do you have any vegetarian dishes?	*¿tienen comida vegetariana/ platos vegetarianos?*
Is there a vegetarian restaurant near here?	*¿hay un restaurante vegetariano por aquí cerca?*
Is this cheese made with rennet?	*¿lleva cuajo este queso?*
Do you have a rennet-free cheese?	*¿tienen queso sin cuajo?*
Do you serve this dish without meat/eggs/cheese?	*¿se sirve este plato sin carne/ huevos/queso?*
Does this sauce/soup contain beef/chicken/fish/meat stock?	*¿lleva caldo de ternera/pollo/ pescado/carne esta salsa/sopa?*
Does this dish contain gelatine/aspic?	*¿lleva gelatina este plato?*
Does this contain organic ingredients?	*¿contiene ingredientes biológicos?*
Do you use GM foods/MSG?	*¿utilizan alimentos genéticamente modificados / glutamato de sodio?*

Useful phrases for people on special diets etc.

I am diabetic	*soy diabético, -a*
Does this dish contain nuts?	*¿contiene frutos secos este plato?*
I am allergic to …	*tengo alergia a …*
I have a peanut/seafood/wheat/ allergy	*tengo alergia a los frutos secos al pescado/al trigo*
I don't eat wheat/gluten	*no como trigo/gluten*

Drinks

Can I see the wine menu, please?	*¿Me trae la carta de los vinos, por favor?*
I would like a/an	*¿Me pone / quiero …?*
aperitif	*un aperitivo*
another	*otro*
I would like a glass of …	*¿Me pone / quiero …?*
red wine	*vino tinto*
white wine	*vino blanco*
rose wine	*vino rosado*
sparkling wine	*vino espumoso*
still water	*agua mineral sin gas*
sparkling water	*agua mineral con gas*
tap water	*agua del grifo (unusual and best avoided in many countries!)*
With lemon	*con limón*

With ice	*con hielo*
With water	*con agua*
Neat	*solo*
I would like a bottle of....	*¿Me trae una botella de ...?*
this wine	*este vino*
house red	*vino tinto de la casa*
Is this wine ...?	*¿Es este vino ...?*
very dry	*muy seco*
dry	*seco*
sweet	*dulce*
local	*de la región*
This wine is ...	*Este vino ...*
not very good	*no es (muy) bueno*
not very cold	*no está (muy) frío*
corked	*sabe a corcho*
I would like a …	*quiero ...*
fruit juice	*zumo de frutas*
lemonade	*limonada*
non-alcoholic beer	*cerveza sin alcohol*
non-alcoholic wine	*vino sin alcohol*
low-alcohol beer	*cerveza baja en alcohol*
low-alcohol wine	*vino de baja graduación alcohólica*
non-alcoholic beverage	*bebidas sin alcohol*
decaffeinated	*descafeinado*
soft drink	*refresco*

Complaints

This is not what I ordered	*Este plato no es lo que yo he pedido*
I asked for …	*Pedí ...*
Could I change this?	*¿Me puede cambiar ...?*
The meat is …	*Esta carne está ...*
overdone	*demasiado hecha*
underdone	*cruda/ poco hecha*
tough	*dura*
I don't like this	*(Esto) no me gusta*
The food is cold	*La comida está fría*
This is not fresh	*(Esto) no está fresco*
What is taking so long?	*Hace rato que esperamos*
This is not clean	*(Esto) no está limpio*

Paying

Could I have the bill?	*¿Me trae la cuenta, por favor?*
I would like to pay	*¿Puedo pagar?*
Can I charge it to my room?	*¿Me lo puede cargar a mi cuenta?*
We would like to pay separately	*¿Nos puede traer la cuenta por separado?*
There's a mistake in the bill	*La cuenta está equivocada*

What's this amount for?	*¿Qué es esta cantidad?*
Is service included?	*¿Está el servicio incluido?*
Do you accept traveller's cheques?	*¿Aceptan cheques de viaje?*
Can I pay by credit card?	*¿Puedo pagar con tarjeta de crédito?*

Numbers

0	*cero*	15	*quince*
1	*uno*	16	*dieciséis*
2	*dos*	17	*diecisiete*
3	*tres*	18	*dieciocho*
4	*cuatro*	19	*diecinueve*
5	*cinco*	20	*veinte*
6	*seis*	30	*treinta*
7	*siete*	40	*cuarenta*
8	*ocho*	50	*cincuenta*
9	*nueve*	60	*sesenta*
10	*diez*	70	*setenta*
11	*once*	80	*ochenta*
12	*doce*	90	*noventa*
13	*trece*	100	*cien*
14	*catorce*	200 etc.	*doscientos*

Spanish-English

abadejo pollack
   abadejo ahumado smoked haddock
abierto open
abrebotellas bottle opener
absenta absinthe
abulón abalone
acedera sorrel
acedias fried baby sole
aceite oil
   aceite de cacahuete groundnut oil
   aceite de girasol sunflower oil
   aceite de oliva olive oil
   aceite de oliva virgen virgin olive oil
   aceite de palma palm oil
   aceite de pepitas de uva grapeseed oil
   aceite de soja soya bean oil
aceite, en in oil
aceituna olive
   aceitunas negras black olives
   aceitunas rellenas stuffed olives
   aceitunas verdes green olives
acelga chard
ácido acidic, sharp
acompañamiento trimmings
aderezo dressing
adobo marinade
adobo, en marinated
agachadiza snipe
agridulce sweet and sour
agrio(a) sour
agua water
   agua con gas sparkling water, fizzy water
   agua de azahar orange or lemon blossom water
   agua de manantial spring water
   agua de Valencia alcoholic beverage from Valencia *[with cava, orange juice and spirits]*
   agua helada iced water
   agua mineral mineral water, bottled water
   agua mineral con gas fizzy mineral water
   agua mineral sin gas still mineral water
   agua potable drinking water
   agua sin gas still water
aguacate avocado
aguado(a) watery
aguardiente brandy
aguaturma Jerusalem artichoke
agulat rock salmon
ahumado(a) smoked

ahumados surtidos   platter of smoked meats
ahumar   to smoke
ají   chilli pepper
ajiaceite   garlic mayonnaise
ajenjo   absinthe
ajillo, al   in garlic sauce
ajo   garlic
   ajoarriero   hot garlic sauce with tomatoes, red peppers and olive oil
ajoblanco   chilled almond soup
al cuarto de hora   mussel soup garnished with hard-boiled eggs
ala   wing
albacora   swordfish
albahaca   basil
albaricoque   apricot
albariño   white wine *[from Galicia]*
albillos   white grapes
albóndigas   meat balls, faggots
   albóndigas con guisantes   meatballs with peas
   albóndigas con sepia   meatballs with cuttlefish
   albondiguillas   small meatballs in tomato sauce
   albondiguillas a la criolla   small meatballs in tomato and pepper sauce
   served with rice pilaff
alcachofa   artichoke
alcaparra   capers
alcaravea   caraway seeds
alergia   allergy
alérgico, -a   allergic
alfajores   small round cakes
alfóncigo   pistachio nut
alga marina   seaweed
algarroba   carob
aliñado(a)   dressed, seasoned
aliño   dressing, seasoning
aliño de atún   tuna fish salad
aliño de gambas   prawn salad
aliño de pulpo   octopus salad
alioli, ali-oli   aïloli sauce *[garlic and olive oil]*
alitán   spotted dogfish
all i pebre   eels stewed in garlic and pepper
almeja   clam
   almejas al natural   clams au naturel *[in brine]*
   almejas marineras   clams in garlic and olive oil sauce
   almejas palourdes   carpet shell clams
almendra   almond
   almendras garrapiñadas   toffee-almonds
   almendras tostadas   toasted almonds
   almendrado   macaroon, almond buiscuit
almíbar   syrup
almíbar, en   in syrup
almidón   starch
almuerzo   lunch
alubias   haricot beans
   alubias blancas, rojas, verdes   white, red, green beans
amargo(a)   bitter
amasar   to knead
americano   black coffee
amontillado   medium dry sherry

anacardos cashews
ananá pineapple
ancas de rana frog's legs
anchoa anchovy
andaluza, a la Andalusian style *[garnished with peppers, tomatoes and aubergine]*
anditos blood sausage with onion
angélica angelica
angelote angel fish
angola sour milk
anguila eel
   anguila ahumada smoked eel
   angula baby eel
anís aniseed
   anís seco dry aniseed
ansario gosling
antojito *[LA]* snack; tortilla filled with meat, tomatoes and onions
añejo aged
aperitivo aperitif, appetizer *[drink or food]*
apio celery
apio-nabo celeriac
arándano cranberry
arándanos bilberries, blueberries
ardilla squirrel
arenque herring, bloater
   arenque ahumado smoked kipper
   arenque ahumado *[y salado]* kipper
   arenque en escabeche pickled herring
aroma aroma
aromáticas *[LA]* herbal teas
aromatizado, -a flavoured
arrayán myrtle, bog myrtle
arrope honey syrup
arroz rice
   arroz a la alicantina fish stew with pepper, garlic, artichoke hearts and saffron, served on rice
   arroz a banda rice and fish cooked together but served separately
   arroz a la cazuela risotto rice
   arroz a la cubana rice with fried egg and tomato sauce
   arroz blanco plain boiled rice
   arroz con almejas rice with clams
   arroz con conejo rice with rabbit
   arroz largo long-grained rice
   arroz con leche baked rice, rice pudding
   arroz parillada mixed meat and vegetables served with rice
   arroz con pollo rice with chicken
   arroz hervido boiled rice
   arroz integral brown rice
   arroz negro paella with squid or cuttlefish ink
   arroz primavera rice with vegetables
   arroz Valencia rice pilaff with meat, peppers, mushrooms
arrurruz arrowroot
arvejas *[LA]* peas
asado(a) roasted
   asado roast *[noun]*
   asado de codorniz roast quail
asadura offal
asar roast

asar a la parrilla to grill
asopao *[LA]* rice stew with meat or fish
ast, al spit-roasted
autoservicio self-service
azafrán saffron
azúcar sugar
   azucarado(a) sweet, with sugar
atún tunny, tuna
   atún blanco tuna
   atún con tomate tuna fish in tomato sauce
avellana hazelnut, filbert
avena oats
   aveno a medio moler coarse oatmeal
aves poultry, fowl
avestruz ostrich
azafrán saffron
azahar orange, lemon blossom
azúcar sugar
   azúcar de caña cane sugar
   azúcar en polvo icing sugar
   azúcar glas icing sugar
   azúcar granulado granulated sugar
   azúcar moreno brown sugar, demerara
   azúcar terciado demerara sugar
   azúcar en cuadrillo sugar lump
babero bib *[child's]*
bacaladilla blue whiting
bacalao cod
   bacalao seco dried salt cod
   bacalao a la vizcaína salt cod cooked in tomato sauce
   bacalao al ajo arriero salt cod cooked in a garlic, pepper and parsley sauce
   bacalao al pil pil salt cod cooked in garlic and olive oil
   bacalao fresco fresh cod
bacon bacon
   bacon ahumado smoked bacon
bacoreta little tunny
baietón bubble and squeak with bacon
bajo en contenido graso low in fat
baldana blood sausage
   baldana de arroz blood and rice sausage
   baldana de cebolla blood and onion sausage
bambú bamboo
barbacoa barbecue
barbacoa, a la barbecued
barbada brill
barbo catfish
barquillo wafer
   barquillos wafer rolls
barra bar
   barra de pan loaf
batata yam
batido creamed; milk shake *[drink]*
   batido de chocolate chocolate milk shake
   batido de fresa strawberry milk shake
   batido de frutas fruit milk shake
   batido de vainilla vanilla milk shake
bebida drink
   bebida alcohólica alcoholic beverage

bebida incluida drinks included
bebida sin alcohol soft drink
becada woodcock
bejel tub gurnard
berberechos cockles
berenjena aubergine, eggplant
berenjenas rellenas stuffed aubergine
berro watercress
berro, mastuerzo cress
berza cabbage
berza marina sea kale
besugo Spanish bream
bicarbonato baking soda
bien hecho well done
biftec steak, beefsteak [US]
bigarro winkle
bikini toasted cheese and ham sandwich
biológico, -a, organic
biscote French toast
bistec steak [beef]
bistec a la pimienta pepper steak
bistec con guarnición steak with trimmings
bistec tártaro steak tartare
bitter non-alcoholic bitter drink
bizcocho sponge cake
bizcocho borracho rum baba
blanco y negro iced milk, coffee and cinnamon
blando(a) soft
blanquear to blanch
bocas [LA] appetizers
bocadillo sandwich
bocadillo de jamón ham sandwich
bocadillo de queso cheese sandwich
bodega cellar
bogavante lobster
bol bowl
bola de helado ice cream scoop
bolillo bun, roll
bollo bun, bread roll
boloñesa vegetariana vegetarian bolognaise
bomba [LA] meatball with chili sauce
bomba helada baked alaska
bombones chocolates
boniato sweet potato
bonito bonito, skipjack
boquerón anchovy
boquerones en vinagre anchovies in vinegar
boquerones fritos fried anchovies
boquitas [LA] small appetizers
borrajas borage leaves
borregos cumin flavoured buiscuits
bote tin
botella bottle
botella de vino bottle of wine
brandada de bacalao creamed salt cod purée with potatoes seasoned with garlic
brasa, a la charcoal-grilled

braseado(a) grilled
brazo de gitano Swiss roll
breca pandora
brécol broccoli
brettone Brussel sprouts
brioche brioche
brocheta kebab, skewer
brócoli broccoli
brut very dry white wine or cava
buccino whelk
budín inglés fruit cake
buey beef
buey de mar crab
búfalo buffalo
buffet buffet
bulavesa fish soup
bull Catalan blood sausage
bullabesa fish stew
buñuelos fritters, blinis
    buñuelos de bacalao salt cod fritters
    buñuelos de cuaresma fritters filled with cream, chocolate or custard
    buñuelos de plátano banana fritters
    buñuelos de viento plain fritters
Burgos soft mild cheese, often sweetened and used as a dessert
burritos *[LA]* stuffed tortillas
butifarra Catalan pork sausage
    butifarra amb mongetes Catalan pork sausage with haricot beans
    butifarra somalla tender cured pork sausage
caballa mackerel
    caballa en escabeche marinated mackerel
caballeros gents *[toilets]*
cabello de ángel vermicelli *[pasta]*
cabeza head
cabeza de cerdo brawn
cabeza de cordero lamb's head
cabra goat
cabrales strong flavoured semi-hard blue cheese
cabrito kid
    cabrito asado roast kid
cabrón goat
cacahuete peanut
cacao en polvo cocoa
café coffee
    café americano black coffee
    café con hielo iced coffee
    café con leche latte coffee, white coffee
    café cortado expresso with a dash of milk
    café corto small expresso
    café descafeinado decaffeinated coffee
    café exprés espresso / expresso coffee
    café instantáneo instant coffee
    café irlandés Irish coffee
    café largo large black coffee
    café ruso Russian coffe
    café solo black coffee
    café vienés coffee with whipped cream
cafeína caffeine
cafetera coffee pot

caja till
calabacín courgette, zucchini *[US]*
   calabacines rellenos stuffed courgettes
calabaza pumpkin
calamar squid
   calamares a la plancha grilled squid
   calamares a la romana squid rings deep-fried in batter
   calamares en su tinta squid in its own ink
   calamares fritos fried squid
   calamares rellenos stuffed squid
caldeirada stewed fish and potatoes, bouillabaisse
caldereta stew, thick fish stew
   caldereta a la pastora, de pastor lamb stew
   caldereta asturiana fish stewed with onions, pepper and spices
   caldereta de langosta lobster stew
   caldereta de pato con patatas duck stew with potatoes
   caldereta gallega vegetable stew
caldero cauldron
caldillo de congrio *[LA]* fish soup from Chile
caldo broth, stock
   caldo a la taza cup of clear soup
   caldo con yema meat broth with egg yolk
   caldo de carne beef tea, meat stock
   caldo de gallina chicken broth
   caldo de perro gaditano white fish stew with Seville orange juice
   caldo de pescado fish broth
   caldo de pollo clear soup
   caldo de verduras vegetable stock
   caldo gallego soup stew with beans, vegetables and meat
caldoso(a) watery, thin
calentar heat up
caliente hot *[not cold]*
callampa *[LA]* *[type of]* mushroom
callos stewed tripe
calostro beestings
calvados calvados
camarera waitress
camarero waiter
camarón shrimp
camote *[LA]* sweet potato
canapés canapés
candelabro, candelero candlestick
canela cinnamon
canelones cannelloni
cangrejo de mar crab
   cangrejo aliñado dressed crab
   cangrejo de rio freshwater crayfish
cantarela chanterelle mushroom
caña glass of beer *[Sp]*; alcoholic beverage made of sugar cane *[LA]*
cañas rellenas custard rolls
canela cinnamon
canelones minced meat
cap i pota stewed calf's head and foot
capón capon
caqui kaki
carabinero large shrimp
caracol, caracoles snail
   caracol de mar whelk, winkle

caracolillos   small snails
carajillo   coffee with brandy *[or other liqueur]*
caramelo   caramel, candy *[US]*, sweet
carbohidrato   carbohydrate
carboncillo   charcoal
carbón   charcoal
carbonada *[LA]*   meat and rice stew with fruits
carbonara   carbonara
cardamomo   cardamom
careta de cerdo   pig's cheeks
carne ahumada   smoked meat
carne   meat
   carne a la castellana   meat served with tomatoes, potato croquettes and
   onion rings
   carne asada   roast beef
   carne asada a la parilla   boiled meat
   carne atada   collared beef
   carne de caballo   horse meat
   carne de cerdo   pork
   carne de cerdo asada   roast pork
   carne de cordero   lamb
   carne de membrillo   quince jelly paste, usually eaten with cheese
   carne de vaca   beef
   carne de venado   venison
   carne en conserva   corned beef
   carne estofada   pot roast
   carne picada/o   minced meat, ground beef
   carnero   mutton
carnicería   butcher's shop
carpa   carp
carquinyolis   dry almond biscuits
carta   menu
   carta de los vinos   wine list
casados   meat cooked with rice, beans and vegetables
cáscara   zest, peel, skin
   cáscara confitada *[cítricos]*   candied peel
   cáscara de limón   lemon zest
   cáscara rallada   grated peel
casero(a)   homemade
castaña   chestnut *[sweet]*
   castaña de agua   water chestnut
cava   champagne
caviar   caviar
cayena   cayenne
caza   game
cazuela   casserole
   cazuela de pescado   fish casserole
cebada   barley
cebiche *[LA]*   marinated fish Mexican style *[with lemon and onions]*
cebolla   onion
   cebolleta   spring onion
   cebollitas   small onions
   cebollinos   chives
cecina   cured meat; pork sausage *[LA]*
cena   supper, dinner
cenicero   ashtray
centeno   rye
centollo, centolla   crab

cerdo pork, pig
cereales cereal *[breakfast]*
cerebro brains
cereza cherry
cerillas matches
cerrado closed
cervecería bar, pub
cerveza ale, beer, lager
    cerveza a presión draught beer
    cerveza con limonada lager shandy
    cerveza de barril draught beer
    cerveza helada iced cold beer
    cerveza negra stout
    cerveza sin alcohol alcohol-free beer
cesta de frutas fruit basket; fruit selection
ceviche *[LA]* marinated raw fish
chabacano *[LA]* apricot
chacinas cold meats, salami, sausages
chacoli white wine *[from Basque region]*
chalote(a) shallot, scallion *[US]*
chalupa *[LA]* deep-fried stuffed tortilla
champaña champagne
champanera wine cooler
champiñón button mushrooms
chanfaina ratatouille, sauce with stewed tomatoes, peppers, onions and
    aubergine or courgette
chanquetes whitebait
chantilly chantilly
chato glass of red wine
chaucha de vainilla vanilla pod/bean
chayote *[LA]* mirliton
chef chef
chicha de manzana apple brandy
chicharos *[LA]* peas *or* chickpeas
chicharra *or* **chicharrón** *[crispy]* crackling
chifa *[LA]* Chinese food
chile chilli, red chilli
    chile con carne *[LA]* chilli-con-carne
    chile en polvo chilli powder
    chile sin carne chilli without meat
    chiles rellenos *[LA]* stuffed peppers
    chilindrón red pepper and tomato sauce with garlic and onions and olives
    chile vegetariano vegetable chili
chimichanga *[LA]* deep fried tortilla filled with spicy meat, beans and chili
chinchón type of aniseed
chipirones fried baby squid
chirimoya custard apple
chiringuito snack bar
chirivía parsnip
chirlas clams
chirmol *[LA]* grilled steak in a tomato and onion sauce
chistorra spicy sausage
chivo *[LA]* kid
chocha woodcock
choco cuttlefish
chocolate chocolate
    chocolate a la taza thick chocolate sauce

chocolate con leche milk chocolate
chocolate con churros thick hot chocolate with churros
chocolatina small chocolate bar
chongos *[LA]* fried bread topped with cheese and sweet syrup
chorizo chorizo *[spicy sausage]*
chucho doughnut filled with custard
chucrut sauerkraut
chufa tiger nut
chuleta chop, cutlet
chuleta de cerdo pork chop
chuleta de cordero lamb chop
chuletas de venado venison cutlets
chuletón rib steak
chupachup lollipop
chupe de mariscos *[LA]* seafood stew
churrasco charcoal grilled meat, barbecued steak
churros fried dough in strips covered in sugar
ciervo deer, venison
cigala langoustine, Dublin bay prawn
ciruela plum
ciruela claudia greengage plum
ciruela pasa prune
cítrico citrus
civet civet
clara shandy
clara de huevo egg white
clarete claret
clavo de olor clove
clementina clementine
coca sweet pastry *[covered in sugar and pine nuts or candied fruits]*
coca mallorquina savoury pastry *[similar to pizza]*
cocada *[LA]* cooked coconut with sugar, egg yolks and sherry
cochinillo suckling pig
cocido(a) cooked
cocido madrileño stewed chickpeas with meat and vegetables
cocina casera home cooking
cocina vegetariana vegetarian cooking
cocinero(a) cook, chef
coco coconut
coco rallado desiccated coconut
cocos fríos *[LA]* chilled coconuts
cóctel de gambas shrimp cocktail
cóctel de mariscos seafood cocktail
codillos pasta shapes *[macaroni]*
codornices rellenas stuffed quails
codorniz quail
cogollo heart *[of lettuce]*
col cabbage
col china Chinese cabbage
col rellena stuffed cabbage
col rizada kale
cola de toro ox tail
coles, colecitas de Bruselas brussels sprouts
coliflor cauliflower
colinabo turnip
colmenilla wild mushroom *[morel]*
comedor dining room

comida lunch, meal
comida frita fried food
comino cumin *[seed]*
complemento supplement
compota jam, stewed fruit
  compota de fruta stewed fruit
con aire acondicionado air-conditioned
con almendras with almonds
con crema creamy
con gas sparkling, fizzy
con helado with ice cream
con hielo on the rocks, with ice
con hueso on the bone
con leche with milk
con mantequilla with butter
con sal salted
con salsa picante devilled
coñac brandy
concha scallop
condimentado(a) seasoned
condimento condiment, seasoning
conejo rabbit
  conejo al rón rabbit with rum
  conejo de bosque wild rabbit
  conejo deshuesado en escabeche marinated filletted rabbit
confitado(a) candied
confitura jam
  confitura de naranja marmalade
  confitura de membrillo quince preserve
congelado(a) frozen
congrio conger eel
conserva jam, tinned food
conserva, en tinned, canned *[US]*
conservas preserves
consomé consommé, clear soup
  consomé frío cold consommé
consumición drink *[in a bar]*
consumición mínima minimum charge
coñac brandy
copa wine glass
copa de helado ice cream sundae
copos flakes
coquina wedge shell clam
corazón heart
cordero lamb, mutton
  cordero lechal baby lamb
coriandro coriander
cortado coffee *[with milk]*
cortado en filetes filleted
cortado(a) sliced, chopped
cortar carve, cut
corteza rind *[cheese]*
  corteza *[de cerdo asado]* pork crackling
corvina *[LA]* sea bass
cosecha vintage
costilla de cerdo spare rib
costillar rack

costillas ribs
costra crust
crema custard, cream
crema, a la with cream or cream sauce
crema catalana caramelized custard cream
crema de espárragos cream of asparagus soup
crema de cacao chocolate liquor
crema de champiñones cream of mushroom soup
crema de coco coconut cream
crema de espárragos cream of asparagus soup
crema de espinacas creamed spinach
crema de guisantes green pea soup
crema de leche single cream
crema de marisco seafood chowder
crema de pollo cream of chicken soup
crema de tomate cream of tomato soup
crema de zanahoria cream of carrot soup
crema quemada caramelized custard cream
cremat coffee with rum and brandy
cremoso(a) creamy
crepería pancake restaurant
crep, crepe pancake
criadillas testicles
criolla creole
criolla, a la with tomatoes, green peppers and spices
crocant, crocante brittle
croissant de chocolate chocolate croissant
croqueta rissole
    croquetas de pescado fish cake
    croquetas de pollo chicken croquettes
crudo(a) raw, underdone, rare
crutón croutons
cuajada curd cheese
cuajo rennet
cuba libre rum and coke
cubertería cutlery
cubierto cover charge
cubiertos cutlery
cubito de hielo ice cube
cubitos, en diced *[cubed]*
cubo de hielo bucket of ice
cuchara spoon
cuchara de servir tablespoon
cuchara sopera soup spoon
cucharada spoonful
cucharadita, cucharilla tea spoon
cucharilla de café coffee spoon
cucharita tea spoon
cuchillo knife
    cuchillo para cortar el pan bread knife
cucurucho cornet *[ice cream]*
cuenco bowl
cuenta account, bill, *[US]* check
cuitlacoche *[LA]* type of mushroom
culantro coriander
culata de contra knuckle, shin
curado cured

curanto *[LA]*   meat with vegetables and fish
cúrcuma   turmeric
curí, cuy *[LA]*   grilled guinea pig
curry   curry
cusuco *[LA]*   armadillo
dados, en   diced *[cubed]*
damasco *[LA]*   apricot
dátil   date
dátiles de mar   date mussels
de crianza   aged
de granja   free-range
de la casa   of the house
de lata   tinned, canned *[US]*
de payés   from a farm
del día   of the day
del país   local
del tiempo   in season
delicias de mar   seafood morsels
delicioso(a)   delicious
dentón al horno   baked denté
desayuno   breakfast
descafeinado(a)   decaffeinated/decaf, caffeine-free
descongelar   defrost
descremado(a)   fat-free
deshuesado(a)   boned *[meat]*; stoned *[fruit]*
deshuesar   debone/fillet *[verb]*
desnatado(a)   skimmed
despojos   offal
desportillado(a)   chipped *[glass, plate]*
destornillador   vodka and orange
diente de ajo   clove of garlic
dieta   diet
dieta de bajo contenido graso   low-fat
discreción del cliente, a la   discretionary
dónut   doughnut
dorada   bream
dorado(a)   browned
dorar   to brown
   dorar a fuego vivo   sear
dulce   sweet, candy *[US]*
   dulces   sweets
dura *[carne]*   tough *[meat]*
durazno *[LA]*   peach
duro   stale, hard
ejotes *[LA]*   green beans
elote *[LA]*   sweetcorn
embuchado   in a sausage
embutidos   cold meat, sausage
empanada   turnover
   empanada de carne y verduras   meat and vegetable pasty
   empanada gallega   fish turnover *[with raisins, olives, onions, peppers and tomatoes]*
   empanadilla   pasty, turnover
empanado   breaded
emparedado   sandwich
empedrat   salad with salt cod or tuna and beans
emperador   swordfish

encebollado   with onions
enchiladas *[LA]*   tortillas filled with meat or cheese in a tomato and chilli
   sauce
encurtidos   pickle
endibia, endivia   chicory
endrina   sloe
endulzante   sweetener
eneldo   dill
enlatado   tinned, canned *[US]*
ensaimada   spiral-shaped bun *[often filled with custard]*
ensalada   salad
   ensalada catalana   mixed salad with cold meats and hard boiled egg
   ensalada de atún   tuna salad
   ensalada de berros   watercress salad
   ensalada de escarola   chicory salad
   ensalada de espárragos   asparagus salad
   ensalada de pollo   chicken salad
   ensalada de tomate   tomato salad
   ensalada mixta   mixed salad
   ensalada templada   warm salad
   ensalada tropical   tropical salad
   ensalada verde   green salad
   ensaladilla rusa   Russian salad *[mixed vegetable and potato salad]*
ensuciar   to soil
entero(a)   whole
entradas   starters
entrante   entrée
entrecot   prime rib, strip steak
entremés   hors d'oeuvre
   entremeses selectos   select hors d'oeuvre
   entremeses variados   assorted hors d'oeuvre
erizo de mar   sea urchin
escabeche   marinated, pickled
escabechado(a)   marinated, pickled
escaldar   blanch
escalfado(a)   poached
escalfar   to poach
escalivada   baked vegetables *[aubergines, peppers, onions, potatoes]*
escalivado   baked, charcoal-grilled
escalopa de ternera   veal escalope
escalope   escalope
   escalopín   fillet, escalope
   escalopines de rape   monkfish escalopes
escarola   endive, frisée *[salad]*
escorpena   scorpion fish
escudella   Catalan meat and vegetable soup
escudella i carn d'olla   broth with pasta followed by the boiled meat and
   vegetables used to make the broth
escupiña   cockle
esencia   essence
   esencia de vainilla   vanilla essence
espaguetis   spaghetti
espalda   shoulder, rack
espárrago   asparagus
espárragos trigueros   wild asparagus
especia   spice
especialidad de la casa   chef's speciality

espinaca spinach
  espinacas a la andaluza spniach with pine nuts and raisins
  espinacas a la catalana spinach with pine nuts, chopped ham and garlic
espinas fish bones
espolvorear sift
esqueixada de bacalao shredded salt cod salad
establecimiento climatizado air-conditioned
estofado stew, hotpot
  estofado de ternera stewed steak
  estofado de ternera a la stroganoff beef stroganoff
estofar braise
estragón taragon, tarragon
esturión sturgeon
fabada asturiana stewed broad beans with pork
faisán pheasant
fajitas *[LA]* sizzling grilled strips of meat or fish served with tortillas
falda saddle
  falda de ternera brisket
farro meat and vegetable soup stew
fécula starch
fiambres cold meats
fideos noodles
  fideos gordos thick spaghetti
fideuá, fideuada paella made with noodles
filete rump steak, tenderloin
  filete de ternera fillet steak
  filete de pescado fish fillet
  filete de salmón salmon steak
finas hierbas herbs
finas hierbas, a las with mixed herbs
fino dry sherry
flamear, flambear flambé
flameado, flambeado flambéed
flamenca, a la with sausage, tomatoes and vegetables *[peppers, onions, peas]*
flan crème caramel, baked custard
  flan con nata crème caramel with cream
flanera individual ramekin *[small container]*
foie gras duck paté
fondant fondant
fondue fondue
fósforos matches
fragancia aroma
frambuesa raspberry
frambuesas con nata raspberries and cream
freir fry
frejoles beans
fresa strawberry
fresa de bosque wild strawberry
fresas con nata strawberries and cream
fresones strawberries
fresco(a) fresh, chilled
fricandó pot roast, grenadine, meat stew with wild mushrooms
frijol flageolet bean, kidney bean, red bean
  frijole negro black bean
frío(a) cold, chilled
fritada fried dish
fritada aragonesa ratatouille

monosódico
fritada de pescado y marisco fried fish and seafood platter
fritura, comida frita fried food
fritura de pescado mixed fried fish
fritura de sangre fried blood
frito(a) fried, deep-fried
fruta fruit
fruta confitada crystallised fruit
fruta de Aragón chocolate coated crystallised fruit
fruta del tiempo fruit in season
fruta en almíbar fruit in syrup
fruta escarchada candied fruit
fruta tropical tropical fruits
frutas del mar shellfish, crustaceans, seafood etc.
frutos secos dried fruits and nuts
fuente platter
fuerte very spicy
fuet dry cured pork sausage
fundido fondue
gachas porridge
galleta biscuit, *[US]* cookies
galletas de almendra almond biscuits
gallina boiling fowl
gallina en pepitoria chicken stew with almonds and/or peppers
gallo de mar lemon sole *[fish]*
gallo pinto *[LA]* beans and rice
gallos *[LA]* tortillas filled with meat and sauce
galupe *[LA]* red mullet
gamba prawn, king prawn, shrimp
gambas al ajillo prawns in a gralic sauce
gambas a la plancha grilled prawns
gambas en gabardina deep-fried prawns in batter
gamo fallow-deer
gandinga *[LA]* spicy kidney, heart and liver
ganso goose
gañiles de atún gills of tuna
garbanzo chickpea
garnacha dessert wine
garobo *[LA]* iguana
garrafa carafe
gaseosa lemonade
gaseoso(a) fizzy
gazpacho gazpacho *[cold tomato soup]*
gazpacho andaluz tomato soup *[with peppers, onions, garlic, cucumber,*
  bread and vinegar served chilled]
gazpacho blanco white gazpacho with almonds
gazpacho malagueño white gazpacho with grapes
gazpacho manchego soup stew with rabbit, vegetables and bread dumplings
gelatina gelatine, aspic
gelatina, en jellied
genéticamente modificado, -a genetically modified *[GM]*
germen de trigo wheatgerm
ginebra gin
girasol sunflower
glacé glazed
glaseado icing
glaseado(a) glacé glazed
glutamato de sodio, glutamato monosódico monosodium glutamate *[MSG]*

golosinas sweets, candy *[US]*
gorditas *[LA]* fried small thick tortillas filled with meat, cheese and vegetables in a chili sauce
gracias thank you
gran reserva vintage wine
granada pomegranate
   granada con moscatel pomegranates soaked in muscatel wine
granizado sorbet, granita
   granizado de café iced coffee drink
   granizado de limón iced lemon drink
granja farm; tea-shop
grano grain, wheat, corn
grasa fat
   grasa de carne asada dripping
gratén, gratinado(a) au gratin *[US]*
gratificación gratuity
grelos turnip tops
grillado *[LA]* boneless
grosella currant
grosella blanca o verde gooseberry
grosella colorada redcurrant
grosella negra blackcurrant
guacamole *[LA]* guacamole *[avocado purée mixed with finely chopped chili and tomatoes]*
guajolote *[LA]* turkey
guanabana *[LA]* custard apple
guarapo *[LA]* spirit
guardarropa cloakroom
guarnición trimmings
guasacaca *[LA]* tomato and avocado relish
guayaba *[LA]* guava
guayoyo *[LA]* long black coffee
guinda glacé cherry
guindilla red chilli
guineo *[LA]* banana
guisado casserole, stew
guisado de carne stew
guisado de cordero lamb stew
guisante pea
guisantes rehogados stewed peas
guiso hotpot
gusto, al to taste
haba bean, broad bean
haba de soja soja bean
habanero *[LA]* very hot chilli pepper
habichuela kidney beans
halibut halibut, black halibut
hamburguesa hamburger
   hamburguesa vegetariana vegetarian burger
harina flour
hecho(a) done
heladería ice cream parlor
helado ice cream
   helado de cucurucho ice cream cone
   helado de fresa, vainilla y chocolate Neapolitan ice-cream
   helado de vainilla vanilla ice cream
   helado en molde bombe

hervido(a) boiled
hervir boil
   hervir a fuego lento simmer
hidrato de carbono carbohydrate
hielo ice
hierbabuena garden mint
hierbaluisa lemon verbena
hierbas finas herbs
hígado liver
   higaditos de pollo chicken livers
higo fig
hinojo fennel
hipogloso halibut
hojaldre puff pastry
hojas de parra vine leaves
hongos wild mushrooms
horchata de almendra cold drink made from ground almonds
horchata de chufa cold drink made from ground tiger nuts
horno oven
horno, al baked
hortaliza vegetables
huachinango *[LA]* red snapper
hueso bone
huevas roe, hard roe
huevera egg cup
huevo egg
   huevo cocido boiled egg
   huevo duro hard boiled egg
   huevo escalfado poached egg
   huevo frito fried egg
   huevo pasado por agua soft boiled egg
   huevo podrido bad egg
   huevos a la flamenca eggs with sausage, tomatoes and vegetables
   huevos a la mallorquina eggs with sobrasada sausage
   huevos a la riojana eggs with chorizo
   huevos al nido eggs in a nest
   huevos al plato shirred eggs
   huevos con jamón eggs with ham
   huevos de codorniz quail's eggs
   huevos de granja farm eggs
   huevos pochés poached eggs
   huevos rancheros *[LA]* fried eggs with a hot tomato sauce
   huevos rellenos stuffed eggs
   huevos revueltos scrambled eggs
   huevos revueltos con jamón scrambled eggs with ham
incluido included
   no incluido not included
infusión herbal tea
ingredientes ingredients
intolerancia a la lactosa lactose intolerance
Irlandés Irish coffee
IVA VAT
jabalí *[wild]* boar
jaiba *[LA]* crab
jalapeño *[LA]* hot green pepper
jalea jam, jelly *[US]*
jamón ham
jamón de jabugo Jabugo cured ham

jamón de pato   duck ham
jamón de York   cured ham, York ham
jamón dulce   cold boiled ham
jamón serrano   dry-cured ham
japuta   pomfret
jarabe   syrup
   jarabe de arce   maple syrup
jardinera, a la   with vegetables
jarra   jug
jarra de agua   jug of water
jarrete   shank
jarrete de cordero   shank of lamb
jengibre   ginger
jerez   sherry
jerez, al   in sherry
jeta   pig's cheek
jibia   cuttlefish
jitomate *[LA]*   tomato
jocoque   sour cream
judía   bean
judía verde   French bean, green bean, string bean
judías blancas   haricot beans
   judías blancas en salsa ketchup   baked beans
judías pintas   pinto beans
judías verdes   green beans
jugo   juice; gravy
jugo, en su   in its own juice
jugo de fruta   fruit juice
jugo de naranja   orange juice
jugo de tomate   tomato juice
jugoso(a)   juicy
juliana   julienne, shredded mixed vegetables or fruits
julivert   parsley
junípero   juniper
ketchup   ketchup
kiwi   kiwi fruit
lacón   cured shoulder of pork
lacón con grelos   cured shoulder of ham with turnip tops
lactosa   lactose
langosta   lobster, crawfish, spiny lobster
langostino   Dublin bay prawns
lanzones   sand eels
lasaña   lasagne
   lasaña vegetariana   vegetarian lasagne
lata   tin
laurel   bay leaf
lavabo   lavatory
lavanda   lavender
lecha   soft roe
lechal   baby lamb
lechaza   soft roe
leche   milk
   leche condensada   condensed milk
   leche de cabra   goat's milk
   leche de oveja   ewe's milk
   leche de vaca   cow's milk
   leche de almendras   almond milk

leche de coco coconut milk
leche desnata, descremada skimmed milk
leche entera full-cream milk
leche fría cold milk
leche merengada milk with lemon, sugar and cinamon
leche natural fresh milk
leche quemada [LA] sweet milk with vanilla and sugar
leche de soja soya milk
leche semidescremada semi-skimmed milk
leche frita fried custard squares
lechecillas sweetbreads
lechón suckling pig
lechona [LA] suckling pig
lechosa [LA] papaya
lechuga lettuce
legumbres legumes, pulses
lengua tongue
lengua de ternera calf's tongue
lengua de ternera fría cold calf's tongue
lengua estofada stewed tongue
lenguado sole, Dover sole, lemon sole
lenteja lentil
lentejas [verdes] **de Puy** Puy lentils
lentejas con chorizo lentils with chorizo
lentejas estofadas stewed lentils
levadura yeast
libritos de lomo pork fillet stuffed with cheese and ham and fried in breadcrumbs
licor liqueur
licuado [LA] milk shake, fruit juice
liebre hare
lima lime
limón lemon, citron
limonada lemonade
limoncillo lemongrass
limpio clean
lionesas de nata profiteroles
lista de precios price list
lista de vinos wine list
llapingachos [LA] mashed potatoes with cheese
llobarro bass, rockfish, sea bass
locrio de cerdo [LA] pork and rice
locro [LA] potato soup with cheese and avocados, corn and meat stew
lombarda red cabbage
lomo tenderloin, fillet
lomo adobado marinated pork loin
lomo curado cured pork sausage
lomo de cerdo mechado spiked pork loin
lomo de conejo saddle of rabbit
lomo embuchado cured loin of pork
lomo relleno stuffed loin of pork
lomo salteado [LA] stir-fried steak
loncha slice
loncha de jamón slice of ham
longaniza Catalan spicy sausage
lubina bass, rockfish, sea bass
lubina a la sal sea bass covered in salt and baked

macarrones macaroni
macarrones con salsa de queso macaroni cheese
macarrón macaroon
macedonia de frutas fruit salad, fruit cocktail
macerado soaked *[fruit]*; marinated *[meat]*; crushed *[garlic]*
macrobiótico, -a macrobiotic
madalena cup cake, muffin *[US]*
madrileña, a la with tomato, pepper, sausage and paprika
maduro(a) ripe
magret de pato duck preserved in its own fat
magro(a) lean, low in fat
mahonesa, mayonesa mayonnaise
maizena cornflour
maíz corn, sweetcorn, maize
málaga sweet dessert wine from Málaga
malo(a) bad
malta malt
malvasia sweet dessert wine
mandarina mandarin
mandioca *[LA]* cassava
mandongo blood sausage with fennel
mango mango
maní *[LA]* peanut
manitas de cerdo pig's trotters
manitas de cordero lamb's trotters
manteca lard
   manteca de cerdo pork lard
manteca de cacao cocoa butter
mantecado powdery biscuit made with lard; type of ice cream
mantel tablecloth
mantequilla butter
mantequilla derretida melted butter
mantequilla dorada brown butter
matequilla negra black butter
mantequilla quemada black butter
mantequilla sin sal unsalted butter
manzana apple
manzana al horno baked apple
manzanilla camomile *[herb]*; manzanilla *[dry sherry]*
mar i muntanya seafood and meat dish
maracuya *[LA]* passion fruit
margarina margarine
margarita tequila with lemon or lime juice; carpet shell clam
marinar to marinate
marinera, a la fisherman style *[usually with mussels]*
mariscada mixed grill of shellfish
marisco; mariscos shellfish; seafood
marmitako tuna casserole
marquesa de chocolate chocolate mousse
marrón *[LA]* strong coffee
masa pastry, dough
   masa para empanadas shortcrust pastry
   masa para pasteles choux pastry
mayonesa mayonnaise
mazapán marzipan
mazorca de maíz corn on the cob
mechado stuffed

medallón medallion
media half
   media botella half bottle
media luna moon-shaped candied turnover
media noche *[LA]* ham and cheese sandwich
media ración half portion
medialuna *[LA]* croissant
mediana half pint of beer
medio asado uncooked
mejillón mussel
   mejillones al vapor steamed mussels
   mejillones de roca rock mussels
mejorana marjoram
mel i mato cottage cheese and honey
melaza treacle
melindres sponge fingers
melocotón peach
   melocotón en almíbar peaches in syrup
melón melon
   melón al oporto melon with port
   melón con jamón melon and ham
membrillo quince
mendo limon lemon sole
menestra de verduras mixed vegetables
menta mint, peppermint
   menta poleo mint tea
menú menu
   menú de la casa house menu, fixed price menu
   menú del día menu of the day, set menu
   menú para niños children's menu
menudillos giblets
menudos offal
mercado market
merengue meringue
merengada *[LA]* fruit milk shake
merienda early evening snack
merluza hake
merluza a la plancha grilled hake
merluza a la romana hake deep-fried in batter
mermelada jam
   mermelada de fresa strawberry jam
   mermelada de naranja marmalade
mero grouper
   mero al horno baked grouper
mesa table
   mesa reservada reserved
mezcal *[LA]* spirit similar to grappa
mezclar blend
michelada *[LA]* beer with lime juice and ice
miel honey
   miel de maple maple syrup
mielga shark
migas breadcrumbs fried in garlic
milanesa, a la fried in breadcrumbs
milhojas puff pastry
minestrone vegetable soup
minuta *[LA]* menu

minutas *[LA]*   iced drink flavoured with honey
mistela *[LA]*   hot punch
moca   mocha
mojama   tuna
mojar   dip
mojete *[LA]*   salt cod salad with peppers and onions
mojito   rum, mint and crushed ice
mojo   sauce *[garlic, oil and hot peppers]*
   mojo colorado   mojo with paprika
   mojo picón   mojo with hot chilli peppers
   mojo verde   green mojo sauce
mole   hot Mexican sauce
moler   grind
molido(a)   ground
moll de roca   red mullet
mollejas   sweetbreads
molusco   mollusc
mondadientes   toothpick
mondado   peeled
mondongo *[LA]*   stewed tripe
montadito   open sandwich
mora   blackberry, mulberry
morcilla   blood sausage similar to black pudding
morcón   spiced blood sausage
morilla   morels
moros y cristianos   black beans and rice
morralla   whitebait, small fry
morro   pig snout *[stewed]*
mortadela   type of salami
moscatel   sweet dessert wine
mostaza   mustard
mosto   grape juice
mousse   mousse
   mousse de chocolate   chocolate mousse
musaca   moussaka
muselina   mousseline
musli, muesli   muesli
muslos *[de pollo o pavo]*   drumsticks
musola   dog fish
muy condimentado   spicy
muy hecho(a)   overdone, well done
muy seco   very dry *[wine]*
nabo   turnip
   nabo sueco   swede
nacatamales *[LA]*   tortillas filled with pork, corn and a sauce wrapped in banana leaves
nachos *[LA]*   tortilla chips with various toppings such as beans, grated cheese and sour cream
naranja   orange
   naranjada   orange juice
nata   cream
   nata batida, montada   whipped cream
   nata para montar   double cream
natillas   custard sauce
natural   natural, fresh, raw
natural, a la   plain
navajas   razor clams

navarra, a la   stuffed with ham
nécoras   small crabs
nectarina   nectarine
negritas   chocolate mousse with whipped cream
negrito *[LA]*   strong black coffee
nieve *[LA]*   sorbet
níscalo   wild mushroom
nixtamal *[LA]*   corn meal dough
noquis   gnocchi
nube   coffee with a drop of milk
nueces con miel   walnuts in honey
nuez   nut
  nuez de nogal   walnut
  nuez del Brasil   brazil nut
  nuez moscada   nutmeg
nyora   dry pepper
oblea   wafer
oca   goose
oca con peras   duck with pears
oliva   olive
olla   pot
olla gitana   vegetable stew
olla podrida   soup-stew
oloroso   full-bodied dark sherry
oporto   port
orégano   oregano
orejas   ears
orejones   dried apricots
orelletes   fried pastry coated with sugar
orgánico, -a   organic
ortiga   nettle
oruga   rocket
orujo   eau-de-vie
ostión   scallop
ostra   oyster
oveja   ewe
pacana   pecan nut
pacharán   sloe gin
pacumutu *[LA]*   beef kebab
paella, a la   pan-fried
paella   paella *[Valencian dish with rice and fish or meat or both]*
  paella de campiña   paella with chicken, bacon, ham and sausage
  paella marinera   seafood paella
  paella mixta   mixed paella *[fish and meat]*
  paella valenciana   paella *[with rabbit and chicken]*
pagel   pandora
paletilla   shoulder
palillo   toothpick
palillo chino   chopsticks
palmitos   palm hearts
palo   éclair
  palo de nata   chocolate eclair
paloma   pigeon
  paloma torcaz   wood pigeon
palomitas de maíz   popcorn
pámpano   vine leaf
pan   bread

pan blanco   white bread
pan con tomate   bread with tomato *[dressed with olive oil and salt]*
pan de almendras   almond loaf
pan de barra   French stick, crusty white bread loaf
pan de hígado   liver loaf
pan de higos   dried fig cake
pan de jenjibre   gingerbread
pan de leche   breakfast bun
pan de molde   bread loaf *[baked in square tin]*
pan de payés   farmhouse loaf
pan de trigo integral   granary loaf
pan de Viena   bread roll
pan griego *[sin levadura]*   pitta bread
pan integral   brown bread, wholemeal bread
pan rallado   breadcrumbs
pan tostado   toast
pana de coco *[LA]*   coconut bread
panecillo integral   brown roll
panaché de fiambres   assorted cold cuts
panadería   bakery
panal de miel   honeycomb
panceta   bacon, streaky bacon
panceta ahumada   smoked bacon
panecillo   bread roll
panellets   traditional sweets eaten on All Saints Day *[made with almonds, mashed potatoes, sugar and egg]*
papa *[LA]*   potato
papas arrugadas   boiled small new potatoes in their jackets served with mojo
papas *[fritas]*   chips; crisps
papaya   papaya
pargo   sea bream
parmesana, a la   with parmesan cheese
parmesano   parmesan *[cheese]*
parrilla   grill
parrilla, a la   grilled, charcoal-grilled
parrilla, brasa   charcoal grilled
parrillada de carne   mixed grill *[meat]*
parrillada de pescado y marisco   mixed grilled fish and seafood platter
parrillada mixta   mixed grill
pasa   raisin
pasa de Corinto   currant
pasado(a)   stale, off
pasado por agua   boiled
pasar por el tamiz   sift
pasar por la licuadora   blend
pasta   dough *or* pastry
pasta alimenticia   pasta
pasta de almendras   almond paste
pasta de anchoas   anchovy butter
pasta fresca   fresh pasta
pasta italiana   spaghetti
pasta para rebozar   batter
pastas secas   biscuits, *[US]* cookies
pastel   cake, gateau, pie
pastel de carne   meat loaf
pastel de chocolate   chocolate cake
pastel de chocolate, nata y cerezas al kirsch   Black Forest gateau

pastel de fresa strawberry pie
pastel de hojaldre puff pastry
pastel de manzana apple tart
pastel de nata cream cake
pastel de pescado fish mousse
pastel de tortillas omelette pie
pastel de verduras vegetable pie
pastelería patisserie
pasticho *[LA]* type of lasagna
pastilla tablet
patata potato
patata al horno baked potato, roast potato
patata asada baked potato, roast potato
patatas a lo pobre pan-fried potatoes with garlic and parsley
patatas bravas pan-fried spicy potatoes
patatas estofadas stewed potatoes
patatas fritas fried potoatoes, chips, crisps
patatas gratinadas scalloped potatoes *[US]*
patatas hervidas boiled potatoes
patatas paja matchstick potatoes
patatas rellenas stuffed potatoes
patatas viudas potatoes roasted in meat fat
paté pâté
patés artesanos homemade pâté
patito duckling
pato duck
pato a la naranja duck with oranges
pato con peras duck with pears
pato confitado duck preserve
pato silvestre wild duck
pavo turkey
pavo al horno roast turkey
pavo asado roast turkey
pavo relleno stuffed turkey
payés farmhouse
pechuga breast
pechuga de pollo chicken breast, breast of chicken
pechuga de pollo rebozada chicken breast in batter
pelado(a) peeled
pelar peel *[verb]*
pelota large meatball *[sausage shaped]*
pepinillo gherkin
pepino cucumber
pepitas seeds
pepito steak sandwich
pepitoria stew sauce
pera pear
percebe goose barnacle
perdiz partridge
perejil parsley
pernil ham
perrito caliente hot dog
pescadería fish shop
pescadilla whiting
pescadito butterfish
pescadito frito fried small fish, whitebait, small fry
pescado fish
pescado ahumado smoked fish

pescado al horno baked fish
pescado de agua dulce freshwater fish
pescado frito fried fish
pestiño honey-coated anise flavoured pastry
pesto pesto
pez espada swordfish
picada paste made of garlic, parsley, olive oil and dried toasted nuts
picadillo minced meat
picado(a) ground
picante hot, spicy
picantón small chicken
picatoste croutons
pichón pigeon, squab
picoso *[LA]* hot, spicy
piel peel, skin
pierna haunch, leg of meat
pierna de cordero al horno roast leg of lamb
pijama creme caramel covered in cream or ice cream and served with tinned fruits
pijotas fried baby hake
pil pil, al cooked in garlic
pimentero pepper mill, pepper pot
pimentón dulce paprika
pimentón rojo red chilli, cayenne pepper
pimienta, a la with pepper
pimienta pepper
pimienta blanca white pepper
pimienta en grano whole pepper
pimienta en polvo ground pepper
pimienta entera whole pepper
pimienta molida ground pepper
pimienta negra black pepper
pimiento pepper, capsicum
pimientos asados y aliñados roast peppers salad
pimientos del piquillo *[rellenos]* tinned red pepper *[stuffed]*
pimiento relleno stuffed pepper
pimiento rojo red pepper
pimiento verde green pepper
pinchito kebab
pincho kebab, skewer
pincho moruno shish kebab
pintada guinea fowl
piña pineapple
piña americana pineapple
piña colada drink with rum, pineapple juice and coconut milk
piña en almíbar pineapple in syrup
piña natural fresh pineapple
piñón pine kernel
pipas sunflower seeds
piquete *[LA]* meat and vegetable stew in a hot spicy sauce
pisco *[LA]* spirit similar to rum
pistacho pistachio nut
pisto ratatouille
plancha, a la grilled
plátano banana
plátanos flameados bananas flambéed
platija plaice, flounder
platillo saucer

platillo de pato   stewed duck
platillo de ternera   veal stew
plato, al   baked in the oven
plato   dish, plate
   plato combinado   set main course
   plato del día   special of the day
   plato principal   main course *or* entree *[US]* *[main course]*
   plato típico   regional dish
plum-cake   fruit cake
poca sal   low-salt
pochas *[LA]*   beans
poco cocido(a)   under-done
poco hecho(a)   underdone, rare, medium-rare
poleo   mint tea
pollito   young chicken
pollo   chicken
   pollo al chilindrón   chicken cooked with onions, peppers and tomatoes
   pollo asado   roast chicken
   pollo borracho *[LA]*   chicken in a tequila sauce
   pollo en pepitoria   casseroled chicken
   pollo frío   cold chicken
   pollo frito   fried chicken
   pollo de granja   farm chickens
polo   ice lolly
polvorón   ground almond biscuit
pomelo   grapefruit
ponche   punch
por favor   please
porcelana   china *[service]*
porción   portion, slice, small helping
postre   dessert, pudding, sweet
postre de músico   toasted nuts and raisins *[served with dessert wine]*
postre de natillas   Bavarian cream
postre helado   parfait
potaje   soup
potaje de garbanzos   chick pea soup
pozole *[LA]*   meat and corn stew
praliné   brittle
precio   price
   precio único   fixed price
primer plato   starter
pringadas   bread dipped in olive oil or fat
productos lácteos   dairy products
profiteroles   profiteroles
prohibido fumar   no smoking
propina   tip
puchero   casserole; Mexican hotpot
puchero canario   meat and chickpea casserole
pudín   pudding
puerco   pig
puerro   leek
pulpitos   baby octopus
pulpitos salteados   sautéed small octopus
pulpo   octopus
puntas de espárragos   asparagus tips
punto, en su   medium rare
pupusas *[LA]*   tortillas filled with meat or beans and cheese

puré mashed
    puré de castañas chestnut purée
    puré de espinacas creamed spinach
    puré de garbanzos hummus
    puré de manzana apple puree, apple sauce
    puré de patatas mashed potatoes, creamed potato *[US]*
purrusalda salt codfish soup-stew with vegetables
quemado(a) burnt
quesada cheesecake
quesito cheese triangle
queso cheese
    queso a las finas hierbas herb cheese
    queso azul blue cheese
    queso blando soft cheese
    queso cabrales strong flavoured semi-hard blue cheese
    queso de bola Edam cheese
    queso de cabra goat's cheese
    queso de oveja ewe's milk cheese
    queso de tetilla soft cheese from Galicia
    queso del país local cheese
    queso fresco green cheese *[unripened]*
    queso graso full fat cheese
    queso manchego strong hard salty cheese
    queso puro de oveja en aceite ewe's milk cheese in olive oil
    queso roquefort strong blue cheese
    queso seco hard cheese
    queso semi seco semi hard cheese
    queso tierno soft cheese
quisquilla shrimp
quitar la mesa clear up
quitar las espinas debone/fillet *[verb]*
rábano radish/radishes
    rábano picante horseradish
rabo de buey oxtail
racimo bunch
ración portion
ragú ragout
raíz root
raja slice
rallado(a) grated
ramito compuesto *[tomillo, perejil, apio, laurel]* bouquet garni
rana frog
ranchero country-style cooking
rancho canario stew with sausage, bacon, beans potato and pasta
rancio stale *or* rancid
rape monkfish, angler fish
ratafía liqueur *[flavoured with extracts from various fruit kernels]*
raviolis ravioli
raya skate
rebanada de pan slice of bread
rebanado, -a sliced
rebozado, -a fried in breadcrumbs, in batter
rebozuelos wild mushrooms *[chanterelles]*
recargo surcharge
receta recipe
reclamación complaint
recocido(a) well-done
refresco soft drink

refrigerio   snack *[light meal]*
refrito   refried *[with garlic and chopped parsley]*
refritos   mashed beans
regaliz   liquorice
rehogado(a)   sautéed
relleno   stuffing
relleno(a)   stuffed
remolacha   beetroot
repollo   cabbage
repostería   assorted small cakes and pastries
   repostería de la casa   house sweets and pastries
requemado   rice pudding with caramelised sugar topping
requesón   cottage cheese
reserva de la casa   vintage wine
reservado   private room
revellón   New Year's Eve party
revuelto   scrambled
   revuelto de bacalao   scrambled eggs with cod
   revuelto de erizos   scrambled eggs with sea urchins
   revuelto de gambas   scrambled eggs with prawns
   revuelto de jamón   scrambled eggs with ham
   revuelto de sesos   scrambled eggs with brains
riñón   kidney
   riñones al Jérez   kidneys cooked with sherry
rioja   Rioja *[wine]*
   rioja de la casa   house Rioja
riojana, a la   with fried chorizo, tomato and parsley
rodaballo   turbot
   rodaballo salvaje   halibut, black halibut
rodaja   slice
rodajas, a   sliced
rollito   roll
   rollitos de col   stuffed cabbage rolls
   rollitos de primavera   spring rolls
rollitos de pescado   fish rolls
rollo de carne   meat loaf
   rollo de primavera   spring roll
romana, a la   deep-fried in batter
romero   rosemary
romesco   hot Catalan sauce *[made with olive oil, garlic, vinegar, ground toasted nuts and dried red pepper]*
ron   rum
ropa vieja *[LA]*   cooked left-overs, shredded beef and green peppers served with rice
rosado   rosé wine
rosbif   roast beef
rosca de reyes   pastry ring filled with candied fruits
roscón   pastry ring
rosquillas   deep fried ring pastries *[similar to small dried doghnuts]*
roto(a)   chipped *[glass, plate]*
rovellón   wild mushroom
ruibarbo   rhubarb
sabayón   zabaglione
sabor   flavor, taste
sacacorchos   corkscrew
sacarina   saccharin
sal   salt

sal, a la   cooked in salt
sal gema   rock salt
sal marina   sea salt
saladitos   appetizers
salado(a)   salted
salazón, en   salted
salchicha   sausage
salchicha de Frankfurt   frankfurter
salchicha vegetariana   vegetarian sausage
salchichón   salami
salmón   salmon
salmón ahumado   smoked salmon
salmonete   barbel/red mullet
salmorejo   chilled soup with tomato, pepper, garlic, olive oil, salt and vinegar
salón   lounge
salón de fiestas   function room
salón para banquetes   function room
salpicón   salad with chopped onion, tomato and peppers
salpicón de mariscos   chopped seafood salad
salsa   sauce
salsa   dip *[noun]*
salsa bechamel   béchamel sauce
salsa criolla *[LA]*   spicy sauce
salsa de almendras   almond sauce
salsa de cebolla   onion sauce
salsa de chocolate   chocolate sauce
salsa de jitomate *[LA]*   hot tomato sauce
salsa de soya   soy sauce
salsa de tomate   tomato sauce, tomato ketchup
salsa Francesa   French dressing
salsa holandesa   hollandaise sauce
salsa Inglesa   Worcestershire sauce
salsa mayonesa   mayonnaise
salsa picante   devilled sauce
salsa roja   red sauce
salsa romesco   hot Catalan sauce
salsa tártara   tartar sauce
salsa vegetariana   vegetarian gravy
salsa verde   parsley sauce
salsera   gravy boat
salteado(a)   sautéed, pan-fried
saltear   sauté
salvado   bran
salvia   sage
samfaina   ratatouille, sauce with stewed tomatoes, peppers, onions and aubergine or courgette
sancochar   par-boil
sancocho *[LA]*   spicy vegetable stew with meat or fish
sandía   water melon
sándwich   sandwich
sangre   blood
sangre encebollada, con cebolla   fried blood with onions
sangría   sangría *[red wine punch]*
sardina   sardine, pilchard
sardineta   sprat
sargo   bream
sartén   frying pan
savenna   clams

sazón   seasoning
sazonar   flavour
sebo   suet
seco(a)   dry, dried
segundo plato   entree *[US]*
semi-seco   medium dry
semilla   seed
   semilla de ajonjoli   sesame seed
sémola   semolina
sémola de maíz   polenta, grits *[US]*
señoras   ladies
sepia   cuttlefish
sepia a la plancha   grilled cuttlefish
sepia con albóndigas   cuttlefish with meatballs
sequillos   hazelnut biscuits
serenata *[LA]*   cod in a vinaigrette sauce served with vegetables
serrano   cured ham
servicio   service
   servicio incluido   service included
   servicio no incluido   service not included
servicios   lavatory
servilleta   napkin, serviette
sésamo   sesame
sesos   brains
   sesos a la romana   brains deep-fried in batter
seta   wild mushroom
   setas confitadas   wild mushroom preserve
setas de cardo   oyster mushrooms
sidra   cider
   sidra, a la   cooked in cider
sidra de peras   perry
sifón   soda water
silla   chair
sin cafeína   decaffeinated/decaf, caffeine-free
sin cáscara   peeled
sin espinas   boned
sin gas   still
sin gluten   gluten-free
sin grasa   fat-free
sin guarnición   plain
sin leche   without milk
sin mantequilla   without butter
sin piel   peeled
sin salsa   plain
sobrasada, sobresada   spicy red sausage from Mallorca
soda   soda water
sofrito   fried with olive oil, gralic, and tomatoes *[optional chopped onion and parsley]*
soja   soy bean, soya bean
sol y sombra   brandy and aniseed liquor
soletas, soletillas   sponge biscuits
solo   neat
solomillo   fillet steak, tenderloin, sirloin
solomillo de ternera a la parrilla   grilled sirloin steak
solomillo mechado al estragón   sirloin stuffed with tarragon
sonsos   sand-eels
sopa   soup

sopa clara   clear soup
sopa de ajo   garlic soup
sopa de albóndigas   meatball soup
sopa de almejas   clam soup
sopa de almendras   almond soup
sopa de arroz y fideos   rice and noodle soup
sopa de cabello de ángel   vermicelli soup
sopa de calabaza   pumpkin soup
sopa de caldo con codillos   broth with macaroni
sopa de caldo de pollo   chicken soup
sopa de cebolla   onion soup
sopa de fideos   noodle soup
sopa de lentejas   lentil soup
sopa de letras   alphabet noodle soup
sopa de maní *[LA]*   roasted peanut soup
sopa de mondongo *[LA]*   soup-stew with tripe
sopa de pescado   fish soup, chowder
sopa de verduras   vegetable soup
sopa del día   soup of the day
sopa espesa   thick soup
sopa juliana   julienne soup *[with mixed vegetables]*
sopa minestrone   minestrone
sorbete   sherbet
soya   soy bean, soya bean
suave   soft
sucio(a)   dirty *[adj]*
suero   whey
suflé   soufflé
suizo   hot chocolate topped with whipped cream
supremas de pescado   fish suprêmes
suquet *[de pescado]*   fish stew
surrullitos *[LA]*   deep fried corn sticks stuffed with cheese
surtido   platter
surtido de embutidos   assorted cold sausages and salamis
surtido de fiambres   assorted cold meats
surtido de quesos   assorted cheese platter
taberna   bar, tavern
tabla de embutidos   assorted cold sausages and salamis
taco *[LA]*   taco
tajada   slice
tajaditas *[LA]*   plantain chips
tallarines   tagliatelle
tamales *[LA]*   mixture of meat, rice, olives and cornmeal wrapped in banana
   leaves
tangerina   tangerine
tapenade   olive and anchovy paste
tapa   appetizer, bar snack
tapioca   tapioca
tarro *[de conservas]*   tin
tarta   pie, flan, tart
tarta con crema   cream cake
tarta de manzana   apple pie, apple tart
tarta de queso   cheesecake
tarta de Santiago   almond tart
tarta helada   ice cream cake
tartaleta   tart
tártara   tartare
taza, a la   in a cup

taza cup
    taza de café cup of coffee
    taza de chocolate cup of cocoa
    taza de té cup of tea
    taza para café coffee cup
    taza para té tea cup
    taza y platillo cup and saucer
tazón bowl
tetera teapot
té tea
    té con hielo iced tea
    té con leche tea with milk
    té con limón lemon tea
    té verde green tea
tejas almond and sugar buiscuits
tellinas wedge shell clam
tembleque *[LA]* coconut pudding
temperatura ambiente room temperature
tenedor fork
tequila tequila
ternasco baby lamb
    ternasco asado roast baby lamb
tenca tench
tentempié snack *[between meals]*
ternera veal, calf
terrina terrine, pâté
tibio(a) warm
tierno(a) tender
tienda shop
tila lime blossom tea
tinta, en su in its own ink
tinto red wine
tirabeque mangetout
tirabuzón corkscrew
tisana herbal tea
tocinillo, tocino del cielo small sweet made of egg yolks and syrup
tocino bacon
    tocino ahumado smoked bacon
toffee toffee
tomate tomato
    tomates cereza cherry tomato
tomillo thyme
toro bull
toronja grapefruit
toronjil lemon balm
torreja, torrija fried egg bread coated with sugar
torta sponge cake
    torta de almendras almond torte
tortilla omelette *[egg]*; tortilla *[maize]*
    tortilla al gusto omelette to taste
    tortilla de ajos tiernos garlic shoot omelette
    tortilla de calabacín courgette omelette
    tortilla de espinacas spinach omelette
    tortilla de finas hierbas omelette aux fines herbes
    tortilla de gambas prawn omelette
    tortilla de jamón ham omelette
    tortilla de patatas Spanish omelette
    tortilla de queso cheese omelette

tortilla francesa   plain omelette
tortuga   turtle
tostada   toast
   tostadas con mantequilla y mermelada   toast with butter and jam
tostado   toasted
tournedo   tenderloin
trigo   wheat
trigo sarraceno   buckwheat
trinchar   carve
tripas   tripe, chitterling *[US]*
triturar   grind
tronco de merluza   baked hake
trozo   slice
trozos, a   chopped
trucha   trout
   trucha a la navarra   trout cooked with ham
   trucha marina   sea trout
   trucha rellena   stuffed trout
trufa   truffle
   trufa de chocolate   chocolate truffle
tuétano   bone marrow
turrón   Christmas nougat, marzipan
   turrón blando   soft nougat *[with ground almonds]*
   turron de Alicante   hard nougat *[with chopped nuts and honey]*
   turrón de chocolate   soft nougat with chocolate *[and nuts]*
   turrón de jijona   soft nougat with ground almonds and honey
   turrón de yema   caramelized soft nougat with egg yolk
   turrón duro   hard nougat *[with chopped nuts]*
untado(a)   greased, spread
   untar con mantequilla   spread with butter
utensilio   utensil
uva(s)   grape(s)
vaca   beef from older stock *[tough]*
vainilla   vanilla
vapor   steam
   vapor, al   steamed
variado(a)   assorted
vaso   glass
   vaso de agua   glass of water
   vaso de vino   glass of wine
   vaso limpio   clean glass
vegetales   vegetables
vegetariano(a)   vegetarian
   vegetariano estricto   vegan
vela   candle
venado   venison
verbena   party, festival
verdura   vegetable
verduras   greens
   verdura hervida   boiled vegetables
   verduras al vapor   steamed vegetables
   verduras enanas   baby vegetables
vermut   vermouth
vieira   scallop
vientre   belly
vinagre   vinegar
vinagreta   vinaigrette, French dressing
vinagreta, a la   in a vinaigrette sauce

vino wine
   vino añejo mature wine
   vino blanco white wine
   vino blanco ligero light *[dry]* white wine
   vino blanco con cuerpo full bodied dry wine
   vino de aguja sparkling wine
   vino de crianza wine aged in barrels
   vino de la casa house wine
   vino de madeira Madeira wine
   vino de mesa table wine
   vino de Oporto port
   vino de postre sweet wine
   vino del país local wine
   vino dulce dessert wine
   vino espumante, espumoso sparkling wine
   vino generoso fortified wine
   vino ligero light-bodied wine
   vino local local wine
   vino muy seco very dry wine
   vino rancio sweet wine for desserts
   vino rosado rosé wine
   vino seco dry wine
   vino tinto red wine
virutas de jamón thin and small slices of ham
vuelta y vuelta rare
whisky escocés Scotch whisky
whisky irlandés Irish whiskey
xató green salad with salt cod and romesco dressing
yaguarlocro *[LA]* potato soup with a local sausage
yema de huevo egg yolk
yerba herb
yogur yoghurt
yogur de fruta fruit yoghurt
yogur desnatado low-fat yoghurt
yogur natural plain yoghurt
zanahoria carrot
zarzamora blackberry
zarzuela fish stew
   zarzuela de marisco y pescado casseroled shellfish
zona de no fumadores non-smoking area
zumo juice
   zumo de frutas fruit juice
   zumo de limón lemon juice
   zumo de manzana apple juice
   zumo de naranja orange juice
   zumo de uva grape juice
   zumo natural fresh fruit juice

Spanish-English

English-Spanish

abalone oreja de mar
absinthe absenta, ajenjo
account cuenta
aged de crianza
aïloli sauce alioli
air-conditioned con aire acondicionado
albacore *[tuna]* albacora, atún blanco
alcohol alcohol
ale cerveza
alfalfa sprouts brotes de alfalfa
allergic alérgico, -a
allergy alergia
allspice pimienta inglesa, pimienta de Jamaica
almond almendra
   almond biscuits galletas de almendra
   almond paste pasta de almendras
   almond tart tarta de almendras, tarta de Santiago
   with almonds con almendras
amandine potatoes patatas a la almendra
anchovy anchoa, boquerón
   anchovy butter mantequilla de anchoas
   anchovy paste pasta de anchoas
angel food cake bizcocho, tarta *[sin yema de huevo]*
angel fish pez ángel, angelote
angel hair pasta cabello de ángel
angels on horseback montado de ostras envueltas en bacon a la parrilla
angelica angélica
angler rape
anise anís
aniseed anís
aperitif aperitivo
appetizer *[US]* aperitivo, tapa
apple manzana
   apple fritter buñuelo de manzana
   apple juice zumo de manzana
   apple pie tarta de manzana
   apple puree puré de manzana
   apple sauce puré de manzana
   apple strudel strudel de manzana *[hojaldre]*
   apple turnover empanada de manzana
   apple tart pastelillo de manzana, tarta de manzana
   baked apple manzana al horno
apricot albaricoque
aroma fragancia, aroma
arrowroot arrurruz
artichoke alcachofa
ashtray cenicero
asparagus espárrago
   asparagus tips puntas de espárragos

aspic   gelatina
assorted vegetables   panaché de verduras
aubergine, eggplant   berenjena
au gratin *[US]*   gratinado(a), al gratén
avocado   aguacate
baby corn *[cob]*   mazorquita de maíz
baby eels   angulas
baby food   papilla
baby leeks   puerros pequeñitos
baby vegetables   verduras enanas
baby's bottle   biberón
bacon   bacon, tocino, panceta
   bacon and eggs   huevos fritos con bacon
bad   malo(a)
   bad egg   huevo podrido
bake   asar, cocer al horno
baked   asado(a), al horno
   baked alaska   bomba helada
   baked apple   manzana al horno
   baked beans   judías blancas en salsa de tomate
   baked custard   flan
   baked potato   patata al horno
   baked rice, rice pudding   arroz con leche
bakery   panadería
balsamic vinegar   vinagre balsámico
bamboo   bambú
banana   plátano *or* guineo
   banana fritter   buñuelo de plátano
   banana split   banana split *[plátano, helado de vainilla, Chantilly, almendras]*
   banana flambé   plátanos flameados
bar *[pub]*   bar
Barbary duck   pato muscovy
barbecue   barbacoa
barbecued   a la barbacoa
barbel/red mullet   salmonete
barley   cebada
   barley sugar   caramelo de azúcar de cebada
   barley water   hordiate *[agua de cebada]*
basil   albahaca
   basil pesto   pesto de albahaca
basmati rice   arroz basmati, arroz indio
bass, sea bass   lubina
baste   rociar con jugo
bathroom   baño, servicios
batter   masa, pasta para rebozar
   in batter   rebozado, -a, a la romana
bavarian cream   postre de natillas
bay leaf   laurel
bean   judía, habichuela, alubia
   bean sprouts   brotes de soja, soja germinada
   broad bean   haba
   French bean, green bean, string bean   judía verde, ejote
   kidney bean, red bean   frijol, habichuela
   runner beans   judía pinta
   soja bean   *[haba de]* soja
béarnaise sauce   salsa bearnesa
béchamel sauce   salsa bechamel

beech nuts   hayuco
beef   *[carne de]* vaca, buey
   beefsteak *[US]*   bistec, biftec
      beef stroganoff   estofado de ternera a la stroganoff
      beef tea   caldo de carne
      beef Wellington   solomillo de buey envuelto en hojaldre
   roast beef   rosbif
beer   cerveza
   draught beer   cerveza de barril, cerveza a presión
beestings   calostro
beetroot   remolacha
bergamot   bergamota
berries   frutos del bosque
bib *[child's]*   babero
big   grande
bilberry   arándano
bill   cuenta
birthday cake   pastel de cumpleaños
biscuit   galleta
bitter   amargo
bitter *[beer]*   cerveza inglesa de barril
black beans   frijoles negros
blackberry   mora, zarzamora
black butter   mantequilla quemada, matequilla negra
black cherry   cereza
black coffee   café, café solo
blackcurrant   grosella negra, casis
Black Forest cake/gateau   pastel de chocolate, nata y cerezas al kirsch
black halibut   halibut
black pepper   pimienta negra
black pudding   morcilla
black truffle   trufa negra
blaeberry   arándano
blanch   escaldar, blanqrear
   blanched   escaldado, -a
blancmange   crema de maizena
blend   mezclar, pasar por la licuadora
blinis   buñuelos
bloater   arenque ahumado
blood   sangre
blueberry   arándano
blue cheese   queso azul
blue whiting   bacaladilla
boar   jabalí
bogue *[fish]*   boga
boil   hervir
boiled   hervido(a)
   boiled egg   huevo pasado por agua, huevo cocido
   boiled ham   jamón cocido
   boiled potatoes   patatas hervidas
   boiled rice   arroz hervido
   boiled vegetables   verdura hervida
   boiling water   agua hirviendo
   hard boiled egg   huevo duro
bombe   helado en molde
bone   hueso
   boned   deshuesado, sin espinas

bone marrow   tuétano
on the bone   con hueso
bones *[of fish]*   espinas
bonito   bonito
book *[a table]*   reservar *[una mesa]*
borage   borraja
bordelaise sauce   salsa bordelesa
borlotti beans   judía
bouquet garni   ramito compuesto *[tomillo, perejil, apio, laurel]*
bottle   botella
bottle opener   abreboteilas
half bottle   media botella
bowl   bol, cuenco, tazón
brains   sesos, cerebro
braise *[verb]*   asar, estofar
braised   asado, -a, estofado, -a
bran   salvado
bran flakes   copos de trigo integral con salvado
brandy   coñac, aguardiente
cherry brandy   aguardiente de cerezas
brawn   carne en gelatina, queso de cerdo
brazil nut   nuez del Brasil
bread   pan
breadcrumbs   pan rallado
bread knife   cuchillo para cortar el pan
bread roll   panecillo
brown bread   pan integral
bread sauce   salsa de miga de pan y leche
breadstick   colín, grisín
breaded   empanado
breakfast   desayuno
breakfast cereal   cereales
bream, sea bream   dorada
breast   pechuga
breast of lamb, veal   costillar de cordero, falda de ternera
chicken breast   pechuga de pollo
brill   rémol
brioche   brioche
brisket *[of beef]*   falda *[de buey]*
brittle   praliné, crocante
broad bean   haba
broccoli   brécol, brócoli
broth   caldo
brown *[verb]*   dorar
brown bread   pan integral
brown butter   mantequilla dorada
brown rice   arroz integral
brown roll   panecillo integral
brown sugar   azúcar moreno
brown sauce   salsa espesa a base de extracto de carne y caldo de verduras con
especias y puré de tomate
Brussels sprouts   coles, colecitas de Bruselas, bretones
bubble and squeak   patata y repollo salteados
buckwheat *[trigo]*   sarraceno
buffet   buffet
buffalo   búfalo
bulgar wheat, bulgur wheat   trigo triturado

English-Spanish

bun bollo, panecillo
burbot rape
burdock bardana
Burgundy *[wine]* vino de Borgoña, burdeos
burn *[verb]* quemar
burnet pimpinela
burnt quemado, -a
butchers shop carnicería
butter mantequilla
   butterfish pescadito
   buttermilk suero de leche
   butter sauce salsa de mantequilla
   with butter con mantequilla
   without butter sin mantequilla
cabbage col, repollo, berza
cabinet pudding púding de molde
Caesar salad ensalada César
café café
caffeine cafeína
   caffeine-free/ decaffeinated descafeinado, -a
cake pastel
   cake shop pastelería
   carrot cake pastel de zanahoria
   cream cake pastel de nata
   fruit cake plum-cake, budín inglés
   sponge cake bizcocho
calamari calamares
calf ternera
   calf's brains sesos de ternera
   calf's liver hígado de ternera
camomile manzanilla
canapés canapés
candied confitado, -a
   candied peel cáscara confitada *[cítricos]*
candle vela
candlestick candelero, candelabro
candy *[US]* caramelo, golosinas, dulces
cane sugar azúcar de caña
canned en conserva, de lata, enlatado
cantaloup *[melon]* melón de Cantalú
capers alcaparra
capon capón
capsicum pimiento, pimentón
carafe garrafa
caramel caramelo
caraway *[seeds]* alcaravea, carvi, comino
carbohydrate hidrato de carbono *or* fécula
carbonara carbonara
carbonated con gas
cardamom cardamomo
carp carpa
carrot zanahoria
   carrot cake pastel de zanahoria
carve cortar, trinchar
cashier caja
cassata helado napolitano, cassata
cashew nut anacardo, castaña de cajú

casserole   cazuela, guiso, guisado
caster sugar   azúcar muy fino
catfish   barbo ferro del norte
cauliflower   coliflor
   cauliflower cheese   coliflor con salsa de queso al gratén
caviar   caviar
cayenne pepper   pimienta de cayena
celeriac   apio-rábano
celery   apio
cereal *[breakfast]*   cereales
chair   silla
Champagne   Champaña, cava
change *[coins]*   cambio, monedas, suelto
change *[verb]*   cambiar
chantilly   chantilly
chanterelle   mízcalo
char   farra *[salmón]*
charcoal   carbón, carboncillo
   charcoal-grilled   a la parrilla, a la brasa
chard   acelga
charlotte   carlota
   apple charlotte   carlota de manzanas
cheap   barato
cheddar *[cheese]*   queso *[inglés]* cheddar
Cheers!   ¡salud!
cheese   queso
   cheese board   tabla para el queso, tabla de quesos
   cheesecake   tarta de queso
   cheese sandwich   bocadillo de queso
   cheese sauce   salsa de queso
   cheese soufflé   suflé de queso
   cheese straw   galletas de queso en forma de paja
   cream cheese   queso crema
chef   chef
cherry   cereza
   cherry brandy   aguardiente de cerezas
   cherry tomato   tomates cereza
chervil   perifollo
chestnut *[sweet]*   castaña
   sweet chestnut   castaña
   water chestnut   castaña de agua
chickpea   garbanzo *or* chicharo
chicken   pollo
   chicken gumbo   sopa de pollo y quingombó
   chicken Kiev   pechugas de pollo rellenas a la Kiev
   chicken liver   hígado de pollo
   chicken salad   ensalada de pollo
   chicken soup   sopa de caldo de pollo
chicory   escarola
children's menu   menú para niños
chilled   fresco, frío
chilli   chile, ají
   chilli con carne   chile con carne
   chilli pepper   pimiento chile
   chilli powder   chile en polvo
   chilli without meat   chile sin carne
china *[service]*   porcelana
china tea   té chino

English-Spanish

Chinese cabbage col China
chipped *[glass, plate]* desportillado, roto
chips patatas fritas, papas
chitterling *[US]* tripas, asadura, menudos
chives cebollino, cebolleta
chocolate chocolate
    chocolate cake pastel, tarta de chocolate
    chocolate croissant croissant de chocolate
    chocolate eclair palo de nata *[lionesas]*
    chocolate mousse mousse de chocolate
    chocolate sauce salsa de chocolate
    chocolate truffle trufa de chocolate
    milk chocolate chocolate con leche
    plain chocolate cholcolate sin leche
choose escoger
chop *[cutlet]* chuleta
chop *[meat]* cortar
chopped *[into pieces]* cortado, a trozos
chopsticks palillo chino
choux pastry masa para pasteles
chowder *[US]* sopa de pescado *[a base de leche]*
Christmas Day Navidad
Christmas dinner comida de navidad
Christmas cake pastel de Navidad *[inglés]*
Christmas Eve nochebuena
Christmas log bizcocho de Navidad en forma de leño
Christmas menu menú de navidad
Christmas pudding púding de Navidad *[inglés]*
cider sidra
    cider vinegar vinagre de sidra
cigar puro
cigarettes cigarrillos
cinnamon canela
citron limón
citrus cítrico
clam almeja
    clam chowder sopa de almejas
claret clarete
clean limpio
clear up quitar la mesa
clear soup consomé, caldo
clementine clementina
clove clavo de olor
    clove of garlic diente de ajo
club sandwich sandwich de dos pisos
cobnut avellana grande
cock-a-leekie *[soup]* sopa de pollo y porros
cockles berberechos
cocktail cóctel
cocoa cacao en polvo
    cocoa butter manteca de cacao
    cup of cocoa taza de chocolate
coconut coco
    coconut cream crema de coco
    coconut milk leche de coco
    desiccated coconut coco rallado
cod bacalao

coffee café
    cappucino coffee capuccino
    coffee parfait parfait de café *[postre helado]*
    coffee pot cafetera
    coffee spoon cucharilla de café
    coffee with whipped cream café con nata
    coffee whitener sucedáneo de leche *[en polvo]*
    decaffeinated coffee café descafeinado
    espresso / expresso coffee café exprés
    filter coffee café de filtro
    instant coffee café instantáneo
    latte coffee café con leche
coke coca cola
cold frío
    cold cuts *[US]* fiambres
    cold drink refresco, bebida fría
    cold meat fiambres
    cold water agua fría
coley palero, faneca plateada *or* abedejo
collared beef carne atada
complimentary gratuito, -a, de obsequio
condensed milk leche condensada
condiment condimento, aliño
confectionery confitería
confectioner's cream nata, crema de pastelero
conger eel congrio
consommé *[soup]* consomé
continental breakfast desayuno continental
cook, chef cocinero, -a, chef
cookies *[US]* galletas, pastas secas
coriander coriandro *or* culantro
corkscrew sacacorchos, tirabuzón
corn maíz
    corn bread pan de harina de maíz
    corn oil aceite de maíz
    corn on the cob mazorca de maíz
    corn syrup melaza, almíbar de maíz
    cornflakes copos de maíz
    cornflour maizena
    sweetcorn maíz
corned beef carne en conserva
cornet *[ice cream]* cucurucho
cos lettuce lechuga *[romana]*
cottage cheese requesón
courgette calabacín
couscous alcuzcuz
cover charge cubierto
crab cangrejo
    dressed crab cangrejo preparado *[aliñado]*
    prepared crab cangrejo preparado
crackling chicharra *or* chicharrón, corteza *[de cerdo asado]*
cranberry arándano
    cranberry sauce salsa de arándanos
crawfish langosta
crayfish cangrejo de rio
cream nata, crema
    cream cheese queso de nata
    cream cake pastel de nata, tarta con crema

cream sauce   salsa bechamel
cream slice   hojaldre *[relleno de nata y mermelada]*
cream tea   té servido con bollitos untados de mantequilla, nata o mermelada
double cream   nata para montar
single cream   crema de leche
sour cream   crema agria
whipped cream   nata montada, chantilly
cream of   crema de
cream of asparagus soup   crema de espárragos
cream of chicken soup   crema de pollo
cream of tomato soup   crema de tomate
creamed   batido con leche o crema
creamed potato *[US]*   puré de patata
creamed spinach   puré de espinacas, crema de espinacas
creamy   cremoso, con crema
crème caramel *[baked custard]*   flan
crème fraîche   nata
cress   berro, mastuerzo
crispbread   tostadita, galleta crujiente
crisps   patatas fritas, papas *[en bolsa]*
croissant   croissant
croquette potatoes   croquetas de puré de patata
croutons   crutón, picatoste
crumble   compota gratinada de azúcar, harina y mantequilla
crumpet   panecillo tostado
crystallised fruit   fruta confitada
cucumber   pepino
cucumber sandwich   sandwich de pepino
cumin *[seed]*   comino
cup   taza
cup and saucer   taza y platillo
cup of coffee   taza de café
cup of tea   taza de té
coffee cup   taza para café
tea cup   taza para té
curd *[cheese]*   requesón
cured   ahumado, salado, curado
currants   pasas de Corinto
curry   curry
curry powder   curry
custard   crema inglesa, natillas
baked custard   flan
custard apple   chirimoya *or* guanabana
custard sauce   crema, natillas
custard tart   tarta de crema
cut   cortar
cutlery   cubiertos, cubertería
cutlet   chuleta
cuttlefish   sepia, jibia
dab   platija, gallo, barbada, limanda nórdica
dairy products   productos lácteos
damson   ciruela damascena
date   dátil
date plum   caqui, fruto del dióspiro
debone/fillet *[verb]*   deshuesar, quitar las espinas
decaffeinated/decaf   descafeinado, sin cafeína
deep-fried   frito

deer/venison   ciervo, venado
defrost   descongelar
delicatessen   charcutería
delicious   delicioso
demerara sugar   azúcar moreno, azúcar terciado
dessert   postre
   dessert spoon   cucharilla *[de postre]*
   dessert wine   vino dulce, vino de postre
devilled   con salsa picante
   devilled kidneys   riñones salteados con salsa picante
   devilled sauce   salsa picante
diced *[cubed]*   en dados, en cubitos
dill   eneldo
   dill sauce   salsa de eneldos
dining car   vagón restaurante, coche comedor
dining companion(s)   comensales
dining room   comedor
dinner   cena
   dinner party   cena, comida
   dinner time   hora de la comida, de la cena
dip *[verb]*   mojar
dip *[noun]*   salsa
dirty *[adj]*   sucio, -a
dirty *[verb]*   ensuciar
discount   descuento
dish   plato
   dish of the day   plato del día
dog fish   alitán, pintarroja, mielga, musola
done   cocido, -a, hecho, -a
   under-done   crudo, -a, poco hecho
   well-done   muy hecho
doner kebab   carne asada en lonchas
dory, John Dory   pez de San Pedro
double *[shot of spirits]*   doble
double cream   nata para montar
dough   masa
doughnut   dónut
   jam doughnut   dónut relleno de mermelada
Dover sole   lenguado
draught beer   cerveza de barril , cerveza a presión
dressing   aliño, aderezo
dried   seco(a)
   sun-dried *[tomatoes]*   tomates secados al sol
drink   bebida
   drink *[verb]*   beber
   drinkable   potable, que se puede beber
   drinking water   agua potable
   drinks included   bebida incluida
dripping   grasa de carne asada
drumsticks   muslos *[de pollo o pavo]*
dry *[wine]* *[vino]*   seco
Dublin bay prawn   cigala
duchesse potatoes   patatas a la duquesa *[canapé]*
duck *[domestic]*   pato doméstico
duck *[wild]*   pato silvestre
duck paté   foie gras
duck with oranges   pato a la naranja

duckling   patito, anadón
dumpling   albóndiga de masa que se añade a las sopas o asados
   potato dumpling   buñuelos de patatas
eat   comer
éclair   palo *[de nata]*
eel   anguila
egg   huevo
   boiled egg   huevo cocido, huevo pasado por agua
   egg and bacon   huevos fritos con bacon
   egg cup   huevera
   egg white   clara *[de huevo]*
   egg yolk   yema de huevo
   eggs Benedict   huevos a la benedictina
   eggs florentine   huevos a la florentina
   fried egg   huevo frito
   hard boiled egg   huevo duro
   omelette   tortilla
   poached egg   huevo escalfado
   scrambled eggs   huevos revueltos
   soft boiled egg   huevo pasado por agua
eggplant/aubergine   berenjena
elderberry   baya del saúco
endive   escarola
enough   suficiente
entree   entrante, primer plato
entree *[US]*   plato principal, segundo plato
escalope   escalope
   turkey escalope   escalope de pavo
   veal escalope   escalope de ternera
espresso   café sólo
essence   esencia
ewe's milk   leche de oveja
   ewe's milk cheese   queso de oveja
excellent   excelente
expensive   caro, -a
extra virgin olive oil   aceite de oliva extra virgen
faggot   albóndiga
falafel   falafel
farm *[eggs, chickens]   [huevos, pollos de]* granja
fast *[not eat]*   ayunar
fat *[adj]*   graso, -a
fat *[noun]*   grasa
   fat-free   descremado(a), sin grasa
feet, trotters   manitas *[de cerdo]*
fennel   hinojo
feta cheese   queso feta
fig   higo
filbert   avellana
fillet   filete, solomillo, lomo *[cerdo]*
   fillet steak   filete de ternera, solomillo
   fillet of beef   filete de buey
   filleted *[cortado]* en filetes
filo pastry   pasta de hojaldre muy fina
filter coffee   café *[de cafetera de filtro]*
fine beans   judías verdes *[finas]*
first course   entrante, primer plato
fish   pescado
   anchovy   anchoa, boquerón

angel fish   angelote
bass, sea bass   lubina
bloater   arenque
bream   pargo, dorada
brill   rémol
burbot   rape
catfish   barbo ferro del norte, siluro
cod   bacalao
coley   abedjo, palero, faneca plateada
conger eel   congrio
crayfish   cangrejo de rio
cuttlefish   sepia, jibia
dog fish   alitán, pintarroja, mielga, musola
dory, John Dory   pez de San Pedro
Dover sole   lenguado
eel   anguila
fish and chips   pescado frito con patatas fritas
fish cake   croqueta de pescado
fish shop   pescadería
fish soup   sopa de pescado
fish stew   bullabesa, guiso de pescado
fish stock   caldo de pescado
fishmonger   pescadería
flounder   platija
flying fish   pez volador, paparda, golondrina de mar
grey mullet   pardete
haddock   abadejo
hake   merluza
halibut   halibut, rodaballo
herring   arenque
kipper   arenque ahumado
lemon sole   gallo
mackerel   caballa
monkfish   rape
pike   lucio
pike-perch   serrano
pilchard   sardina
redfish   gallineta nórdica
red mullet   salmonete de fango, salmonete de roca
rockfish   lubina
roe   huevas
sea bass   lubina
sea bream   pargo
sea trout   trucha marina
shark   tiburón
skate   raya
skipjack   bonito
smelt   eperlano
sole   lenguado
sturgeon   esturión
swordfish   emperador, pez espada
tench   tenca
trout   trucha
tunny, tuna   atún
turbot   rodaballo
whitebait *[sprats]*   morralla, chanquetes
whiting   pescadilla, plegonero
fisherman's pie   pastel de pescado

fixed price   precio único
  fixed price menu   menú turista
fizzy   con gas, gaseoso, -a
flageolet *[beans]*   frijol
flakes   copos
flambé   flambear
flan   tarta
flat fish   pez plano
flavour   sazonar
  flavoured   aromatizado, -a
flounder   platija
flour   harina
flying fish   pez volador, paparda, golondrina de mar
fondant   fondant
fondue   fondue
food   comida, alimentos
  food poisoning   intoxicación alimentaria
fool   mousse de frutas y crema
fork   tenedor
fowl   aves
  boiling fowl   gallina
frankfurter   salchicha de Frankfurt
free *[of charge]*   gratis
free-range   de granja
French beans   judías verdes
French dressing   vinagreta
French fries *[US]*   patatas fritas, papas fritas
French toast   tostada *[en paquete]*, biscote, torrija
fresh   fresco(a)
freshwater *[fish]*   pescado de agua dulce
fried   frito(a)
  fried chicken   pollo frito
  fried egg   huevo frito
  fried fish   pescado frito
  fried food   fritura, comida frita
  mixed fried fish   fritura de pescado
frisée *[salad]*   escarola
fritter   buñuelo, tortita
  apple fritter   buñuelo de manzana
frog's legs   ancas de rana
frozen   congelado(a)
fruit   fruta
  fruit bread/loaf   pan de frutas
  fruit cocktail   macedonia de frutas
  fruit juice   zumo de frutas
  fruit salad   macedonia de frutas
fry   freír
fudge   caramelo, dulce de azúcar y chocolate
full *[restaurant]*   lleno
full *[after eating]*   lleno, -a
full-bodied wine   vino con cuerpo
full-cream milk   leche entera
full-fat *[cheese]*   queso *[no descremado]*
fungi   hongo
galantine   galantina *[fiambres]*
galeeny   pintada, gallineta

game caza
   game pie pastel de caza
gammon jamón fresco
garden mint menta, hierbabuena
garden peas guisantes
garlic ajo
   garlic bread pan tostado con mantequilla y ajo
   garlic mayonnaise aioli
   garlic mushrooms setas al ajillo
garlicky a ajo *or* con ajo
garnished con guarnición
gateau pastel
gazpacho gazpacho
gelatine gelatina
general store/grocer's tienda, almacén
genetically modified *[GM]* genéticamente modificado, -a
gents' toilets lavabo, servicio de caballeros
ghee mantequilla clarificada *[cocina india]*
gherkin pepinillo
giblets menudillos
gin ginebra
   gin and tonic gin tonic
ginger jengibre
   ginger beer cerveza al jengibre
   gingerbread pan de jenjibre
   ginger cake pastel de jengibre
glacé cherry cereza confitada, guinda
glass vaso
   clean glass vaso limpio
   glass of water vaso de agua
   wine glass copa
glazed glaseado, glacé
gluten-free sin gluten
GM *[genetically modified]* genéticamente modificado, -a
gnocchi ñoquis
goat cabra
   goat's cheese queso de cabra
   goat's milk leche de cabra
good bueno, -a
goose ganso, oca
   goose liver hígado de ganso
gooseberry grosella espinosa
goulash estofado húngaro
gourmet gourmet, gastrónomo, -a
granary loaf pan de trigo integral
granita granizado
granulated sugar azúcar granulado
grape(s) uva(s)
grapefruit pomelo, toronja
grapeseed oil aceite de pepitas de uva
grated rallado
gratuity gratificación
gravy salsa a base del jugo de la carne asada
   gravy boat salsera
grease grasa
Greek yoghurt yogur griego
green beans judías verdes, ejotes

greengrocer   verdulero, -a
green olives   aceitunas verdes
green peas   guisantes
green pepper   pimiento verde
green salad   ensalada verde
green tea   té verde
greengage *[plum]*   claudia *[ciruela]*
Greenland halibut   halibut, rodaballo de Groenlandia
greens   verduras
grenadine   granadina, fricandó
grey mullet   pardete
grill *[verb]*   asar a la parrilla
grill *[noun]*   parrilla
   mixed grill   parrillada de carne
grilled   a la parrilla
grind   moler, triturar
gristle   cartílago
grits *[US]*   sémola de maíz
groats   cereal, avena molida
grocery   tienda de comestibles, tienda de ultramarinos
ground   molido(a), picado(a)
   ground beef   carne picada
   ground coffee   café molido
groundnut oil   aceite de cacahuete
grouper   mero
grouse   urogallo
guacamole   guacamole
guava   guayaba
gudgeon   cabot
Guinea fowl   pintada, gallina de Guinea
gumbo   sopa a base de pollo o marisco y verduras
gurnard   arete
haddock   abadejo
hake   merluza
half   medio, -a
   half a litre   medio litro
   half a pint   media pinta
   half bottle   media botella
   half done   medio hecho
   half-cooked   medio crudo
halibut   halibut, rodaballo
ham   jamón, pernil
   boiled ham   jamón *[cocido]*, jamón de York
   ham sandwich   bocadillo de jamón
   slice of ham   loncha de jamón
hamburger   hamburguesa
hangover   resaca
hard   duro, -a
hard boiled egg   huevo duro
hard cheese   queso *[seco]*
hard roe   huevas
hare   liebre
haricot beans   judías blancas, alubias
hash browns *[US]*   salteado de patatas y cebolla
haunch   pierna
hazelnut   avellana
health   salud

health shop tienda de productos naturales, herbolario
healthy sano, -a
heart corazón
heat up calentar
herbs hierbas
herbal tea infusión, tisana
herring arenque
hickory nut pacana
highchair trona, silla alta
high-fibre alto contenido en fibra
hollandaise sauce salsa holandesa
home-made casero, -a
hominy grits *[US]* maíz descascarillado y molido
honey miel
honeycomb panal de miel
honeydew melon melón
hors d'oeuvre entremeses
horse mackerel jurel,chicharro
horse meat carne de caballo
horseradish rábano picante
hot *[not cold; strong]* caliente *[no frío]*; picante *[fuerte]*
hot dog perrito caliente
hot drink bebida caliente
hot water agua caliente
hotpot estofado, guiso
house specialities especialidades de la casa
hummus puré de garbanzos
hungry hambriento
ice hielo
   bucket of ice cubo de hielo
ice cream helado
   ice cream cone helado de cucurucho
   ice cream scoop bola de helado
   with ice cream con helado
ice cube cubito de hielo
ice lolly polo
iceberg lettuce lechuga repollada
icing glaseado, fondant
   icing sugar azúcar glas, azúcar en polvo
ide *[fish]* cacho, cachuelo
ingredients ingredientes
inside dentro
instant coffee café instantáneo
Irish stew estofado de cordero, patata y cebollas a la Irlandesa
Irish whiskey whisky irlandés
jam confitura, mermelada, compota, conserva
Japanese tea té japonés
jellied en gelatina
jelly *[savoury]* gelatina, aspic
jelly *[sweet/pudding]* gelatina
Jerusalem artichoke pataca, aguaturma
John Dory, dory pez de San Pedro
jug jarra
jugged hare estofado de liebre
juice zumo, jugo
   juicer exprimidor, juguera, licuadora
julienne juliana

kaki caqui
kale col rizada
kebab pincho, brocheta
kedgeree arroz con pescado y huevo duro
ketchup catsup, ketchup, salsa de tomate
kettle hervidor de agua
key lime pie tarta de lima
kidney riñón
kidney beans frijoles
king prawn gamba
kipper arenque ahumado *[y salado]*
kitchen cocina
kiwi fruit kiwi
knife cuchillo
knuckle jarrete, codillo
kohlrabi colinabo
kosher plato preparado siguiendo estrictamente los principios de la dieta judía

kumquat naranjita china
label etiqueta
lactose lactosa
   lactose intolerance intolerancia a la lactosa
ladies fingers quimbombos
ladies' toilets lavabo, servicio de señoras
ladle cucharón
lager cerveza *[rubia]*
   lager shandy clara, cerveza con limonada
lamb cordero
   lamb chop chuleta de cordero
lamb's lettuce valeriana
langoustine cigala
lard manteca, grasa de cerdo
lark alondra
lasagne lasaña
latte *[coffee]* café con leche
lavatory lavabo, servicios
lavender lavanda, espliego
lean magro, -a
leek puerro
leg pierna, muslo *[pollo]*
   leg of lamb gigote, pierna de codero
legumes legumbres
lemon limón
   lemon balm toronjil
   lemon grass limoncillo
   lemon juice zumo de limón, limonada
   lemon sole lenguado
   lemon zest cáscara de limón, peladura
   lemonade limonada
lentil lenteja
lettuce lechuga
lime lima
ling maruca, arbitán
light-bodied wine vino ligero
liqueur licor
liquorice regaliz
litre litro

liver hígado
   liver sausage embutido de paté de hígado
loaf pan, barra de pan
   meat loaf pan de carne, rollo de carne
   white loaf pan blanco
lobster langosta, bogavante
   lobster bisque sopa de langosta
local local
   local cheese queso local
   local specialities especialidades locales
loganberry frambuesa americana
loin *[of veal, pork, venison]* lomo
long-grained rice arroz largo
low-fat *[diet]* *[dieta]* de bajo contenido graso
low in fat magro, bajo en contenido graso
low-salt que contiene poca sal
lunch almuerzo, comida
luncheon meat fiambre *[de cerdo]*
lunchtime hora del almuerzo
lychee lichi
lythe abadejo
macadamia nuts macadamia
macaroni macarrones
   macaroni cheese macarrones con salsa de queso
macaroon macarrón, almendrado
mace macia
mackerel caballa
macrobiotic macrobiótico, -a
madeira *[vino de]* madeira
   madeira cake bizcocho de mantequilla
   madeira sauce salsa de madeira
maids of honour pastelitos de almendras *[franchipán]*
main course plato principal
maize maíz
mallard pato real
malt malta
mandarin mandarina
mangetout tirabeque
mango mango
mangosteen mangostán
maple syrup jarabe de arce
maple sugar azúcar de arce
margarine margarina
marinade adobo
   marinated en adobo, en escabeche
marjoram mejorana
market mercado
marmalade mermelada de naranja, confitura de naranja
marrow *[vegetable]* calabaza en forma de calabacín
marrow bone hueso con tuétano
   bone marrow médula
marsala wine vino de marsala
marshmallow malvavisco
marzipan mazapán
mashed puré
mashed potatoes puré de patatas
matches cerillas, fósforos

English-Spanish

matchstick potatoes patatas paja
mature [*wine*] añejo
mayonnaise salsa mayonesa
mead hidromiel, aguamiel
meal comida
meat carne
   meat ball albóndiga
   meat loaf pan de carne, rollo de carne
   meat pie empanada de carne
   medium-rare poco hecho(a), en su punto
   rare crudo(a), poco hecho, vuelta y vuelta
   well done muy hecho(a)
medallion medallón
medlar níspero, níspola
medium cooked en su punto
medium rare [*steak*] poco hecho, -a
medium wine semi seco
melon melón
melted butter mantequilla derretida
menu menú, carta
meringue merengue
mild suave
milk leche
   cow's milk leche de vaca
   ewe's milk leche de oveja
   goat's milk leche de cabra
   milk chocolate chocolate con leche
   milkshake batido de leche
   poached in milk escalfado en leche
   semi-skimmed milk leche semidescremada, leche semidesnatada
   soya milk leche de soja, de soya
   with milk con leche
   without milk sin leche
minced meat carne picada, picadillo
mincemeat picadillo de frutos secos para pastelería
mince pie pastelito picadillo de frutas
mineral water agua mineral
   fizzy mineral water agua mineral con gas
   still mineral water agua mineral sin gas
minestrone [*soup*] sopa minestrone
mint menta
   mint sauce salsa de menta
   mint jelly jalea de menta
   mint tea poleo
mixed grill parrillada de carne
mixed herbs hierbas provenzal
mixed salad ensalada mixta
mixed vegetables menestra de verduras
mollusc molusco, marisco
monkfish rape
monosodium glutamate [*MSG*] glutamato de sodio, glutamato monosódico
morels morilla
moussaka musaca
mousse mousse
muesli musli, muesli
muffin [*UK*] bollo de pan que se sirve tostado
muffin [*US*] mollete, madalena
mug taza grande [*sin platillo*]

mulberry   mora
mullet   pardete, capitán, lisa, mújol
mulligatawny *[soup]*   sopa muy condimentada de origen indio
mushroom   seta, hongo
   button mushrooms   champiñón
mushy peas   puré de guisantes
mussel   mejillón
mustard   mostaza
mutton   cordero, carnero
napkin   servilleta
natural   natural
Neapolitan ice-cream   helado de fresa, vainilla y chocolate
neat / straight *[US]*   solo, sin hielo ni agua
nectarine   nectarina
nettle   ortiga
no smoking   prohibido fumar
noisettes   avellanas *[fruto]*; filete, medallón *[carne]*
non-alcoholic drink   bebida sin alcohol
non-smoking area   zona de no fumadores
noodles   fideos
   noodle soup   sopa de fideos
nut   fruto seco *[nuez, almendra, avellana...]*
   almond   almendra
   brazil nut   nuez del Brasil
   cashew nut   anacardo, nuez de la india, castaña de cajú
   chestnut   castaña
   cobnut   avellana grande
   coconut   coco
   hazelnut   avellana
   peanut   cacahuete
   pecan nut   pacana
   sweet chestnut   castaña
   walnut   nuez *[de nogal]*
nutmeg   nuez moscada
oatcake   galleta de avena
oatmeal   harina de avena
oats   avena
   porridge/rolled oats   copos de avena
octopus   pulpo
off [*food, wine*]   pasado, -a
offal   despojos y vísceras, asaduras, menudos
oil   aceite
okra   quingombó *or* kimbombó
olive   aceituna, oliva
   black olives   aceitunas negras
   green olives   aceitunas verdes
   olive oil   aceite de oliva
omelette   tortilla francesa
on the rocks *[with ice]*   con hielo
onion   cebolla
   onion soup   sopa de cebolla
open *[verb]*   abrir
orange   naranja
   orange juice   zumo de naranja, naranjada
   orange sauce   salsa de naranja
oregano   orégano
organic   biológico, -a, orgánico, -a
ostrich   avestruz

English-Spanish

outdoors/outside al aire libre
oven horno
overdone recocido(a), muy hecho
oxtail rabo de buey
   oxtail soup sopa de rabo de buey
ox tongue lengua de buey
oyster ostra
oyster mushroom champiñón, pleurota
pancake crep, crepe, tortita
pan-fried salteado, a la paella
papaya papaya
paprika pimentón dulce, paprika
par-boil sancochar
parfait postre helado
Parma ham jamón de Parma
Parmesan *[cheese]* *[queso]* Parmesano
parsley perejil
   curly parsley perejil de hoja rizada
   flat parsley perejil de hoja plana
   parsley sauce salsa de perejil
parsnip chirivía
partridge perdiz
party fiesta
pasta pasta alimenticia
   fresh pasta pasta fresca
pastry masa *[para pasteles]*, pasta
   filo pastry pasta de hojaldre muy fina
   puff pastry hojaldre
pasty empanada *[de carne y verduras]*
pâté paté
   liver pâté paté de hígado
pawpaw papaya
pay *[verb]* pagar
pea guisante *or* chicharo
   green peas guisantes
   green pea soup crema de guisantes
   split peas guisantes secos
   pea soup *[with split peas]* crema de guisantes secos
peach melocotón, durazno
peanut cacahuete
   peanut butter mantequilla de cacahuete
pear pera
pearl barley cebada perlada
pease-pudding puré de guisantes secos
pecan nut pacana
   pecan pie tarta de pacanas
peel *[verb]* pelar
peel *[noun]* cáscara, piel
   grated peel cáscara rallada, ralladura
peeled sin cáscara, sin piel, pelado(a)
pepper *[spice]* pimienta
   black, green, white pepper pimienta negra, pimienta blanca
   ground pepper pimienta en polvo, pimienta molida
   whole pepper pimienta entera, en grano
   pepper mill molinillo de pimienta *or* pimentero
   pepper pot pimentero
   pepper steak bistec a la pimienta
pepper *[vegetable]* pimiento

English-Spanish

    green pepper pimiento verde
    red pepper pimiento rojo
    stuffed pepper pimiento relleno
peppermint menta
perch perca de agua dulce
perry sidra de peras
persimmon caqui
pesto pesto
pheasant faisán
pickled cabbage choucroute *[conserva de col salada y fermentada]*
pickled cucumber pepinillo en vinagre al eneldo
pickled herring arenque en escabeche
pickled onion cebollitas en vinagre
pickles encurtidos
picnic picnic
pie empanada, tarta, pastel
piece porción, trozo
pig cerdo, puerco
    suckling pig cochinillo, lechón
pigeon pichón
pig's trotters manitas de cerdo
pike lucio *[sollo]*
pike-perch serrano
pilchard sardina
pine nuts piñones
pineapple piña, ananá
pinto bean alubia pinta, frijol pinto
pistachio nut pistacho
pitcher jarro, jarra
pitta bread pan griego *[sin levadura]*
pizza pizza
plaice platija
plain sin salsa, sin guarnición
    plain chocolate cholcolate sin leche
plantain plátano
plat du jour dish of the day
plate plato
plum ciruela
plum pudding plum púding, púding de frutos secos
plum tomato tomate *[de]* pera
poach escalfar
poached escalfado
poached egg huevo escalfado
polenta sémola de maíz, polenta
pollack abadejo
pomegranate granada
popcorn palomitas de maíz
porcini mushroom seta, carne de puerco
pork cerdo
    pork chop chuleta de cerdo, costilla de cerdo
    pork crackling chicharrón, corteza *[de cerdo asado]*
porridge gachas, copos de avena
port vino de Oporto
pot roast carne estofada
potato patata
    baked potato patata asada, al horno
    fried potoatoes patatas fritas

    mashed potatoes puré de patatas
    new potatoes patatas tempranas
    potato chips patatas fritas, papas chips
    potato crisps patatas fritas, papas *[en bolsa]*
    potato dumpling buñuelo de patatas
    potato salad ensalada de patatas
potted shrimp camarones en conserva
poultry aves
pound cake pastel *[que contiene partes iguales de harina, huevos, mantequilla y azúcar]*
poussin pollito
prawn gamba
preserves conservas
price precio
    price list lista de precios
prime rib entrecot
profiteroles lionesas de nata, profiteroles
protein proteína
prune ciruela pasa
pudding *[savoury]* pudding, budín, pudín
pudding *[sweet]* postre, pudding, budín, pudín
pudding rice arroz de grano redondo
pudding wine vino dulce, vino generoso, vino de postre
puff pastry pastel de hojaldre
pulses legumbres
pumpkin calabaza redonda
pure puro, -a
purée puré
purslane verdolaga
puy lentils lentejas *[verdes]* de Puy
quail codorniz
    quail's eggs huevos de codorniz
quality calidad
quark quark *[queso fresco blando]*
quarter cuarto, -a
quiche quiche *[tarta de huevos francesa]*
    quiche lorraine quich lorena *[tarta de huevos con jamón]*
quince membrillo
quorn sustituto de carne a base de proteína
rabbit conejo
rack espalda, costillar
    rack of lamb costillar de cordero
    rack of ribs costillar
radicchio escarola roja
radish/radishes rábano
ragout estofado *[de carne]*
rainbow trout trucha *[arco iris]*
raisin pasa
ramekin *[food]* tartaleta de queso
ramekin *[small container]* flanera individual
rancid rancio, -a
rare *[steak, meat]* crudo, -a, poco hecho, vuelta y vuelta
raspberry frambuesa
ravioli ravioles
raw crudo, -a
receipt recibo
recipe receta

recommend   recomendar, aconsejar
red cabbage   lombarda
red chilli   pimentón rojo, chile, guindilla
redcurrant   grosella roja
   redcurrant jelly   jalea de grosellas
redfish   gallineta nórdica
red mullet   salmonete de fango, salmonete de roca
red pepper   pimienta, pimentón rojo
red wine   vino tinto
reindeer   reno, corzo
rennet   cuajo
reservation   reserva
   reserve *[verb]*   reservar
restaurant   restaurante
rhubarb   ruibarbo
ribs   costillas
   rack of ribs   costillar
   ribs of beef   costilla de buey
   spare ribs   costillas de cerdo
rice   arroz
   long-grained rice   arroz largo
   rice paper   papel de arroz
   rice pudding   arroz con leche
   risotto rice   arroz italiano *[a la cazuela]*
   wild rice   arroz silvestre
rind *[cheese]*   corteza
ripe   maduro, -a
rissole   croqueta
river   río, de agua dulce
roast *[verb]*   asar
roast *[noun]*   asado
   roast beef   rosbif, carne asada
   roast chicken   pollo asado
   roast meats   carne asada
   roast pork   carne de cerdo asada
roasted   asado, -a
rock salt   sal gema, sal de grano
rocket   oruga *[planta para ensaladas]*
rockfish   lubina
roe   huevas
   hard roe   huevas
   soft roe   lecha, lechaza
roll *[bread]*   panecillo, bollo, bolillo
rolled oats   copos de avena
rollmop herring   arenque encurtido, arenque adobado
romain *[lettuce]*   lechuga romana
room temperature   temperatura ambiente
root   raíz
rosé *[wine]*   *[vino]* rosado
rosehip   escaramujo
rosemary   romero
roulade   roulade
rum   ron
   rum baba   *[bizcocho]* borracho
rump steak   filete
runner bean   judía pinta
rusk   galleta, bizcocho *[tostado]*

English-Spanish

rye centeno
rye bread pan de centeno
rye whisky whisky de centeno
saccharin sacarina
saddle lomo, falda
safflower cártamo
saffron azafrán
sage salvia
sago sagú
saithe palero, faneca plateada, carbonero
salad ensalada
   green salad ensalada verde
   mixed salad ensalada mixta
   salad bowl ensaladera
   salad cream mayonesa agridulce *[inglesa]*
   salad dressing vinagreta, aliño
   side salad ensalada verde *[acompañamiento]*
salami salami
salmon salmón
   salmon steak filete de salmón
salmon trout trucha salmonada
salsify salsifí
salt sal
   low-salt poca sal
   salt cellar salero
   salt mill molinillo de sal
   salted salado, -a, con sal
   salty salado, -a
sand sole lenguado
sandwich bocadillo, emparedado, sándwich
   cheese sandwich bocadillo de queso
   club sandwich sandwich de dos pisos
   ham sandwich bocadillo de jamón
sardine sardina
sauce salsa
   white sauce salsa bechamel
saucer platillo
saury paparda
sausage salchicha, embutido
   liver sausage embutido de paté de hígado
   sausage roll salchicha envuelta en hojaldre
sauté saltear, sofreir
   sauté pan sartén para saltear
   sautéed salteado, -a
saveloy salchicha gruesa y corta muy sazonada
savoury *[plato]* salado, comida no dulce
savoy cabbage repollo rizado, col rizada *[de Milán]*
saxifrage saxífraga
scald escaldar
scallion *[US]* cebolleta, chalote, -a, cebollín
scallop vieira, concha, ostión
scalloped chicken *[US]* escalopa de pollo
scalloped potatoes *[US]* patatas gratinadas
scampi colas de cigala rebozadas
scone *[UK]* bollito *[se sirve con mantequilla, confitura o nata]*
scorpion fish escorpena, cabracho
Scotch *[whisky]* escocés

Scotch broth   sopa escocesa *[contiene cordero, verduras y cebada]*
Scotch egg   huevo escocés *[huevo duro envuelto en carne picada y rebozado]*
scrambled eggs   huevos revueltos
sea bass, bass   lubina, corvina *[LA]*
sea bream   pargo
sea view *[i.e. table with]*   mesa con vistas al mar
seafood   mariscos
sear   dorar a fuego vivo
sea salt   sal marina
seasonal   estacional
seasoning   condimento, sazón
   seasoned   condimentado, -a, sazonado, -a
seat   asiento
sea trout   trucha marina
seaweed   alga marina
second course   segundo plato
selection   selección
sell-by-date   fecha de caducidad
semi-dry   semi seco
semi-hard cheese   queso semi duro
semi-skimmed milk   leche semidescremada, leche semidesnatada
semi-soft cheese   queso semiblando
semolina   sémola
service   servicio
   discretionary   a la discreción del cliente
   included   incluido
   not included   no incluido
   service charge   servicio
serviette   servilleta
sesame seeds   semillas de sésamo, semilla de ajonjoli
set menu   menú del día
shad   saboga, sábalo
shallot   chalote, chalota
shallow-fry   freír en una sartén
shandy   clara, cerveza con limonada
   a half of shandy   una clara
shank   pierna
shark   tiburón
sharp   fuerte, ácido
shell *[fish]*   concha
shell *[nuts]*   cáscara
shellfish   marisco
shepherd's pie   pastel de carne picada y puré de patata
sherbet   sorbete, granizado
sherry   jerez
shiitake mushroom   seta
shish kebab   brocheta, pincho de cordero asado
shop   tienda
shortbread   galleta dulce de mantequilla
shortcrust *[pastry]*   masa para empanadas y pasteles
shoulder   paletilla, espalda
shrimp   camarón, quisquilla, gamba
   shrimp cocktail   cóctel de gambas
shut/closed   cerrado, -a
side dish(es)   acompañamiento, guarnición
sift   pasar por el tamiz *[o la criba]*, espolvorear

silverside corte de carne redondo para asados
simmer hervir a fuego lento
single cream crema de leche
sippets picatoste, crutón
sirloin solomillo
skate raya
skewer brocheta, pincho
skimmed milk leche desnata
skin piel, cáscara, nata *[leche]*
skipjack listado, barrilate
slice loncha, rodaja, tajada
    slice of bread rebanada de pan
    slice of pie porción, trozo de pastel
    slice of ham loncha de jamón
sliced cortado(a), a rodajas
sloe endrina
    sloe gin licor de endrinas, pacharán
smell olor
smelt eperlano
smoke *[a cigarette]* fumar
    smoker fumador, -a
smoke *[food]* ahumar
smoke *[noun]* humo
smoked ahumado(a)
    smoked bacon bacon ahumado, tocino ahumado, panceta ahumada
    smoked cheese queso ahumado
    smoked eel anguila ahumada
    smoked fish pescado ahumado
    smoked haddock abadejo ahumado
    smoked kipper arenque ahumado
    smoked meat carne ahumada
    smoked salmon salmón ahumado
snack *[between meals]* tentempié
snack *[light meal]* refrigerio, tentempié
snail caracol
snipe agachadiza
soda bread pan *[de levadura de polvo]*
soda water sifón, agua de seltz, soda
soft suave, blando, -a
soft-boiled egg huevo pasado por agua
soft cheese queso blando
soft drink refresco, bebida sin alcohol
soft roe lecha, lechaza
sole lenguado
sorbet sorbete, granizado
sorghum sorgo, zahína
sorrel acedera, hierva salada
soufflé suflé
    cheese soufflé suflé de queso
soup sopa, potaje
    beef tea caldo de carne
    broth caldo
    chowder sopa de pescado *[a base de leche]*
    fish broth caldo de pescado
    fish soup sopa de pescado
    mulligatawny sopa de curry
    onion soup sopa de cebolla
    soup of the day sopa del día

soup spoon cuchara *[de sopa]*, cuchara sopera
vegetable soup minestrone, sopa de verduras
vichyssoise vichyssoise *or* sopa de porros
sour agrio, -a
    sour cream crema agria
    sour dough masa fermentada
    sweet and sour agridulce
soy bean, soya bean, soja bean soya, soja
soy sauce, soya sauce salsa de soya, salsa de soja
soya milk leche de soja, leche de soya
spaghetti espaguetis
    spaghetti bolognese espaguetis a la boloñesa
Spanish omelette tortilla de patatas
spare ribs costillas de cerdo
sparkling con gas
    sparkling water agua con gas
    sparkling wine vino con gas
speciality especialidad
spice especia
spicy picante, muy condimentado
spinach espinaca
spiny lobster langosta
spirits licores
sponge biscuits galletas, soletillas, soletas
sponge cake bizcocho
spoon cuchara
    spoonful cucharada
sprat espadín
spring greens hojas de col temprana
spring lamb cordero lechal
spring onion cebolleta, cebollino
spring rolls rollitos de primavera
spring water agua de manantial
sprouts *[Brussels]* coles, colecitas de Bruselas
squab pichón
squash calabacín, calabaza
squid calamar
stale pasado(a); duro *[pan]*; rancio *[queso]*
starch fécula, almidón
starter entrante, primer plato
steak *[beef]* bistec
steak and kidney pie pastel de bistec y riñones
steak and kidney pudding púdin de bistec y riñones
steam *[verb]* cocer al vapor
steamed al vapor
    steamed vegetables verduras al vapor
stew *[meat]* estofado, guisado de carne
    lamb stew guisado de cordero
stewed estofado, guisado *[carne]*; en compota *[fruta]*
    stewed fruit compota de fruta
    stewed steak estofado de ternera
stilton queso *[azul]* stilton
stir-fry saltear al estilo chino *[con poco aceite y revolviendo]*
stock caldo
    fish stock caldo de pescado
    vegetable stock caldo de verduras
stout cerveza negra

stove   cocina, hornillo
straight [US]   solo, sin hielo ni agua
strawberry   fresa
   strawberry jam   mermelada de fresa
   strawberry shortcake   torta de fresas y nata
streaky bacon   panceta, bacon, tocino
strip steak   entrecot
strong   fuerte
stuffed   relleno
   stuffed olives   aceitunas rellenas
stuffing   relleno
sturgeon   esturión
suckling pig   cochinillo, lechón
suet   grasa, sebo
sugar   azúcar
   caster sugar   azúcar muy fino
   granulated sugar   azúcar granulado
   icing sugar   azúcar glas, azúcar en polvo
   sugar-coated almonds   peladillas
sugar snap peas   tirabeques
sultanas   pasa de Esmirna
sundae   sundae, helado con frutas
sun-dried   secado al sol
sunflower   girasol
   sunflower oil   aceite de girasol
   sunflower seeds   pipas, semillas de girasol
supermarket   supermercado
supper   cena
supplement   complemento
swede   nabo sueco
sweet   dulce, caramelo
   sweet [wine]   vino dulce, vino generoso, vino de postre
   sweet chesnut   castaña
   sweet potato   boniato, batata
   sweet trolley   carrito de los postres
   sweets [candy]   caramelos, golosinas
sweet and sour   agridulce
sweetbreads   mollejas, lechecillas, criadillas
sweetcorn   maíz tierno, elote
sweetener   endulzante
Swiss roll   brazo de gitano
swordfish   emperador, pez espada, albacora [LA]
syllabub   dulce a base de leche, azúcar, licor y zumo de limón
syrup   almíbar, jarabe
table   mesa
   table by the window   mesa al lado de la ventana
   tablecloth   mantel
   tablespoon   cuchara de servir
   table wine   vino de mesa
tagliatelle   tallarines
tangerine   mandarina, tangerina
tap water   agua del grifo
tapioca   tapioca
taragon, tarragon   estragón
tart   tarta, tartaleta
tartar sauce   salsa tártara
tartare   tártara

taste sabor
tasty sabroso, -a
tea té
    afternoon tea té *[de las cinco]*
    beef tea caldo de carne
    cup of tea taza de té
    green tea té verde
    herbal tea infusión, tisana
    high-tea merienda que se toma acompañada de té
    iced tea té con hielo
    lemon tea té con limón
    teacake bollito *[tostado y untado de mantequilla]* que se sirve con el té
    tea spoon cucharita, cucharilla
    tea with milk té con leche
    tea-time la hora del té
    teapot tetera
tench tenca
tender tierno, -a
tenderloin filete, lomo, solomillo
terrine terrina
thick grueso, -a, espeso, -a
thirsty sediento, -a
thrush tordo
thyme tomillo
tin lata, bote, tarro *[de conservas]*
tinned en lata, enlatado, -a, en conserva
tip propina
toad in the hole buñuelo o empanada de salchichas *[al horno]*
toast tostada, pan tostado
    French toast tostada, biscote
toast *[tribute]* brindar
toasted tostado, -a
toffee toffee
tofu queso de soya, queso de soja
toilet(s) servicios
toilet paper papel higiénico
tomato tomate
    cherry tomato tomates cereza
tomato juice jugo de tomate
tomato ketchup catsup, ketchup, salsa de tomate
tomato purée concentrado de tomate
tomato salad ensalada de tomate
tomato sauce salsa de tomate
tongue lengua
tonic water tónica
toothpick palillo, mondadientes
tope rosada, cazón, tintorera
tough *[meat]* *[carne]* dura
treacle melaza
    treacle tart tarta de melaza
trifle sopa inglesa *[postre de bizcocho, fruta y jerez cubiertos de crema y chantilly]*
trimmings guarnición, acompañamiento
tripe tripas, callos, mondongo
trolley carrito
trout trucha
truffle trufa

English-Spanish

chocolate truffle [sweet] trufa de chocolate
truffle butter mantequilla de trufas
tuna, tunny atún
turbot rodaballo
turkey pavo, guajolote
roast turkey pavo al horno, pavo asado
turmeric cúrcuma
turnip nabo, colinabo
turnip tops grelos
turnover empanada
uncooked crudo, -a, medio asado
underdone poco hecho, crudo, -a
unsalted butter mantequilla sin sal
upside-down cake pastel al que se le da la vuelta para servirlo
use by usar antes de, fecha de caducidad
vanilla vainilla
vanilla essence esencia de vainilla
vanilla ice cream helado de vainilla
vanilla pod/bean vaina, chaucha de vainilla
vanilla sugar azúcar aromatizado con vainilla
veal ternera
veal escalope escalopa de ternera
vegan vegetariano estricto
vegetable verdura
vegetable chili chile vegetariano
vegetable oil aceite vegetal
vegetable soup sopa de verduras, minestrone
vegetable stock caldo de verduras
vegetarian vegetariano, -a
vegetarian bolognaise boloñesa vegetariana
vegetarian cooking cocina vegetariana
vegetarian gravy salsa vegetariana
vegetarian lasagne lasaña vegetariana
vegetarian burger hamburguesa vegetariana
vegetarian sausage salchicha vegetariana
venison carne de venado
venison cutlets chuletas de venado
vermicelli fideos finos, cabello de ángel
very dry [wine] [vino] muy seco
very rare, [meat] poco hecho
very sweet muy dulce
victoria sponge [cake] bizcocho inglés
vinaigrette vinagreta
vinegar vinagre
vine vino
vine leaves hojas de parra
vintage cosecha
virgin olive oil aceite de oliva virgen
vol au vent volován, vol-au-vent
chicken vol au vent vol-au-vent de pollo
wafer barquillo, oblea
waffles wafles, gofres
waiter camarero
waitress camarera
Waldorf salad ensalada Waldorf [manzana, apio, nueces y mayonesa]
walnut nuez de nogal
warm [salad etc.] tibio, -a [ensalada tibia]
water agua

English-Spanish

bottled water   agua mineral
glass of water   vaso de agua
iced water   agua helada, agua muy fría
jug of water   jarra de agua
sparkling water/fizzy water   agua con gas
spring/mineral water   agua de manantial
still water   agua sin gas
watercress   berro
water melon   sandía
wedding cake   tarta, pastel de boda
well done *[meat]*   muy hecho(a), bien hecho
Welsh rarebit, rabbit   pan tostado con queso derretido
whale   ballena
wheat   trigo
wheat flour   harina de trigo
wheatgerm   germen de trigo
whelk   caracol de mar, buccino
whipped cream   nata montada, chantilly
whisky   whisky escocés
whitebait *[sprats]*   morralla, chanquetes
white *[wine, meat]*   *[vino]* blanco; *[carne]* blanca
white bread   pan blanco
white truffle   trufa blanca
white wine   vino blanco
whiting   pescadilla, plegonero
whole   entero, -a
whole grain mustard   mostaza *[de grano entero]*
wholemeal bread   pan integral
wholewheat   integral
wholewheat flour   harina de trigo integral
whortleberry   arándano
wild   silvestre
wild boar   jabalí
wild mushrooms   setas
wild rice   arroz silvestre
wild strawberry   fresa de bosque, fresa silvestre
window table   mesa al lado de la ventana
wine   vino
wine cooler   champanera
wine list   carta de los vinos
wine vinegar   vinagre de vino
wine waiter   sumiller, escanciador
bottle of wine   botella de vino
glass of wine   vaso de vino
house wine   vino de la casa
local wine   vino local, vino del país
red wine   vino tinto
sparkling wine   vino de aguja, vino espumante
sweet/pudding wine   vino dulce, vino generoso, vino de postre
white wine   vino blanco
winkle   bígaro, caracol de mar
with ice cream   con helado
woodcock   chocha, becada
Worcestershire sauce   salsa inglesa
yam   boniato, batata
yeast   levadura
yoghurt   yogur
plain yoghurt   yogur natural

English-Spanish

Yorkshire pudding Yorkshire pudding *[buñuelo inglés de harina, huevo y leche que se sirve con el rosbif]*
zabaglione sabayón
zest cáscara, peladura
zucchini *[US]* calabacín